# 斑斓阅读 · 外研社英汉双语百科书系典藏版

**新近推出：**

斑斓阅读·**外研社英汉双语百科书系**

**典藏版**

**通识读本**

# 古代亚述简史
# Ancient Assyria
## A Very Short Introduction

Karen Radner 著
颜海英　常洋铭 译

**外语教学与研究出版社**
FOREIGN LANGUAGE TEACHING AND RESEARCH PRESS
北京 BEIJING

京权图字：01-2020-2803

**图书在版编目 (CIP) 数据**

古代亚述简史：英汉对照 ／（奥）卡伦·拉德纳著 ；颜海英，常洋铭译. —— 北京：外语教学与研究出版社，2020.11
（斑斓阅读·外研社英汉双语百科书系：典藏版：通识读本）
书名原文：Ancient Assyria: A Very Short Introduction
ISBN 978-7-5213-2161-6

Ⅰ.①古… Ⅱ.①卡… ②颜… ③常… Ⅲ.①英语－汉语－对照读物②亚述学 Ⅳ.①H319.4；K107.8

中国版本图书馆 CIP 数据核字 (2020) 第 215882 号

地图审图号：GS (2020) 3279

出 版 人　徐建忠
项目负责　姚　虹　周渝毅
责任编辑　都楠楠
责任校对　徐　宁
封面设计　牛茜茜　曾新蕾
版式设计　吕　茜
出版发行　外语教学与研究出版社
社　　址　北京市西三环北路 19 号（100089）
网　　址　http://www.fltrp.com
印　　刷　三河市北燕印装有限公司
开　　本　650×980　1/16
印　　张　17.5
版　　次　2020 年 11 月第 1 版　2020 年 11 月第 1 次印刷
书　　号　ISBN 978-7-5213-2161-6
定　　价　42.00 元

购书咨询：（010）88819926　电子邮箱：club@fltrp.com
外研书店：https://waiyants.tmall.com
凡印刷、装订质量问题，请联系我社印制部
联系电话：（010）61207896　电子邮箱：zhijian@fltrp.com
凡侵权、盗版书籍线索，请联系我社法律事务部
举报电话：（010）88817519　电子邮箱：banquan@fltrp.com
物料号：321610001

记载人类文明
沟通世界文化
www.fltrp.com

# Contents

# 目录

# List of illustrations

IV

# 图目

To Amélie, with love and admiration

# Acknowledgements

I wish to thank Luciana O'Flaherty, Andrea Keegan, Jenny Nugee, Emma Ma, and Carrie Hickman at OUP who oversaw the book's genesis from conception to completion as well as the anonymous expert and editorial readers who commented astutely and encouragingly on the proposal and the manuscript. I am indebted to Hartmut Kühne, Julian Reade, and Michael Roaf for their kind permission to reproduce, respectively, two images of the Tell Sheikh Hamad Project, an original drawing and a site plan, and to Alessio Palmisano for creating the map at short notice.

Frans van Koppen and Erika Radner read the first complete draft of the book, with Dieter Radner providing some key suggestions for Chapter 1, while Amélie Kuhrt read the final manuscript. I am very grateful for their suggestions and continual support. My thanks extend to Paul, Dibbes, and Mita for their energizing and calming influence on my study's atmosphere.

# Preface to the Chinese translation

Assyria is an ancient country in Western Asia, with its centre situated in what is today the north of Iraq. This state has a long and sometimes extremely well-documented history that begins in the second half of the third millennium BC and in China corresponds broadly to the periods of the Xia Dynasty, the Shang Dynasty and the first part of the Zhou Dynasty. Assyrian history is well known because the Assyrians relied for millennia on small tablets formed of clay as their main writing materials. Such clay tablets tend to survive very well—unlike paper, for example, which decays easily. Therefore, although the Assyrian Empire was conquered in the late 7th century BC and never rose again, the hardy clay tablets tell us a lot about the ancient Assyrians who used them to write down all sorts of things: poetry and songs, narratives celebrating their rulers' deeds, prayers, rituals and incantations, debt notes and sale contracts, testaments and adoption agreements, business and family letters, state correspondence, recipes for food and medicines, and much more.

Because fire conserves the already durable clay tablets even better there are certain periods in Assyria's long history about which we are especially well informed: whenever an Assyrian city was catastrophically destroyed by fire, the writings of the last two or three generations are conserved. For example, a period of 80 years, some four thousand years ago at the beginning of the second millennium BC, is documented in great detail because of the destruction of the city of Kanesh in modern-day Turkey where several generations of Assyrian merchants had entertained the headquarters of their import-export firms. Or the 7th century BC, some three thousand years ago, is known very well because when the great cities in the central region of the Assyrian Empire were destroyed in the fights marking the end of that state, the palaces of the capital city of Nineveh with the voluminous imperial archives and the private residences of many families serving the most important Assyrian temple in the city of Assur went up in flames, too. Had the Assyrians written on paper, these fires of destruction would have devoured their documents together with many of their other possessions. But as they used clay the fire baked their tablets like pottery bowls and made them even more durable.

Abandoned in the ruins, the clay tablets survived until European explorers and adventurers first started to excavate the long-forgotten ancient cities of Assyria in the 19th century AD, guided by their mention in the Hebrew Bible/Old Testament. Among the remains of temples, palaces and private houses, they found very many clay tablets. These are inscribed in the so-called cuneiform script, which is created by impressing a reed stylus into the still soft clay to form complex characters that stand for words and syllables—conceptually quite similar to the way the Chinese script works. This script had fallen out of use two thousand years ago, and at first, no one could read it. But already the first attempts of decipherment showed that the script documented a language (Akkadian), which was related to languages like Arabic and Hebrew that are still spoken today in the Middle East. This realisation allowed the lost language's relatively quick decipherment. And with the ability to read the clay tablets came the opportunity to reconstruct an almost entirely forgotten civilisation that had, however, deeply shaped the world documented in the Hebrew Bible and the writings of Greek historians like Herodotus.

While the Assyrian writing system might perhaps have seemed relatively familiar for an accidental visitor from China, some other hallmarks of Assyrian culture would have been quite alien. Let's start with food. Assyrian cuisine is deeply rooted in bread-making and diary-consumption, with rice cultivated only very late in its history and never on a large scale. The most important cereals were wheat and barley, which were used to make bread, porridge and beer—the staples of Assyrian everyday food. The Assyrian central region in northern Iraq is part of the area where cattle, sheep and goats were first domesticated, and all these animals were kept for their milk products and meat; the latter also applied to the pig, which was separately domesticated in China and Western Asia. While the Assyrians bred various birds for their eggs and meat, including ducks and geese, they did not yet keep chickens, which only arrived in the region from the east after the end of the Assyrian Empire. They also ate fish but caught it wild and didn't breed it. The amount of meat an Assyrian consumed was directly linked to his or her social standing: while the members of the royal court had it every day (and can be shown to have developed various illnesses connected to the consumption of too rich food, such as gout and tooth decay), others only ate meat when they were offered it during religious and state holidays. The same was true for wine made from grapes, which were also first domesticated close to the Assyrian heartland: while the influential and wealthy drank wine every day (albeit always mixed with water) Assyrians of simpler means may have had a taste only at very rare occasions and otherwise stuck to the omnipresent beer. The Assyrians also grew vegetables such as onions, lentils and beans and fruit including apples, pomegranates, figs and plums (but not yet peaches and cherries which arrived in their region only later). To sweeten their dishes the Assyrians used honey or date-syrup. Although tea is widespread in the modern Middle East, you would not have found it anywhere in Assyrian times. You can judge for yourself whether you would have enjoyed Assyrian cuisine.

What about clothes and personal grooming? Most garments were made of sheep's wool, which was the traditional fibre of the region; the highly developed textile industry could produce very thin and very colourful fabrics. Linen was also known since ancient times but far less popular than in Egypt, where it was the most common fabric. Silk started to be available to the wealthiest Assyrians in the 8th and 7th centuries BC through long-distance trade all the way from China; at that time, also cotton fabrics became more widespread among the members of the elite and the plant may have even been cultivated locally. Whatever fabrics were used, the Assyrians of both sexes favoured a style of dress that typically consisted of an undergarment that resembles a long, tight T-shirt and a shawl-like overgarment in the shape of a large rectangle of cloth that was draped around the upper body, shoulders and arms, hanging down over the legs. The undergarment was worn with a belt while the overgarment was held in place with large pins. The Assyrians did not know loose trousers although they wore woollen tights against the cold. Depending on the season, they wore sandals or long boots made of leather. All Assyrian houses had their own source of water and a bathroom. Washing and bathing was culturally very important, especially when connected to worship and temple service. If a man fulfilled certain cultic roles at a temple he had to be clean-shaven of all body hair. Otherwise, men did not shave at all and wore their beards and hair at shoulder-length. Women, too, wore their hair long. Archaeological finds and depictions show that personal jewellery did not differ between the sexes, with both men and women wearing earrings and bracelets; but the materials used offer a very clear indication of the owner's social status. Gold, lapis lazuli and ivory were the most valued materials.

If much regarding food, clothes and grooming would have been entirely alien, the key concepts underpinning Assyrian architecture would have seemed quite familiar to a visitor from China: the use of enclosed open spaces, the importance of symmetry and directional hierarchies, the emphasis on a building's width rather than its height, and the incorporation of cosmological, mythological and symbolic allusions into the decorative scheme are typical of both Assyrian and Chinese architecture. However, because there was a general lack of building timber in Assyria wood never played a prominent role in construction and was routinely only used for doors and roof beams, and very occasionally for columns. Instead, Assyrian architecture relied heavily on mud-brick and the resultant buildings were therefore very sturdy and bulky. Colourful glazed ceramic elements were popular as building decoration, but not as roof tiles because the roofs were generally flat. Despite sharing many key concepts with Chinese architecture, Assyrian buildings therefore take a very different form due to the use of very different materials in the two traditions. But our Chinese visitor would have appreciated the Assyrian love of horticulture and the beautifully designed gardens attached to the palaces that brought together trees and plants collected from near and far.

We have already mentioned the Assyrian temples. The beings that were worshipped in these shrines were not ancestors but gods and goddesses that represented natural phenomena such as the sun, the moon or the weather, cultural concepts such as writing, medicine or warfare, or a place (usually the god's city). These deities were imagined and depicted in human form, and in the temples' inner sanctum, their statues were displayed to the worshippers. These statues were carved from precious woods, clothed in the richest garments and adorned with priceless jewellery. Every day, the deities were washed and dressed and served lavish meals that were prepared specifically for this purpose, but afterwards eaten by the people holding cultic offices as the gods were thought to have consumed the essence of their feast by smell. The deities also enjoyed the entertainment offered by musicians and singers but differently from the royal court, whose ceremonial greatly resembled temple service, all temple personnel were exclusively male. No women or eunuchs (who were very common in the ruler's service) were allowed into the divine statues' immediate presence, making the Assyrian temples an entirely male-dominated domain—despite the fact that the gods were habitually conceived as part of a family: a temple's occupants were typically imagined as a divine couple living with their divine son and heir and thus formed an idealised nuclear family unit that was well suited for a society where inheritance passed exclusively through the male line.

In the pages of this book, you will encounter a diverse selection of individuals from Assyrian history. Men, women and eunuchs, kings, princes and priests, scholars, merchants and scribes, people born into slavery and people enslaved by war or debt. Now that you know what they would have eaten and drunk and how they would have dressed and lived I hope that you can imagine them as vividly as I did when I wrote about their fates, based on the information offered by the clay tablets that underpin all our knowledge of these people of a far-away time and place.

# 中文版序

　　亚述是一个西亚文明古国，它的核心地域位于今日的伊拉克北部。它悠久且记录翔实的历史可以一直追溯到公元前3千纪的后半叶，存续时间大致与中国的夏代、商代以及西周重合。亚述历史之所以为人熟知，是因为亚述人数千年来都用小小的泥板作主要的书写材料。这些泥板通常可以完好地留存至今，不像纸张等材料那样容易损毁。因此，虽然亚述帝国在公元前7世纪末被征服，而且从此一蹶不振，但这些坚硬的泥板依然可以向我们讲述关于古代亚述人的诸多情况——他们在泥板上写下了各种内容：诗篇和歌曲、歌颂统治者言行的文章、祷词、仪式和咒语、欠条和销售合同、遗嘱和收养协议、商务信函和家庭信件、国务信件、食谱和药方等，不一而足。

　　因为火的焙烤能够更好地保存这些已经很耐久的泥板，所以在亚述悠久的历史中，我们对一些时期的了解格外详细：每当一座亚述城市毁于大火，最后两三代居民的书写文件都会被保存下来。例如，在大约4000年前，即公元前2千纪伊始，现位于土耳其境内的卡奈什城被毁，一段长达80年的历史被详尽地记录了下来。在这一时期，数代亚述商人将自己的进出口商行的总部设在了卡奈什。又比如大约3000年前的公元前7世纪，这一时期的信息也相当丰富。原因在于，在那场标志着亚述帝国灭亡的战争之中，帝国核心地域的大城市接连被毁，首都尼尼微的宫殿连同其中保存的大量帝国档案都被付之一炬，供职于亚述城中最重要的亚述神庙的许多家庭的私人住宅也被烧毁。如果亚述人的书写材料是纸，火焰会将他们的档案连同大量其他家产一道化作灰烬。但由于他们使用的是黏土制成的泥板，大火反而像烧陶碗一样，将它们焙烤得更加牢固。

这些泥板被遗弃在废墟之中，直到公元 19 世纪，欧洲旅行家和探险家在《希伯来圣经》/《旧约圣经》中相关描述的指引下，开始发掘这些被遗忘已久的亚述古城，泥板才得以重见天日。在神庙、宫殿和私人住宅的遗迹中，他们发现了许多泥板，上面刻着所谓的楔形文字。这种代表单词和音节的复杂字符由芦苇笔在依然柔软的黏土板上压写而成，从概念上来讲，它们与汉字极为相似。这种文字在 2000 年前就已经不再使用，在被发现之初，无人能够读懂。不过，首次破译的结果表明，这种文字记录的是阿卡德语，与阿拉伯语、希伯来语等至今仍在中东使用的语言密切相关。这一发现使得这门失传的语言相对快速地得到破译。在读懂泥板的基础上，再现一个几乎完全被遗忘的文明成为可能，而在当时，这一文明深刻地塑造了《希伯来圣经》和希罗多德等古希腊历史学家的著作中记载的世界。

对于偶然到访的中国来客来说，亚述的书写体系可能看起来比较熟悉，不过，亚述文化其他的一些特色可能是相当陌生的。我们先来谈谈食物。亚述烹饪起源于面包的制作和乳制品的使用，水稻种植在很晚才出现，而且一直是小规模种植。在亚述，最重要的谷物是小麦和大麦，它们被用来做面包、熬粥、酿啤酒，这三样是亚述人的日常主食。现位于伊拉克北部的亚述核心地域所在的区域属于人类最早驯养牛、绵羊和山羊的地区，饲养这些动物是为了获得乳制品和肉；猪也是肉类的来源之一，中国和西亚地区也曾驯养猪。为了获取蛋和肉，亚述人还会饲养包括鸭和鹅在内的各种禽类动物，但他们这时候还没开始养鸡——鸡是在亚述帝国覆灭后才从东方来到这一地区的。亚述人也吃鱼，但他们只捕野生鱼，并没有开展集中养殖。亚述人吃肉的数量与他／她的社会地位直接相关：王室成员每天都可以吃肉（他们因饮食过于营养而患上各种疾病，如痛风和蛀牙，这一点便可作证），而其他人只有在宗教节日和国家假日才能吃到肉。亚述核心地域附近也是最早驯化栽培葡萄的地方。葡萄酒的饮用也同食肉一样：位高权重的富贵人家每天都能喝到葡萄酒（尽管总是掺水饮用），而亚述平民可能只有在极少数场合才能尝上一口，平时只能喝普遍流行的啤酒。亚述人也种植洋葱、豆类等蔬菜，以及苹果、石榴、无花果和李子等水果（但当时此地还没有桃子和樱桃）。亚述人用蜂蜜或椰枣糖浆为菜肴添加甜味。尽管茶在现代中东很普遍，但在亚述时期，你们完全找不到它的踪影。现在，你们可以判断自己是否会喜欢亚述美食了。

那衣服和个人打扮呢？亚述的大部分服装都是用绵羊毛制成的，绵羊毛是该地区传统的纺织纤维；当地高度发达的纺织业可以生产出极其轻薄华美的面料。亚麻布也是当地自古以来就有的面料，但远不如在埃及那么流行。在埃及，亚麻布是最常见的面料。公元前 8 至前 7 世纪，丝绸经长途贸易从中国远道而来，开始供应给那些最富有的亚述人；当时，棉织物也愈加受到精英阶层青睐，亚述当地可能也已经开始种植棉花。无论衣服用的是哪种面料，亚述男女都喜欢一种衣着搭配，这种搭配通常包括一件内衣——类似于一件又长又紧的 T 恤衫，和一件像披肩一样的外套——一块很大的长方形的布，盖住上身、肩膀和手臂，垂至双腿。内衣上系着腰带，外套则用大大的别针固定住。亚述人虽然会穿羊毛紧身衣御寒，却并不会穿宽松的裤子。根据季节变化，他们会换上皮革制成的凉鞋或是长靴。亚述人的房屋都有自己的水源和浴室。在亚述文化中，清洁和沐浴是非常重要的，特别是在祭拜神祇和从事神庙里的工作的时候。如果一个人在神庙里担任某种宗教类的职务，他必须把所有的体毛都剃光。除此情况，男人无须剃须，通常留着齐肩的胡子和长发。女人也留长发。考古发现和文物中的描述表明，珠宝首饰不分性别，男女都佩戴耳环和手镯，但首饰所用的材料非常清楚地表明了主人的社会地位。黄金、青金石和象牙是最为珍贵的材料。

对于中国访客而言，亚述的食物和衣着打扮可以说是非常陌生的，不过，亚述建筑的核心理念应该就相当熟悉了：使用与外界隔绝的开放空间，重视对称性和方位所反映的等级差别，强调建筑的宽度而不是高度，在装潢中融入宇宙学、神话和具有象征意义的典故——这些都是亚述和中国古代建筑的典型特征。然而，由于亚述普遍缺乏木材，因此，木材在建筑中从未发挥过突出的作用，通常只用来做门，当房梁，偶尔也被用作柱子。取而代之的是泥砖，亚述的建筑极为依赖这种材料，建成的楼宇也因此非常坚固和庞大。色彩斑斓的釉陶物件是一种流行的建筑装饰，但它们并不是用来作屋顶瓦的，因为亚述的屋顶通常都很平。尽管亚述建筑与中国古代建筑有许多共同的核心理念，但由于两者使用的材料截然不同，因此在外观上也相差甚远。不过，我们的中国来客定会赞赏亚述人对园艺的热爱：宫殿周围附有设计精美的花园，汇集了从各处寻来的花草树木。

我们此前提到了亚述神庙。这些神殿中供奉的并非祖先，而是象征着日月、天气等自然现象，书写、医药或战争等文化观念，或是某地（通常是神所守护的城市）的男神和女神。这些神祇被想象和描绘成人类的模样，他们的雕像被安置在神庙的内殿里，向崇拜者展示。这些雕像通常用珍贵的木材雕刻而成，穿着最华丽的衣服，饰以价值连城的珠宝。人们每天都会清洗和打扮神祇的雕像，并呈上专门为他们准备的美味佳肴。但在祭祀仪式之后，这些食物会由神职人员吃掉，因为人们认为众神靠嗅闻气味来享用宴席。众神同样可以享受乐手和歌手提供的娱乐表演，宫廷里的仪式与之相差无几。不过，前后两种表演的不同之处在于，所有在神庙供职的人员都是男性。（宫内常见的）侍女或宦官不准进入神像所在的圣地，亚述的神庙也因此成为一个完全由男性主导的领域——尽管众神通常被视为一个家庭的一部分：神庙里的住户通常被想象成一对神祇夫妇与他们圣子暨继承人这样的组合，如此一来便形成了一个理想化的核心家庭单位，非常符合一个遗产单传男性的社会。

在这本书中，你们会读到历史中各种各样的亚述人：男人、女人和宦官，国王、王子和祭司，学者、商人和书吏，生而为奴的人和因战争或负债而沦为奴隶的人。泥板所提供的信息支撑起了我们对这些来自遥远的时代和地方的人的所有认知。在此基础上，我写下了他们的命运。读到这里，你们已经知道他们吃什么、喝什么、穿什么、住什么，现在，我希望你们能像我在写作时那样，对他们展开生动的想象。

# Chapter 1
# Introducing Assyria

Ancient Assyria is just one of many states flourishing in the
Middle East in the millennia before the beginning of the common
era, but the long-lived kingdom was certainly one of the most
influential. Looking back at an eventful history already spanning
over a millennium, this state emerged in the 9th century BC as the
first world empire. Decisions made in the imperial capital cities
in present day northern Iraq influenced lives from the Nile to the
Caspian Sea while its political, administrative, and infrastructural
heritage profoundly shaped the subsequent history of the wider
Mediterranean region and the Middle East.

Assyrian culture is at once familiar and strange. We may share
the Assyrian taste for good wines, but perhaps would not choose
locusts on a stick for nibbles. A fresh water supply, indoor toilets,
and a well-functioning sewage system in the family home are as
important to us as to urban Assyrians, but we may find it less
essential to have an underground burial chamber accessible from
the living room. We may congratulate Assyrian buyers on enjoying
consumer protection and extended warranties, but are perhaps
taken aback to find that these extended to the purchase of people
who were subject to a 100-day guarantee against epilepsy and
mental instability. The foldable parasol was a practical Assyrian
invention, but carrying one was dangerous: its use was exclusively

reserved for royalty and without entitlement was an act of treason. We, too, enclose letters in envelopes, but they are not made out of clay.

Since the archaeological rediscovery of Assyria in the mid-19th century, its cities have been excavated extensively in Iraq, Syria, Turkey, and Israel, with further sites in Iran, Lebanon, and Jordan providing important information. It is because of the fact that durable clay was the Assyrians' most common writing material that we know so much about these idiosyncrasies and many other details of their culture.

## The city-state of Aššur

Assyrian history begins in the city of Aššur which was founded early in the third millennium BC, most likely as a trading emporium to supply the Sumerian cities in the south of modern Iraq with merchandise from the north. From the mid-third millennium BC onwards, textual sources document how the city was periodically integrated into large states centred in the south. The city was part of the realms of the kings of Akkad, then under a local ruler, and later of the kings of Ur. During the latters' time, a career official was dispatched from the south to govern the city: Zarriqum later rose to an even more prestigious post as the regent of Elam in Iran.

After the disintegration of the Ur kingdom around 2000 BC, Aššur was again an independent city-state. Its inhabitants spoke Assyrian. It is a Semitic language, like modern Arabic and Hebrew. Assyrian is a distinct language, albeit closely related to Babylonian, which was used in the regions south of Aššur. In antiquity, only the latter was called 'Akkadian', although today both Assyrian and Babylonian are often described as Akkadian dialects. The cuneiform script was used to record both languages, but the respective signs look quite different and are easily distinguished by experts.

After independence, hereditary local rulers once again governed the city, but they did not style themselves as kings, as the overlords from Akkad and Ur had done. Instead, they asserted that 'Aššur is king and Silulu is representative of Aššur', as one ruler's inscription of the early second millennium BC puts it. The city's god, who shared its name and was the divine manifestation of the site, was conceived as the sovereign in whose name the human ruler governed. In the 7th century BC, King Aššurbanipal still used the phrase in a praise hymn to the god: 'Aššur is king, Aššur is king and Aššurbanipal is his representative!' The regent of Aššur shared power with the collective citizen body in the city assembly and with an official chosen yearly called *līmum*, whose name was used to date the year (e.g. '*līmum* of Ennam-Aššur' for 1760 BC), in a practice attested elsewhere in the ancient world in communities with a strong tradition of collective government (Athens, e.g. 'archonship of Solon' for 594 BC; Rome, e.g. 'consulship of Caesar and Bibulus' for 59 BC). Especially well attested is the period of the 19th century BC when family-run merchant firms based in Aššur established a network of profitable trading colonies in Anatolia. Throughout that time the designation 'Assyrian' referred only to the city of Aššur and its inhabitants.

## The birth of Assyria

From the 18th century BC onwards, Aššur came again under the direct control of larger regional states but retained a strong cultural identity. The age of the city-state embedded in larger political structures came to an end when Aššur's last sovereign power Mittani (Hanigalbat to the Assyrians) went into decline in the 14th century BC. The rulers of Aššur used the power vacuum to establish their city as the centre of a territorial state that incorporated most of what is today northern Iraq. For the first time, they adopted the title of king. Their realm became the dominant power of northern Mesopotamia as they deftly played the game of international diplomacy, carefully navigating relations with states like Babylonia and Egypt to further their own ends.

The triangle between Aššur, Nineveh, and Arbela constituted the heartland of a state that subsequently governed much of the Middle East. Whenever regions were integrated as provinces, their inhabitants were counted as 'Assyrians', justified ideologically by their contribution to the worship of the god Aššur. By the late 13th century BC, Assyria controlled most of Mittani's former holdings. The western borders of the kingdom reached the Euphrates and the realm asserted itself politically and on the battlefield over its competitors in the south and north-west, the Babylonian and Hittite kingdoms.

When these states weakened and, in the case of the Hittite kingdom, completely disintegrated during the time of the great migrations marking the end of the Late Bronze Age, the political and social organization of their former territories changed drastically. Assyria, too, incurred territorial losses but maintained control over its well-protected heartland without any significant threats to the Assyrian monarchy and the kingdom's structure. In political discourse, the Arameans, one of the populations attested by sources of the 11th century BC to have been on the move, were cast in the role of the destructive intruders, whose unlawfully snatched territories must be absorbed back into the kingdom of Assyria, their rightful owner.

## The creation of an empire

Unlike the adjoining regions, Assyria had never lost its chariot troops and could afford to maintain this specialized branch of the armed forces financially and socially. This and the realm's extent, greatly exceeding that of the neighbouring states, gave the kingdom an advantage in its subsequent wars of conquest. They began in the 10th century, when contemporary Assyrian sources prominently cite the duty to recreate the lost realm and to rescue those Assyrians who had been left behind the retreating borders. By the mid-9th century BC, Assyria's former maximum extent had been re-established. The state in the resultant form is today called the 'Assyrian Empire'. Its political organization was profoundly transformed in the king's favour by the creation of the mega-city Kalhu as the imperial centre and a sustained and extensive programme of relocating its populations to best serve state interests.

A three-decade long period of territorial expansion meant that by 700 BC, the lands from the Mediterranean shore to Hamadan (Ecbatana) in Iran, from Cappadocia to the Persian Gulf were under direct Assyrian control. Until the late 7th century BC, the empire was the unrivalled political, economic, and cultural power of the Middle East and the wider Eastern Mediterranean region.

## The end of the empire

Then, however, Nabopolassar, king of the recently independent former client kingdom of Babylonia, and a Median army led by Cyaxares, began a decade-long war. In 614 BC the city of Aššur was captured and the temple of its god destroyed, followed in 612 BC by the loss of the then capital Nineveh and the life of the last rightful king Sin-šarru-iškun, who died defending his city and empire. Based in the city of Harran, the defence of the empire continued under the crown prince for a few more years. However, as he could no longer be crowned in the Aššur temple, the sacred custom that confirmed the king as the deity's representative and served as the ideological backbone of the imperial claim to power was painfully disrupted. As Aššur-uballit II, a name surely deliberately chosen to invoke the first Assyrian king of the 14th century BC, this last ruler was crowned in the temple of the moon god of Harran, one of the greatest Assyrian deities. But while this was good enough for Babylonian commentators, contemporary Assyrian sources suggest that he was still only considered the crown prince. The lack of Aššur's blessing must have severely damaged the authority of this last Assyrian ruler and not even the military support of allies from Egypt and the Iranian kingdom of Mannea could save the empire.

Most of the Assyrian heartland's population was resettled in Babylonia where Nabopolassar and his successor Nebuchadnezzar transformed their capital Babylon into an imperial centre to rival its Assyrian prototypes in Kalhu, Dur-Šarrukin, and Nineveh. No one took over the maintenance of these cities, whose enormous size and population could only be upheld with extensive and expensive regional irrigation systems supporting the fresh water supply. Without upkeep, the canals and aqueducts soon became dilapidated, never to be used again. At Nineveh, the bodies of those killed defending the city were never cleared away, as gruesome discoveries at Nineveh's Halzi Gate illustrate. At Kalhu, bodies of executed men were dumped in the well providing the citadel with drinking water, which illustrates a desire to destroy and spoil, rather than appropriate, the Assyrian heartland.

## Assyrian history after the empire

Assyrian history was not over, though. On the one hand, it continued in exile. In the southern Babylonian city of Uruk, a group of Assyrian expatriates maintained in the 6th century BC a small shrine devoted to god Aššur, and much later, in the 2nd century BC, when the city was part of the Seleucid Empire, typical Assyrian traditions in cult and scholarship were still practised. And in Aššur, the temple of its god was re-established after 539 BC, albeit on a much more modest scale. According to the Cyrus Cylinder, having conquered Babylonia, Cyrus the Great, king of Persia, granted permission to do so:

> From Babylon I sent back to their places, to the sanctuaries across the river Tigris whose shrines had earlier become dilapidated, the gods who lived therein: to Aššur, Susa, Akkad, Ešnunna, Zamban, Meturan, Der, as far as the border of Gutium (i.e. Zagros mountain range). I made permanent sanctuaries for them. I collected together all of their people and returned them to their settlements.

In this small shrine, documents pertaining to the god and his sanctuary from the early second millennium BC until its destruction in 614 BC were assembled and demonstrate a keen awareness and appreciation of the city's glorious past. In the 1st century AD, when Aššur had found wealth and prominence as a trading centre in the kingdom of Hatra, the shrine was again rebuilt on monumental scale.

At that time, there was already a well-established Christian community at Hatra (Bardaisan, *Liber legum regionum* 46), and perhaps Christianity was also practised in Aššur. In any case, while the new temple and Aššur's cult fell victim to the Sassanian conquest of the kingdom of Hatra in about AD 240, the Eastern Churches flourished subsequently and local Christian traditions found new roles for prominent figures and sites of Assyrian history, quite separate from the information recorded in the Bible. Hence, the city of Aššur and King Sennacherib appear in the legend of the 4th century AD martyr, Saint Behnam, who converted to Christianity after local holy man Saint Matthew (in Aramaic, Mar Mattai) had miraculously healed his sister. Sennacherib was cast as Behnam's royal father who ordered the prince's execution. In turn, the king was struck by a disease and only cured when he agreed to be baptized by Saint Matthew in the city of Aššur. Grateful, Sennacherib then founded the monastery of Deir Mar Mattai near Mosul, one of the centres of the Maphrianate of the East (i.e. the Syriac Orthodox Churches east of the Euphrates). Today, Syriac Christian groups of the Eastern Church from the former Assyrian heartland (Nestorians and Jacobites) identify themselves as 'Assyrians'. The origins of this view remain a matter of debate but they pre-date the spectacular archaeological discoveries of the mid-19th century that put Assyria on the map for the rest of the world.

# Chapter 2
# Assyrian places

In this chapter we encounter the city where everything started and the city where the empire of the first millennium first came together: Aššur and Kalhu are two of Iraq's most significant archaeological sites. A glimpse at the trading colony at Kaneš in Central Turkey will enable us to investigate Assyrian history of the early second millennium BC further afield, while Dur-Katlimmu, an important provincial centre in Syria, will serve to emphasize the impact of Assyria's expansion from the 13th century BC onwards. The story of the exploration of those key sites will give insight into Assyria's rediscovery since the mid-19th century.

## Aššur: the god and his sacred city

The city of Aššur (Figure 1) is situated at the southern edge of the core region of the Assyrian kingdom, a triangle formed by its three most important cities: Aššur, Nineveh in the north, and Arbela in the east. The Assyrian heartland covers an area of roughly 4,000 square kilometres and corresponds in size to, for example, the US state of Rhode Island (4,000 km²) or, in Britain, the county of Suffolk (3,800 km²). At the triangle's northern tip, underneath the urban sprawl of northern Iraq's largest city Mosul, lie the ruins of ancient Nineveh which have been excavated, on and off, since 1842. Nineveh oversees an important ford across the Tigris that is the natural terminus of the overland route leading along the

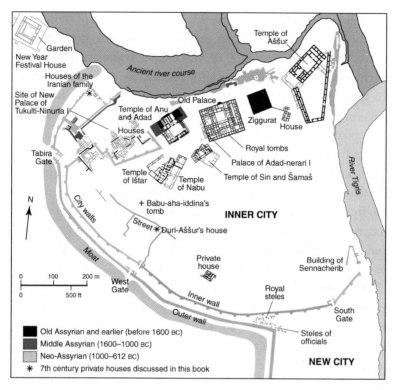

**1. The city of Aššur.**

southern foothills of the Taurus mountain range to the
Mediterranean coast and into Anatolia. At the triangle's eastern
tip, Arbela has kept its ancient name until today; as Erbil, it is
now the capital of the Kurdish Autonomous Region of Iraq. The
exploration of its archaeological heritage began only recently in
2006. Arbela is located on the western fringes of the Zagros
mountain range and controls various routes across the mountains
into Iran. Like Nineveh, the city of Aššur lies at an important
Tigris ford, but on the western riverbank. Situated in a
strategically excellent position on a rocky outcrop rising high over
a bend in the river, the site is a natural fortress. From there, one
controls the overland route leading west across the steppe into the
valleys of the Khabur and the Euphrates, and from there into
western Syria or across the Taurus mountains into Anatolia.

The Assyrian heartland occupied an important node of the overland trade network for the metals indispensable to the Middle Eastern economy. Tin, together with copper, was essential for the manufacture of the binary alloy bronze, the preferred material for tools and weapons from the fourth until well into the first millennium BC. From the Central Asian mines in what is today Afghanistan, Uzbekistan, and Tajikistan, tin was transported across Iran and into modern Iraq within easy reach of the Assyrian triangle. Silver was the preferred currency of the ancient Middle East and came primarily from Anatolian deposits, the fabled 'Silver Mountains'. The regions immediately to the north and east of the Assyrian heartland are occupied by the mountain ranges of Taurus and Zagros, which offer iron ore, timber, and stone as well as pasture for cattle and horses. Westwards lie the steppe lands of al-Jezira (the 'island' between Euphrates and Tigris); good grazing grounds for sheep. To the south lies Babylonia in the flood plain of Euphrates and Tigris whose promise of prosperity is closely linked to its ability to maintain large-scale and labour-intensive artificial irrigation through a network of canals, and therefore to the political organization of the region.

With the notable exception of Aššur, the Assyrian heartland lies on the eastern bank of the Tigris. Part of the Mediterranean climate zone, its agriculture is rain-fed and therefore fundamentally different from that of Babylonia, which is entirely dependent on artificial irrigation. The region is a natural breadbasket, nourished by very good soils in a flat physical environment favourable for large-scale cultivation. The main crops were barley and wheat, which were harvested in autumn. Aššur is situated on a geo-ecological border where the favourable Mediterranean climate gives way to the arid steppe zone. As the only central Assyrian city situated on the western bank of the Tigris, Aššur was a key contact point with the pastoralists who made use of this dry region with their sheep flocks, and its geographical position favoured its function as a trading centre. The city emerges as an important emporium most clearly in the texts dating to the early second millennium BC. The relatively limited material available from Aššur is complemented by the extremely rich textual sources from one of its trading colonies in Anatolia at the city of Kaneš.

## The god Aššur

Assyria's self-designation from the 14th century BC onwards is the 'land of Aššur' (*māt Aššur*). We call this state Assyria, using the Greek term. This obscures some of the nuances of its original name that refers as much to the city of Aššur, the state's original centre and the place of origin of its ruling dynasty, as to the deity of the same name whose ancient temple dominated that city. The god Aššur and the city of Aššur are inseparable, as the deity is the personification of the rocky crag called Qal'at Sherqat in Arabic that towers high above a bend of the river Tigris. Shaped like the prow of a ship, the roughly triangular crag rises 40 metres above the valley, providing shelter and opportunities for the people who settled there since at least the mid-third millennium BC. As the city developed, the natural defences provided in the north and east by the rock cliffs and the Tigris below were completed with a crescent-shaped fortification wall, resulting in an enclosed area of *c.*65 hectares.

Popular Assyrian names, such as Aššur-duri, 'The god Aššur is my fortress'; Dur-makî-Aššur, 'A fortress for the weak is the god Aššur'; Aššur-nemedi, 'The god Aššur is my base'; or Aššur-šaddî-ili, 'The god Aššur is a divine mountain', illustrate that the deity could be perceived as a very concrete space. A stone relief from the early second millennium BC (Figure 2) depicts Aššur accordingly: using the typical scale design reserved for mountains in Assyrian art, it shows the god as a rocky peak from which the torso of a bearded man emerges, accompanied by two deified fountains and sprouting plants that nourish two goats, the emblematic animals of the deity.

Aššur's shrine at the top of the crag was the heart of the city and later the land of Aššur. It was known under several names: as

**2. Stone relief depicting the god Aššur and two deified springs. From Aššur.**

Eamkurkurra 'The House of the Wild Bull of the Lands' in the early second millennium and as Ehursagkurkurra 'House of the Mountain of the Lands' in the later second millennium, and as Ešarra 'House of the Universe' in the first millennium BC. These names are all in the Sumerian language that was spoken in the south of Iraq in the third millennium, when the city of Aššur was first founded, and later continued to be used in ritual and scholarship.

As the site of the one and only temple of the god, the city of Aššur was the nucleus of his realm and for millennia, and the inhabitants cared for the sanctuary until its last manifestation was destroyed in *c.* AD 240. In the 12th century BC, a ruler called Ušpia, thought to have lived a millennium earlier, was credited with the construction of the earliest version of the huge temple complex that at that time occupied the top of the crag. The Assyrian ruler was considered Aššur's human agent, invested by the deity's grace with the power to rule and at the same time also his head priest, lending him religious as well as political authority. Ušpia and his successors had the privilege and duty to care for the god's temple and numerous inscriptions found in the sanctuary celebrate building work undertaken at the sanctuary.

## Excavating Aššur

The sanctuary of Aššur was explored during the German excavations from 1903 to 1914 led by Walter Andrae who lived and worked there for over a decade, investigating Aššur and nearby sites with the help of a few assistants, usually, like Andrae himself, architects by training, and hundreds of local workmen. In Iraq, specialized archaeological excavators are called Sherqatis because the profession originated with Andrae's workers at Qal'at Sherqat. Most of the objects unearthed during these excavations are now in the Vorderasiatisches Museum in Berlin and in the Oriental Museum in Istanbul, as the finds were divided between the German Oriental Society that funded the work and the Ottoman authorities who controlled Iraq at that time. In addition to some German excavations, Iraqi teams have continued sporadically with the exploration of Aššur since 1978, but it is Andrae's many years of uninterrupted work at the site that forms the basis of our detailed knowledge of the city. Andrae excavated the northern part of the site where the Aššur temple complex, including its massive stepped tower, is surrounded by other sanctuaries and the royal palaces. Trained as an architect, his main objective was to recover the ground plans of these monumental structures and to reconstruct their building history. But he also wanted to understand the city as a whole and therefore methodically excavated trenches, 10 metres wide, across the entire site, one every 100 metres. In this way, he uncovered parts of many private houses from the last period of the Assyrian Empire. When Aššur was captured in 614 by the forces of Cyaxares, king of the Medes, many of these houses were set on fire—in contrast to the monumental buildings which were thoroughly looted before their destruction, the excavation of the private quarters has yielded a great many finds, including clay tablets that were baked in the fires and thus ideally conserved. These texts, in the main legal documents but also letters and in some cases substantial libraries of scholarly and literary compositions, provide exceptional insight into the lives of Aššur's inhabitants in the 7th century BC. We will encounter some of them in chapters 3 and 5.

The houses had underground tombs where the dead of the family were buried, usually constructed underneath the innermost room where the family's archive was kept. The crypts were preserved even when the houses were rebuilt or razed. Andrae uncovered several dating back to the second millennium BC, including in 1908 the very rich burials of men and women of the family of Babu-aha-iddina ('Tomb 45'), part of whose archive was discovered near the entry shaft leading to the underground vault. The letters and administrative texts document the private business activities of this high-ranking state official who served under several kings in the 13th century BC and draw attention to the household's broad range of specialized manufacturing, which concentrated on creating expensive finished products such as perfumes, chariots, composite bows, and luxury leather and textile goods, using rare materials procured over large distances. The beautiful objects with which two bodies, thought to be Babu-aha-iddina and his wife, were placed on the remains of the earlier family burials include elaborate jewellery of gold and precious stones, intricately carved ivory combs, pins, and containers, and sumptuously decorated stone vessels—giving a vivid impression of the luxurious lifestyle that the Assyrian elite enjoyed at a time when the kingdom had become the leading political power of the Middle East.

## The one temple of the god Aššur

One of the main objectives of Walter Andrae's excavations was the exploration of the Aššur temple. But his investigation barely reached the earlier parts of the sanctuary because they are covered by massive later constructions, all executed in mud-brick, the traditional Middle Eastern building material. The oldest connected structures that Andrae was able to uncover date to the beginning of the second millennium BC, at a time when income from the booming trade colonies in Anatolia swelled the coffers of the city. The earliest building inscriptions recovered from the temple date to the period of the foundation of these colonies and were written in the name of Erišum I. They describe how this ruler dedicated a new throne for the god Aššur and how private houses were cleared away in order to increase the area reserved for the sanctuary. About the Aššur shrine, Erišum writes:

> The name of that temple is 'Wild Bull', the name of the door is 'Protective Goddess', the name of the lock is 'Be Strong!' and the name of the threshold is 'Be Alert!'

The sanctuary and its constituent parts were considered animate, even sentient. They and all objects used in the temple were created and maintained by expert craftsmen: builders, carpenters, smiths, goldsmiths, scribes, and others. The temple craftsmen were also responsible for the fashioning and awakening (with a ritual called the 'Opening of the Mouth') of the statues of Aššur and the other gods revered at the city. Some had their own temples, like Ištar, the goddess of sex and battle, of whose repeatedly rebuilt shrine Andrae's excavations managed to expose the inner sanctuary of the early third millennium, with the stone statues of the goddess's worshippers lining its walls. The storm god Adad and the sky god Anu shared a temple as did the moon god Sin and the sun god Šamaš, but most deities were worshipped in Aššur's vast sacred complex.

Over time, as the Assyrian realm grew, more and more gods came to 'live' in the Aššur temple, in part the result of the practice of seizing the divine statues of defeated enemies and relocating them in Aššur's shrine. So long was the list of the temple's occupants by the first millennium BC that a learned text called today the Divine Directory of Aššur was composed to chart the complex topography of the sanctuary. The statues of gods were seen as manifestations of the deities, and by staying as Aššur's guests, or hostages, in his home, these gods accepted, for all to see, Aššur's sovereignty. When in c.700 BC King Sennacherib, for example, captured statues of Attar-šamayin, Day, Nuhay, Rudaw, Abir-ilu, and Attar-qurumâ, 'the gods of the Arabs', from the oasis of Adummatu (Dumat al-Jandal in Saudi-Arabia) and placed them in the Aššur temple, this had immediate political implications for the Arab tribes. They found themselves deserted by their gods who moreover seemed to recognize Aššur as their host and overlord. The strategy of god-napping was designed to persuade enemies or reluctant allies to follow their deities' lead and to accept Assyrian dominion. It was often successful, as in this case.

It was the privilege and duty of the servants of Aššur to provide their god with regular sacrifices that were presented to him in the form of a daily feast. Sheep, cattle, and poultry and other ingredients for these meals, namely barley, wheat, emmer (hulled wheat), sesame, honey, and seasonal fruit including apples and figs, were periodically delivered from all regions of his dominion to the sanctuary. These ingredients were not especially rare and could easily have been procured by other means. That they had to be provided, in relatively small quantities but regularly, from all across the realm, sometimes over vast distances, may have made little logistic sense but was of paramount ideological importance: all subjects of Aššur had to participate jointly in the care for the god. In this way, the realm was defined as the community of Aššur's worshippers. Conversely, the refusal to provide for the god's meal was of course considered an act of treason.

Once the ingredients arrived at Aššur, the temple's butchers, bakers, brewers, and oil-pressers—all of them men—processed the materials and prepared the dishes that were then served to Aššur. Culinary specialists may perhaps not immediately match commonly held connotations of priesthood, but in a context where the ritual preparation and celebration of a daily feast in honour of the deity was at the core of temple worship, they were naturally among the priestly personnel. Like the craftsmen responsible for temple and cultic objects, all kitchen staff had to be ritually pure in order to interact so intimately with the deity. As a visible marker of their purity, all temple staff had to be clean-shaven. Whereas other Assyrian men typically sported shoulder-length hair and full beards (except for the eunuchs who served the empire in key roles from the 9th century BC onwards), the temple staff had to be bald and without facial hair. Only in the 7th century BC were these rules somewhat relaxed, and some of Aššur's kitchen staff 'stood with hair' for several years before they were shaven.

In 1911 Andrae found more than 650 clay tablets in one of the buildings of the temple complex for Aššur, archived in ten large ceramic containers, which held parts of the records of four successive temple administrators responsible for the organization of the god's meals in the 12th and early 11th century BC. When the building was structurally modified at a time when these records were no longer relevant, the heavy pots were simply left in place and buried within the new construction. As the documents record deliveries from all twenty-seven provinces constituting the kingdom, they allow the detailed reconstruction of the political organization of

Assyria, encompassing at that time the lands from the Euphrates to the Lower Zab. Even when the royal court and the centre of political power and government were moved away from Aššur in the imperial period—to Kalhu in 879 BC, then to Dur-Šarrukin in 706 BC, and finally to Nineveh around 700 BC—the feast of Aššur continued to be organized in the established way by involving all provinces (about seventy-five by the 670s BC). As administrative texts found at the royal palace in Nineveh demonstrate, organizing Aššur's menu remained a matter of state importance.

As gods were thought to consume their meals by smelling, the 'leftovers' of Aššur's feast, as the dishes were called once they had been removed from the offering table, could be further distributed. A strict protocol governed who received which parts of the leftovers, with cuts of meat being considered the most prestigious. The Assyrian ruler, regarded as the earthly representative of the god Aššur, naturally topped the list of recipients that embraced temple staff and dignitaries from across the realm, including the provincial governors. In order to reach these, the dishes had to be transported over considerable distances, just as had previously the ingredients from which they had been prepared. That the food was no longer fresh was not an issue, as to eat from the divine feast was a blessing rather than a culinary experience: 'Whoever eats the leftovers will live,' as one royal official put it in the 7th century BC. Partaking in Aššur's meal in this manner was a huge privilege and bound the Assyrian officials together and to the god, no matter how far away from his temple they were based. Even when abandoned as the political centre after 879, the city of Aššur never lost its fundamental ideological importance.

## The city of Aššur after Assyria

The temple quarter of Aššur was called Libbali 'Heart of the City', a designation first attested in texts of the 13th century BC, although very likely older. The name came to be used as a synonym for the entire city, presumably as this avoided confusion with god and country. According to the geographical compendia of Ptolemy of Alexandria (2nd century AD; as Labbana) and Stephen of Byzantium (6th century AD; as Libana) and possibly also the Tabula Peutingeriana (AD 1200 copy of an original Roman map; misspelt as Sabbin), the city was still known under this name much later in the Roman imperial period when it was part of the kingdom of Hatra. At that time, the cult of Aššur (now called Assor) continued to be practised according to the by now millennia old traditions and festival calendar, albeit with a contemporary veneer. The temple had been rebuilt in modern Parthian-style architecture and the inhabitants of the city now invoked the deity with their Arabic, rather than Assyrian, names. But the cult was of local importance only and it was the city lords, rather than the kings of nearby Hatra, who were the patrons of the sanctuary. They saw themselves firmly in the tradition of the Assyrian kings of old, as perhaps best illustrated by the inscribed steles erected in the gateway leading to the Assor temple. They share the typical rounded shape of the Assyrian royal steles (see Figure 8) and show city lords like R'uth-Assor ('Joy of Aššur') in the same gesture of prayer as the Assyrian kings on their monuments, albeit in a Parthian-style trouser suit rather than the traditional Assyrian shawl garment and with an inscription in alphabetic Aramaic instead of Assyrian cuneiform (Figure 3).

The invasions of the kingdom of Hatra under the Sassanian kings Ardashir I and Shapur I from AD 240 onwards led to the violent destruction of the Assor temple and the entire city and the dispersal of its inhabitants. In later periods, the crag often served as a fortress, most recently in Ottoman times—small wonder, given its excellent strategic position. But the sanctuary and the cult of Aššur were never revived, although the desolate remnants of the ruined stepped tower of the Assyrian temple serve even now as a haunting reminder of the time when this great shrine was the religious hub of an empire stretching from the Mediterranean to Central Iran.

3. Stele of R'uth-Assor, Master (Maryo) of Labbana/Assor.

# Kaneš: a 'harbour' in Central Turkey

Long before sacrifices for the god Aššur reached his city from regions beyond the Taurus Mountains, treaties were sworn in his name to protect the interests of his city and its inhabitants. According to these, Aššur is not the unrivalled master of the universe who stipulates his will. Instead, he stands on equal footing with the deities who were thought to guide and guard the other parties: the rulers of the Anatolian principalities in the early second millennium BC. As agreed in these treaties and protected by oath, the local leaders allowed the Assyrian traders free passage and, depending on the location, the right of residency in a trading colony in return for a cut of their profits.

One of the most important treaty partners was the ruler of Kaneš, today one of the best-explored archaeological sites in Central Turkey. It is situated about 20 kilometres from the modern city of Kayseri and dominates a fertile plain where several long-distance routes meet that connect western and northern Anatolia with Syria. The site's modern name Kültepe means 'ash mound'. This refers to the fact that during its long existence from *c.*3000 BC to the early Roman period, the ancient settlement was repeatedly destroyed by fire, which left behind huge ash layers. As always in this case, this proved beneficial for the survival of the clay tablets used as writing material by the city's inhabitants in the early second millennium BC, because they were baked and conserved in this way. In 1881 the first cuneiform texts from Kültepe came to the attention of scholars who called them 'Cappadocian tablets', after the classical name for the Central Anatolian plateau, as this was all that was known about their origin. Written in an early dialect of Assyrian and in a particular form of the cuneiform script that used fewer than 200 characters, the tablets' contents allowed them to be linked to the city of Aššur. The realization that merchants from northern Iraq had established colonies some 1,000 kilometres away from their city caused great interest in the tablets and in the puzzle of their origin.

But for over forty years, the local people who periodically dug the tablets up at Kültepe (Figure 4) and sold them to antiquities dealers managed to keep their source a secret, despite the fact that several archaeological missions investigated the site, always focusing their attention on the high mound. The locals had discovered the tablets when digging for ancient mud-brick, traditionally used throughout the Middle East as fertilizer and building material—to the dismay of archaeologists, as this practice is very destructive. Some 2,500 tablets were unearthed and bought up by various European and American museums and private collectors. Only in 1925, the mystery of the origin of the Cappadocian tablets was solved by the drunken indiscretion of a local coachman in the employ of Bedřich Hrozný, the Czech orientalist famous for his decipherment of Hittite, which he identified as an Indo-European language. Hrozný had recently started excavations at Kültepe and when his driver revealed that the tablets did not come from the

4. Satellite image of Kültepe, showing the extent of the excavations: the palaces and temples of Kaneš on the circular high mound and the merchant quarters in the lower town adjoining the mound in the north-east.

mound but from a site in the lower town, his team quickly found over a thousand tablets in what turned out to be the ruins of the Assyrian merchant quarters. Since 1948 the mound and the lower town have been investigated in yearly excavations under the auspices of Türk Tarih Kurumu, the Turkish Historical Society founded by Mustafa Kemal Atatürk in 1930 to promote the study of Turkey's past. The exploration of Kültepe is among the organization's flagship activities and profoundly shaped by the life's work of Ankara archaeologist couple Tahsin and Nimet Özgüç who excavated there from 1948 to 2005. The finds from the site are kept in the Museum of Anatolian Civilizations at Ankara, with highlights on display in the fine gallery devoted to Kültepe.

The Assyrian tablets allow the identification of Kültepe with the city of Kaneš. With an area of over 20 hectares and a height of c.20 metres, its circular high mound is one of the largest in central Anatolia. The walled enclosure of a lower town takes up a crescent-shaped area of more than 100 hectares surrounding the high mound from the north, east, and south. The settlement is therefore considerably larger than the city of Aššur. Judging from the limited area of just under 9 hectares where Assyrian clay tablets are being found, the merchants from Aššur inhabited a particular quarter of this extensive lower town that was in the main populated by local people. The texts identify the Assyrian quarter as 'The Harbour' (kārum) of Kaneš, using the usual Assyrian word for a trading post; in the Middle East these were typically established in a waterside setting, albeit not in the case of Kaneš. In contrast to the three-millennia long occupation of the mound, the lower town was used only in the first part of the second millennium BC for a period of about three centuries. It was rebuilt several times and the houses of the Assyrian traders date to the lower town's settlement level II and, after a massive fire had engulfed the lower town, level Ib. The tablets found in these buildings constitute the archives of the Assyrian trading firms based at Kaneš. Assyrian texts from this period have been found elsewhere at a few sites in central Anatolia but amount to merely *c.*150 tablets and fragments in total, a tiny number compared to the staggering figure of 23,500 clay tablets recovered so far from Kaneš. The vast majority of these texts date to a period of about fifty years in the 19th century BC. Only 4,500 tablets have been published, mostly the early finds, with preliminary editions of another 5,000 texts from the Turkish excavations awaiting publication. Much remains to be done.

## Assyrian trade in Anatolia

The archives of the Assyrian merchants at Kaneš allow the reconstruction of their business and private activities in amazing detail. They document the traders' lives at Kaneš, and especially the organization of their business enterprises, but also give insight into contemporary Aššur, where only very limited evidence for this period has been uncovered due to the fact that massive later occupational levels cover the relevant archaeological layers. Most of what we know about Aššur's political and social circumstances derives from the Kaneš material. Fortunately for us, the Assyrians based abroad were keen to stay closely informed about news from home and corresponded extensively with family members and business associates in Aššur, usually simply called 'The City' (*ālum*). The majority of known documents from Kaneš are letters. They consist of an inner tablet with the text, around which a thin coat of clay was wrapped as an inscribed envelope that identified sender and addressee and was impressed with the sender's seal but otherwise protected the confidentiality of the letter. This format is generally used for Assyrian letters and also in evidence for the later cuneiform correspondence of the second and first millennium BC.

During the roughly two centuries of the Assyrian traders' residence there, Kaneš was the capital of a regional state whose ruler, designated as 'prince' (*ruba'um*) by the Assyrians, resided in a palace on the fortified high mound. The lower town was structured by open squares and paved streets, underneath which sewage drains led away the wastewater. Six to eight two-storey houses, built back to back, formed the building blocks that made up the lower town's residential quarters. By far the best explored is the quarter inhabited by the Assyrians whose houses were built in the local style. Private buildings had a residential part with living rooms and kitchen and a smaller, lockable part where valuables were kept, including the cuneiform documents of the Assyrians, which were filed according to content and stored on shelves or inside containers (pots, wooden chests, or bags). The dead were typically buried with their grave goods in coffins or cist graves (resembling a stone-built box) underneath the houses, and this is also attested for the buildings occupied by Assyrians, although the texts indicate that they typically hoped to die and be laid to rest in Aššur.

The Assyrian traders specialized in the import of tin, procured in Aššur from distant supplies, and luxury textiles produced in that city and elsewhere by domestic manufacture. They transported these goods overland with caravans of donkeys, each carrying *c.*65 kilograms (=130 minas) of tin. The small but very heavy ingots were wrapped up in bales of fabric that were carefully balanced across the donkeys' backs and sides in order to spare them from discomfort and their owners from the expense of replacing ruined animals. Four-wheeled, ox-drawn carts with loading capacities of between 300 and 1,500 kilograms were used whenever good enough roads were available. Once at Kaneš, the merchants deposited their merchandise in the spacious storerooms of the palace up on the citadel, which, as the texts show, were used as central storage facilities. The strong-rooms in the traders' private houses will have mainly served to keep the silver and gold safe, into which the Assyrian traders converted their returns for the transport back to Aššur. But much of their economy functioned without cash purely on the basis of credit, anticipating key strategies employed in much more recent times by merchant banks.

The prince of Kaneš collaborated closely with the merchants, as he took a cut of all their business in return for residency rights and protection within his territory, both for the caravans and the Assyrians living there. They were not regarded as his subjects, as the merchant quarter was politically and legally considered an extraterritorial part of the city-state of Aššur. Even during local hostilities the caravans were to pass unharmed—the Assyrians, who had little military power (and certainly none in Anatolia), were keen to protect their neutrality. In turn, as stipulated by treaty, the prince was entitled to taxes of *c*.3 per cent on the imported tin (that is, 4 minas per donkey load) and of 5 per cent on the textiles, with the option of buying another 10 per cent of the fabrics at market price. The prince's treaty partner was 'the city of Aššur, the citizens of Aššur and the "harbour"', which was not just the physical location of the Assyrian trading quarter at Kaneš but also the name for the collective body of traders operating there.

The agreements between the prince of Kaneš and the Assyrian merchant collective can be reconstructed from references in various texts but are also laid down in detail in an original treaty tablet that was found in 2000 in one of the houses of the second occupational phase of the Assyrian merchant quarter (level Ib). The trader collective also conducted treaties with the rulers of the kingdoms that the caravans traversed on their way to Kaneš, such as Apum (region of modern Qamishli in north-eastern Syria) and Hahhum (region of the modern Turkish city of Samsat), where another Assyrian 'harbour' was located, this time indeed waterside near an important ford across the Euphrates. Recorded in another original treaty tablet found together with the one concerning Kaneš, the stipulations assuring free passage and protection intriguingly include a guarantee not to sabotage the ferry and sink the merchandise—an indication that such acts of river piracy might have otherwise come to pass. Instead of an outright entitlement to levy taxes, the dignitaries of Hahhum were given the right to buy certain quantities of the Assyrian caravans' tin and fabric at discounted prices.

Its favourable position in the overland route network made Kaneš a very good choice for the Assyrians to use as the central base of their commercial activities, with a network of smaller outlets administrated from there. It took the caravans five to six weeks to cover the distance of c.1,200 kilometres from Aššur to Kaneš. But the traders operated on a much larger geographical scope and maintained similar bases elsewhere at the capitals of over a dozen Anatolian realms. The most important are the 'harbours' at the cities of Durhumit, perhaps situated close to sizable copper deposits and the Black Sea in the plain of Merzifon (250 kilometres north of Kaneš), and Purušhaddum, now thought to correspond to Üçhöyük near Bolvadin (385 kilometres west of Kaneš). Transport costs and taxes, rather than time and distance, determined where business was going to be profitable. If the price was right the Assyrian merchants were willing to travel very far. Aššur's involvement in Anatolia ceased when the emergence of large territorial states robbed the trader collective of the legal and political basis making long-distance trade lucrative.

## Kalhu: a capital fit for an empire

In 879 BC the city of Aššur was stripped of its traditional role as the seat of political power and state administration when King Aššurnasirpal II moved the court to a new location. His choice fell on Kalhu (Figure 5), an ancient city that was transformed into the unrivalled imperial centre during his reign and that of his son and successor Shalmaneser III.

Whereas Assyria's extent in the 9th century mirrored its boundaries in the 12th century BC, before the migrations at the end of the Bronze Age, its role in the wider region was now markedly different. It was an imperial power, no longer surrounded by states of comparable size and manpower but by much smaller principalities. Once Assyria had reclaimed the territories it had lost in the west and north, the state exceeded its

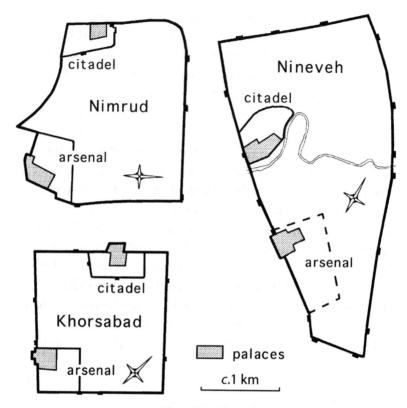

5. The Assyrian capital cities Kalhu (Nimrud), Dur-Šarrukin (Khorsabad), and Nineveh.

neighbours in extent and manpower many times over. The success of the reconquest allowed the Assyrian king to assume a new role of hegemon over his neighbours. Kalhu was conceived and created as the capital city for the new imperial power, its architecture designed to overwhelm and impress.

Kalhu is situated in a uniquely central position in the Assyrian heartland. It is very advantageously positioned inside the triangle formed by the three most important cities of Central Assyria and well connected to all of them: Aššur in the south, Nineveh in the north, and Arbela in the east. The city lies on the eastern bank of the Tigris, controlling a ford just north of its confluence with the Upper Zab. It has therefore direct access to the two principal waterways of the region and moreover a crossing over the Tigris, linking it to the west. On that river, Kalhu is located between Nineveh and Aššur and, thanks to a canal linking the city with the Upper Zab, there is also a direct river connection with Arbela. The distance from Kalhu to Aššur is *c.*70 kilometres, to Arbela *c.*60 kilometres, and to Nineveh *c.*35 kilometres as the crow flies. Travelling to and from either of these cities, therefore, takes a day, two at most, depending on the direction and the mode of travel, but in any case about half the time it takes to cover the distance between any of the three cities themselves. Moreover, Kalhu held an important position in the long-distance traffic network, both over land and on the rivers. It was a stop on the north–south route along the Tigris and controlled a key route leading in eastern direction via Arbela towards the Zagros Mountains and, along their western fringes, southwards into Babylonia.

## Excavating Kalhu

Today, Kalhu's ruins are known as Nimrud, after a local tradition that connected the site to the Biblical figure of Nimrod, a grandson of Noah, who was the first human to claim kingship and credited with the foundation of Assyria. Nimrud is one of Iraq's most important archaeological sites.

Its investigation started in November 1845 with the British explorer Austen Henry Layard whose subsequent books on his travels and discoveries were extremely popular at the time of their publication and remain among the most readable travelogues documenting the Middle East. Inspired and guided by the work of pioneering Frenchman Paul-Émile Botta at what turned out to be Sargon II's capital city of Dur-Šarrukin, Layard's very first scrapings on Nimrud's citadel mound immediately yielded inscribed stone reliefs from what was afterwards identified as the palace of King Aššurnasirpal II. By employing an approach borrowed from mining, Layard was able to explore much of that building through a system of tunnelling, despite the very modest funding available for his activities. This way of working had little in common with the careful archaeological excavation methods that Andrae first used in Aššur some sixty years later, but yielded fast and spectacular results, especially in the form of intricately carved wall reliefs and other stone sculptures. Layard at first mistakenly thought that he had found Nineveh at Nimrud, but he later excavated at the actual city of Nineveh, digging on the Kuyunjik mound. He continued his digs until 1851, mainly with the goal to find as many antiquities as possible that could be transported back to Britain.

For a few decades, Assyria captured the imagination of 19th century audiences. A stream of newspaper articles kept the public abreast of the discoveries of Layard, his associate Hormuzd Rassam, and other pioneers taking up work on Assyrian sites. The first public showing of Assyrian objects was held in 1847 at the Louvre in Paris, followed in 1852 by the exhibition of Layard's finds at the British Museum, both pulling enormous crowds. Subsequently, stone sculptures from Nimrud were put on permanent display in the Assyrian Gallery of the British Museum and elsewhere in the world, as surplus materials were passed on to other European and American museums and collections. When the first Assyrian artefacts arrived in Europe, the craze of public interest led to the mass manufacture of various Assyrian-inspired luxury products such as jewellery, silver cutlery, and fireplace ornaments.

The general curiosity in all things Assyrian and the quick publication of the Assyrian inscriptions found at Nimrud and elsewhere made attempting to decipher the cuneiform script a favourite challenge for the linguistically minded, greatly aided by the realization that Assyrian was a Semitic language, like Hebrew and Arabic. By 1857, a competition organized by the Royal Asiatic Society in London served to demonstrate publicly the decipherment of Assyrian. Since these heady days of Assyromania, excavations at Nimrud have continued, on and off, mainly conducted by British and Iraqi archaeologists, and while they tended to concentrate on the citadel mound, there has also been work conducted on Tell Azar, the second citadel mound, and in the lower city.

Nimrud's most famous excavator since Layard was arguably not a professional archaeologist but crime novelist Agatha Christie, whose husband Max Mallowan directed the British excavations between 1949 and 1957. She photographed and registered finds and notably repurposed her expensive skin lotion to clean and strengthen the fragile ivory carvings that once decorated elaborate palace furniture and luxury objects. By writing murder mysteries such as 'They Came to Baghdad' on site, she continued Layard's tradition of authoring best-sellers inspired by work at Nimrud. The excavations during the 19th century only resulted in the discovery of a single cuneiform clay tablet, presumably because the unfired clay tablets were not recognized. During Mallowan's time at Nimrud and afterwards, Kalhu yielded a number of important textual finds. Particular highpoints are the so-called Nimrud Letters, some 300 letters from the Assyrian state correspondence of kings Tiglath-pileser III and Sargon II, unearthed in 1952, and multiple copies of the covenant imposed in 672 BC by King Esarhaddon on his subjects, found in 1955.

The most spectacular discoveries at Nimrud are the result of routine conservation measures undertaken by the Iraqi Antiquities Service which led in 1988 and 1989 to the unexpected detection of three undisturbed royal tombs underneath Aššurnasirpal's palace. These housed the burials of several Assyrian queens of the 9th and 8th centuries BC whose sumptuous grave goods include over fifty kilograms of intricately crafted gold jewellery and luxury vessels made of gold and rock crystal, many with inscriptions. When excavated, bodies and garments were in relatively good condition, but although anthropological and fibre analyses were quickly initiated, the start of the Gulf War in 1990 and subsequent trade sanctions have prevented the burials from being studied in the scientific detail that this extraordinary discovery merits. So far, the precious finds have only ever been on public display for very short periods of time. Most of the time they have been locked away in a bank vault, but in this way, they have survived Iraq's tumultuous recent history relatively unscathed. Whenever the time comes for the Iraq Museum in Baghdad to put these objects on permanent display, they will hopefully attract the public attention they so richly deserve.

Most of the archaeological exploration of Nimrud so far has concentrated on the first millennium BC. Only occasionally, earlier materials have been exposed. While the foundation of the settlement is thought to go back to the sixth millennium BC, small-scale excavations on the citadel mound have succeeded in unearthing pottery and flint finds going back to the beginning of the third millennium BC. But it is in the early second millennium BC, during the time of Samsi-Addu, that the city emerges clearly as a site of trans-regional significance. Known at the time as Kawalhum, it appears in texts from the palace archives of Mari in Syria, where Samsi-Addu had appointed his younger son as regent, as an important port on the Tigris, and a richly equipped stone tomb with a bronze battle-axe, found in 1854 on the citadel mound, dates to that same period. Once the kingdom of Assyria was established in the 14th century BC, the city was the capital of a province, a status that it held until the end of the 7th century BC when the state ceased to exist.

## The king's city and the king's people

Kalhu's position within Assyria was most prominent during the time from 879 to 706 BC, when it was the political centre of the empire. The city was elevated to its new role not only at the expense of Aššur, which it replaced as the main residence of the king, but also at the expense of Nineveh and Arbela. Due to

Aššur's peripheral location within the Assyrian state, these cities were economic and political centres in their own right, of almost the same importance as Aššur and, at least in Nineveh's case, with their own royal palace. Just as the cult of Aššur regularly demanded the king's attention and presence, the special significance of the cults of Ištar of Nineveh and Ištar of Arbela for the state required the king to spend considerable amounts of time in these cities in order to take his place in their festivals. By elevating Kalhu to the new imperial centre, the influence of all three cities, and their inhabitants, within the state was substantially weakened.

One can easily argue that the creation of the new centre was part of a larger strategy designed to strengthen the position of the king at the expense of the old urban elites. While they had previously played an important role in the political life of the Assyrian state, the highest administrative and military offices were from now on reserved for a new cadre of civil servants, the eunuchs (*ša rēši*, literally 'He of the head', i.e. 'personal attendant' of the king, contrasted with uncastrated officials called *ša ziqni*, 'He of the beard'). It is unclear today what qualities or qualifications were looked for in a boy or who made the fundamental decision to turn him into a eunuch. Nor is anything known about the eunuchs' original family backgrounds—but there is no reason to think that being made a eunuch was considered a terrible fate and one cannot necessarily assume that future eunuchs were forced into this life. It is quite possible that the eunuchs were in fact members of the same old families who previously held political offices, perhaps younger sons who could not expect to inherit much. Being a royal eunuch guaranteed high social status and a place in the king's household for life. But by sacrificing their ability to father children, the eunuchs gave up family life for good. They did not marry and were without any distraction at the state's and the king's disposal—the perfect employees. In return, the royal family shouldered the obligations normally expected from one's family, including the funeral and the subsequent offerings necessary to guarantee well-being in the afterlife. Yet despite being so very close to royal power, a eunuch could never hope to become king. Assyrian kingship required a man to be perfect in all respects, and a eunuch, with his mutilated body, was therefore categorically excluded.

The residents of the new imperial centre were handpicked by one of the royal eunuchs, the Palace Overseer Nergal-apil-kumu'a, whom Aššurnasirpal appointed by edict to oversee the move to Kalhu. The city's development changed settlement patterns not only in the Assyrian heartland but all over the empire, as suitable settlers were chosen from all provinces. We can safely assume that only those who had showed enthusiasm for the king and his plans for the Assyrian state were picked, thus creating in 879 BC not just a new political centre, but one that was populated by loyal supporters of king and empire. By creating new patterns of authority and allegiance, both socially and geographically, Aššurnasirpal was successful in changing the power structures that had previously defined Central Assyria. The move to Kalhu reinforced and secured the pre-eminence of the king and the state administration and provided the emerging Neo-Assyrian Empire with one unrivalled centre and a guaranteed power base of loyal supporters.

Architecturally, the ancient city of Kalhu was completely transformed. In order to provide the water needed for the maintenance of the new mega-city, a regional canal system was constructed. No expense was spared as the gigantic building project was calculated to show off Assyria's wealth to the world. The old settlement mound, having grown to a substantial height in the course of its long occupation, was turned into a fortified citadel that housed the royal palace and temples. But despite its size, it occupied only a small part in the south-western corner of the much larger city. With an area of about 360 hectares, Aššurnasirpal's Kalhu covered an area the multiple of the surface of Aššur and was surrounded by a 7.5 kilometre-long fortification wall. A second fortified citadel mound in the south-eastern corner of the city housed the arsenal where military equipment was stored and the army mustered. This basic plan was used also for the subsequent Assyrian capitals. The temples established at Kalhu were dedicated to the most important deities of Assyria, such as Ištar (but in the guise of the Lady of Kadmuri, distinct from her manifestations in Nineveh and Arbela), Ninurta, and Nabu, but there was no shrine for Aššur whose only sanctuary remained in the city of Aššur. Kalhu's purpose was to celebrate the king, not Aššur, as the nucleus of the empire.

At the time of Aššurnasirpal, Kalhu's most impressive building was certainly his new royal palace, called today the Northwest Palace due to its position on the citadel. With a length of 200 metres and a width of 130 metres, this gigantic building dominated its surroundings and, in an inversion of the topography of Aššur, dwarfed the neighbouring temples. Colossal human-headed winged bulls, perhaps the most iconic expression of Assyrian imperial architecture (Figure 6), guarded the monumental gates and provided Layard with a formidable logistical challenge when he shipped some of them back to London. Cedar trunks imported from Lebanon, with a length of up to 30 metres they were the longest roof beams available anywhere, allowed the construction of halls of unprecedented dimensions. The palace was organized around three courtyards with state apartments, an administrative wing, and the private quarters of the royal family, where the underground tombs of the queens were uncovered. This ground plan became the template for representative buildings all over the Assyrian Empire, such as the mansion of Šulmu-šarri at Dur-Katlimmu (see Chapter 3). Huge alabaster slabs with engraved figures and inscriptions celebrated the king's achievements and lined the walls of the palace's state apartments (see Figure 12). In particular, the throne room where Aššurnasirpal received dignitaries from all over the empire and beyond was decorated with scenes of heroic conquest and its results, the spoils, tribute, and gifts from the subdued adversaries. According to the inscription of a stele that was erected

6. Colossal winged human-headed bull from King Aššurnasirpal II's Northwest Palace at Kalhu, excavated by A. H. Layard.

inside the palace, 69,574 persons participated in the inaugural celebrations for the new city, the inhabitants of Kalhu joined by people from all over the empire and 5,000 foreign dignitaries from the adjacent states. Aššurnasirpal wined and dined his guests for ten days in a feast whose menu is preserved on the stele: 17,000 sheep and cattle and twice as many ducks, geese, and pigeons were slaughtered, meaning that every participant could expect to eat half a bird and a very sizeable portion of mutton and beef. These main courses were supplemented by venison, fish, and (less to our taste) rodents, enormous quantities of vegetables, fruit, and spices, and a broad range of dairy products, while 10,000 tubs of beer and 10,000 skins of wine provided relief for the thirsty.

Kalhu served as the main residence of all Assyrian kings up to Sargon II, who moved the court to his new imperial capital of Dur-Šarrukin, 'The Fortress of Sargon', in 706 BC. Several of Aššurnasirpal's successors established their own palaces in addition to the Northwest Palace that continued to be used as the provincial governor's residence. Iraqi archaeologists only recently excavated the palace of Adad-nerari III in 1993. The palace of Tiglath-pileser III is today known prosaically as the Central Palace, but this does not do its ancient name justice: 'Palaces of joy which bear abundance and bless the king who made their structure everlasting.' The ceremonial name given to the palace gateway makes it clear how Kalhu was seen not just as the centre of Assyria but of the entire world:

> Gates of justice which pass fair judgement on the rulers of the four corners of the world, which offer the tribute from the mountains and the sea, which admit the produce of mankind before the king, their lord.

The stone parts of both these palaces were ransacked in the 7th century to provide building materials for a new palace of Esarhaddon who spent much time in Kalhu. His building remained unfinished, but its unusual columned halls highlight Egyptian cultural influence after the conquest in 671 BC.

## Dur-Katlimmu: life in the western provinces

To the Assyrians, Tell Sheikh Hamad, located on the eastern bank of the Khabur River in north-eastern Syria, was the city of Dur-Katlimmu, a provincial centre of importance in the kingdom of Assyria since the 13th century BC. When the wealthy dignitary Šulmu-šarri (see Chapter 3) resided there in the 7th century the city was also known under the Aramaic name Magdala ('Tower'). This reflects the fact that Aramaic, rather than Assyrian, was the language most widely spoken in the Assyrian Empire of the first millennium BC. This West Semitic language is closely related to Hebrew and Phoenician, and any speaker of Assyrian, also a Semitic language, would have been able to understand Aramaic fairly well—without necessarily mastering its grammatical nuances—and vice versa. Outside the Assyrian heartland, Aramaic was very probably also the most frequently used written language. But in contrast to the Assyrian-language texts that were recorded in cuneiform on clay tablets, Aramaic was written in alphabetic script on paper-like materials such as leather or papyrus: these only survive in very dry contexts, such as the caves in the Judaean desert where the vast majority of early Aramaic documents have been found (but from much later dates), and disintegrate otherwise.

From at least the 9th century BC, the Assyrian state employed both Assyrian and Aramaic for government purposes as a direct consequence of the integration of the western states where this language was widely spoken. The use of Aramaic is documented in the Assyrian heartland from the reign of Shalmaneser III onwards: characters of the Aramaic alphabet are painted on the glazed bricks used for his buildings in the capital city of Kalhu, probably as fitters' marks. In addition, palace reliefs and door decorations routinely depict pairs of scribes, one writing with a pen on a scroll and the other impressing signs with a stylus into the surface of a clay tablet or a multi-leaved wax-covered wooden tablet. These devices, too, did not usually survive the ravages of time. Some luxury versions made from ivory have been recovered from Aššur and Kalhu, but without the wax layer and therefore the text. Such wax tablets closely correspond to the famous Vindolanda Tablets from Hadrian's Wall, Britain's oldest surviving handwritten documents from the 1st and 2nd centuries AD; cuneiform scribes routinely used them ever since the third millennium BC.

The most important indications of the widespread use of Aramaic as a written language in the Assyrian Empire are, first, the alphabetic annotations incised or written in ink on clay tablets that record the transfer of property. These short notes summarize the content of the cuneiform contract, apparently for the benefit of those who could read Aramaic but were less familiar with Assyrian cuneiform (Figure 7). Secondly, there is a particular type of clay tablet that was inscribed with Aramaic text only. These debt notes use a very specific, triangular shape and were formed around a knotted string. It is unclear what was fixed to the other end of that string but most likely it was a version of the same debt note on an Aramaic-language scroll. The reason for this assumption is that the more frequently attested alternative format for debt notes consists of an inner tablet enclosed in a sealed clay envelope, both inscribed with identical text. The Aramaic clay triangles, too, are sealed and may therefore fulfil the function of the envelope vis-à-vis the hypothetical scroll. Whatever they are, very many such tablets as well as contracts with Aramaic annotations have been found at Dur-Katlimmu and they are also known from other sites in the western Assyrian provinces. In the heartland, they are considerably less frequent, presumably reflecting the much wider knowledge of cuneiform. Although the scribes writing private legal documents in Dur-Katlimmu produced very handsomely shaped and elegantly written tablets, they were certainly not native Assyrian speakers: their frequent

7. Property sale contract from Dur-Katlimmu in Assyrian cuneiform, with two lines of summary in alphabetic Aramaic incised above and below the two stamp seal impressions.

and very characteristic grammatical mistakes indicate that they were used to expressing themselves in a West Semitic language, most likely Aramaic.

## Integrating the west into the kingdom of Assyria

A German team led by Hartmut Kühne has been exploring the site of Tell Sheikh Hamad in annual excavation campaigns since 1978, after the archaeological team mapping the Khabur valley's many sites in 1977 learned that local people had found a group of clay tablets. It turned out that when constructing a water reservoir on the settlement mound they had unwittingly exposed rooms of a building complex from where the city and its region were managed in the last part of the second millennium BC. In total, some 400 tablets have been recovered of an administrative archive of the 13th and early 12th century BC that deals with the running of the agricultural estates supporting the provincial government. The tablets were baked in the fire that had destroyed the building. Some texts were rendered illegible, as they came too closely into contact with the flames, and others were lost to the river when local children used the earliest finds, in an ingenious repurposing of the flat clay tablets that comfortably fit into one's hand, as skipping stones. The surviving texts also contain references to wooden writing boards, which of course have not been preserved.

Most of the extant texts are administrative documents that give much insight into the economic situation at Dur-Katlimmu, which lies in the 'risk zone' between the climate zones of the Mediterranean and the steppe. A local irrigation canal system supported the rain-fed agriculture and fostered production of good harvests of barley, wheat, and sesame, supplemented by vegetables and herbs. The work was performed by the 'farmers of the palace', managed by the provincial government. They maintained two herds of donkeys, totalling 150 head, as pack animals. Cattle, used in pairs to drag the seeder-ploughs and to supply milk and meat, grazed in the meadows by the river while shepherds took the flocks of sheep and goats into the steppe: their wool and hair (for felt) was the backbone of the local textile industry.

The Dur-Katlimmu documentation and the agricultural activities recorded therein closely correspond to what is known from the capital Aššur and other sites in the provinces, such as the nearby city of Harbe (Tell Chuera in Syria) and the smaller fortified settlements called *dunnu* at modern Giricano (Dunnu-ša-Uzibi; near the Turkish city of Diyarbakir) or Sabi Abyad (in the Syrian Balikh valley). This illustrates one aspect of how the expanding kingdom of Assyria brought its way of life to the newly integrated territories. The governor and his staff were dispatched from the centre to the provinces where they introduced administrative routines using the Assyrian language and script, as well as typical standard forms for all sorts of documents to organize the provincial government's economic base. A set amount of taxes had to be delivered from the provincial centres to the capital, including the ideologically important contributions of ingredients for the daily feast prepared for the god Aššur.

Within the kingdom of Assyria in the late second millennium BC, Dur-Katlimmu had a special position, as it was not merely the centre of a province but the pre-eminent city of the realm's western half. The second-highest dignitary of the kingdom resided here, the Chief Chancellor (*sukallu rabiu*) of Assyria, whose courtesy title was 'King of Hanigalbat', after the Assyrian designation for its former overlord Mittani. The first to hold this title was Ibašši-ili, a younger son of King Adad-nerari I and brother of his successor Shalmaneser I. Both these kings waged war against Mittani and brought its territories under Assyrian control. At that time, rather than appropriating one of the old Mitanni centres, Dur-Katlimmu was established as the centre of government. This ancient settlement was linked to the city of Aššur through a direct route (later part of the 'King's Road' network; see Chapter 6) that was the shortest connection from the

capital to the new holdings in the Khabur valley. This gave
the incentive for the city's elevation under Shalmaneser I who
founded a temple for the god Salmanu there, a deity closely
associated with the Assyrian royal family and celebrated by this
king's name, which in Assyrian is rendered Salmanu-ašared 'The
god Salmanu is eminent'. Salmanu's name means 'The Kind One'
and perhaps he was merely a deified aspect of the god Aššur,
whose intimate connection to the city of Aššur made building
other temples in his own name awkward. A stele dating to the
early 8th century BC, of which the first piece was recovered from
Tell Sheikh Hamad in 1879 by Austen Henry Layard's associate
Hormuzd Rassam, records how King Adad-nerari III and the
local governor Nergal-ereš renovated the temple, using cedar logs
procured from Lebanon during a military campaign to the
Mediterranean:

> The old temple, which Shalmaneser (I), my ancestor (literally 'my
> father'), had built, had become dilapidated and I, in a stroke of
> inspiration, built this temple from its foundations to its parapets.
> I placed the cedar roof beams from Mount Lebanon on top.

Shalmaneser's brother Ibašši-ili passed on his new and powerful
office of King of Hanigalbat to his descendants. When the main
line of the Assyrian royal house became extinct in 1183 BC, after
old King Tukulti-Ninurta I, who had occupied the throne for
thirty-seven years, was assassinated by his sons who then became
embroiled in violent succession conflicts, his great-great-grandson
Ninurta-apil-Ekur became king of Assyria. So powerful was the
new king's father Ili-pada that a Babylonian king addressed him
and the actual king Aššur-nerari III, one of Tukulti-Ninurta's
short-lived sons, insultingly as 'the kings of Assyria' in a letter that
ridicules Assyrian impotence in the aftermath of the regicide:

> The god Aššur has made you, Aššur-nerari and Ili-pada, because of
> (your) irresponsibility, constant drunkenness and inability to make
> decisions, go crazy. There is no one among you who has any sense.

It was a Babylonian intervention that brought Ili-pada's son to the throne after his death, and all subsequent kings, until the end of the empire, were his descendants. When the 8th century ruler Adad-nerari III claimed Shalmaneser I as 'his father' in the stele from Dur-Katlimmu, a designation that Assyrian kings generally used for their predecessors, he was factually wrong as he was descended from Shalmaneser's brother Ibašši-ili.

In the period of the reconquest of the lost western regions in the 10th century BC, Dur-Katlimmu played a crucial strategic role as an Assyrian enclave. In the 9th century BC, a sizeable fortified lower town was added to Dur-Katlimmu, transforming it from a relatively small town into a 60-hectare large city with a fortification wall of almost 4 kilometres, traversed by a canal 9 metres wide—modest when compared to contemporary Kalhu with its 360 hectares, but by far the biggest settlement on the Khabur. Much of the archaeological work since 1978 has focused on this lower town, unearthing enormous mansions modelled on the imperial palace architecture. The best known of these, the so-called Red House (see Figure 9), dates to the 7th century BC and was the residence of military man and wealthy landowner Šulmu-šarri. The activities of Šulmu-šarri's heirs were documented even during and after the disintegration of the Assyrian Empire and illuminated the political situation in Dur-Katlimmu at the time. At first, just after 612 BC, the population was loyal to the Assyrian crown, but local power rested now in the hands of a 'city lord' rather than the members of the previous city administration. A decade later, the city accepted Babylonian sovereignty: four private legal documents that otherwise conform entirely to the Assyrian traditions are dated according to the regnal years of Nebuchadnezzar II. As the mention of his priest in two of these texts indicates, the temple of the god Salmanu was still active at the time.

# Chapter 3
# Assyrians at home

The following sketches illustrate the great variety of living
conditions and human experiences in the Assyrian Empire. They
have two things in common: they all date to the 7th century BC, the
period when the source material is most numerous and diverse, and
they all are situated in an urban context. This is not coincidental
as the available sources all come from cities and tend to concern
themselves with matters of urban life. We encounter a king, two
scholars of a leading learned family, a wealthy landowner, and a
wine merchant, as well as their families and households.

## Master of the universe: King Esarhaddon

Of all kings of Assyria, Esarhaddon (Figure 8) is the one emerging
most clearly as an individual from the available sources. Most
Assyrian rulers are known primarily from their royal inscriptions.
Written on the kings' behalf to commemorate their deeds, these
texts were either inscribed on monuments (statues, steles, rock
reliefs) or written into the fabric of temples, palaces, and city walls,
visibly on walls and gates or ritually buried in foundation deposits.
Their Assyrian designation means 'written names' and their
purpose was to perpetuate their protagonists' existence beyond
their physical existence. Their authors, royal scholars headed by
the Chief Scribe, concentrated unashamedly on the king and his

8. Stele of Esarhaddon, king of Assyria, showing him on the front with the subjugated rulers of Tyre and Kush and on the sides his sons Aššurbanipal and Šamaš-šumu-ukin as crown princes of Assyria and Babylon, respectively.

deeds, focusing on what was expected of a ruler and pleasing to the gods: the building and maintenance of temples, palaces, and cities and the protection and expansion of the realm. Written during their protagonists' lifetime and with their authorization, such compositions present a sympathetic reading of their heroes' life and times, excluding what did not serve to celebrate and impress.

For most of Assyrian history, royal inscriptions are our most prominent yet biased source. But this is not the case in the 8th and 7th centuries BC, when contemporary correspondence and administrative documents survive from the palaces at Kalhu and Nineveh, and from elsewhere; the 670s, when Esarhaddon ruled the empire, are an especially well-documented decade.

Esarhaddon was a younger son of Sennacherib, as indicated by his name, which means 'The god Aššur has given a brother (to the existing siblings)'. He became king of Assyria in 681, despite the fact that he had not been the original crown prince—the heir apparent to the throne, chosen by the king, confirmed by the gods, and appointed in public. When making Esarhaddon crown prince in 683, Sennacherib first had to dismiss his previous choice, heir apparent to the empire for well over a dozen years. This son, Urdu-Mullissi, remained at court, so it is unlikely he had fallen from grace completely, but Sennacherib's motives are unknown. He did not realize that his decision endangered his life, for Urdu-Mullissi now assembled supporters for a *coup d'état*. The plot was almost uncovered when an official, whom the conspirators had approached in vain, sought an audience with the king, but so widespread was the conspiracy that Urdu-Mullissi's cronies were able to intercept him. According to a letter later sent to Esarhaddon,

> They asked him: 'What is your appeal to the king about?' He answered: 'It is about Urdu-Mullissi.' They covered his face with his cloak (as was the custom when meeting the king) and made him stand before Urdu-Mullissi himself, saying: 'Look! Your appeal is being granted, say it with your own mouth!' He said: 'Your son Urdu-Mullissi will kill you.'

The conspirators promptly disposed of him and their plot came to fruition: in 681, Urdu-Mullissi and a brother stabbed their father to death. But the aftermath of the regicide saw friction between the conspirators and Urdu-Mullissi's coronation was delayed.

Nineveh was in chaos when Esarhaddon, absent at the time of the assassination, marched on the capital. He managed to drive out the murderers and ascended the throne two months after his father's death. These events caused a stir all over the ancient world, best illustrated by the Biblical accounts that also report the flight of the murderous princes to Urartu (2 Kings 19:37; Isaiah 37:38).

For well over a century, the empire had been locked in conflict with its northern rival and now, by sheltering pretenders with a good claim to the throne, Urartu gained substantial influence over Assyrian politics. Esarhaddon could not touch the leaders of the *coup d'état* and steered clear of Urartu throughout his reign. At home, he made every effort to ensure that his brothers had no powerful allies left, should they ever try to return from exile. Officials high and low who were suspected of sympathy for the enemy were replaced throughout the empire. Archival records from Nineveh and Kalhu show, for example, that the entire palace security staff was dismissed, and we may suspect that they were not sent into early retirement but executed. His bloody ascent to power shaped the new king profoundly and Esarhaddon was distrustful of all around him. Routine inquiries made every three months to the all-seeing sun god Šamaš, patron of justice and divination, were supposed to establish whether anyone wished him ill. But problematically, the prime suspects were those who were meant to support him in governing: state officials, members of the extended royal family, the military, palace staff, and the Assyrian allies who provided auxiliary troops for the empire's army. This is one of many such queries from late in Esarhaddon's reign, filed in copy together with the expert report on the autopsy of the liver of a sacrificed lamb that was thought to reveal the divine answer:

> Will any of the eunuchs or bearded officials, the king's courtiers, the members of the royal line, senior or junior, or any other relative of the king, or the military officers, recruitment officers, team

commanders, the royal guard, personal guards or the king's
charioteers, the keepers of the inner or outer gates, stable attendants,
domestic staff, cooks, confectioners, bakers, craftsmen, or...(various
foreign) auxiliaries, or their brothers, sons or nephews, their friends
(literally, 'masters of salt and bread') or anyone who is acquainted
with them, be they eunuchs or bearded, any enemy at all, whether
by day or by night, or in the city or in the country, whether while
(Esarhaddon is) sitting on the royal throne or chariot or rickshaw,
walking, going out or coming in, eating or drinking, dressing or
undressing or washing himself, whether through deceit or guile or
any other means, make an uprising and rebellion against Esarhaddon,
king of Assyria?...I ask you, great lord Šamaš, whether from today
6/XII to 5/III of the coming year they will rise and rebel against
Esarhaddon, king of Assyria, whether they will act in a hostile
manner against him or kill him.

The Assyrian allies listed in this query indicate that the empire's
power was greater than ever before. By force or by treaty, and often
both, the empire had acquired new partners that extended Assyrian
influence as far as the Caspian Sea and Sudan and deep into the
Arabian Peninsula. Our text lists Elam and the Cimmerian horse
nomads in Iran, the polities along the Nile, including the kingdom
of Kush and Arabian tribes such as the Qedarites, who all became
tied to the empire. The completion of a peace treaty with Elam,
Assyria's long-standing rival in Iran, in 674 was a skilful political
manoeuvre that secured the empire's eastern borders. This provided
the first chance ever to invade Egypt, whose politically fragmented
landscape was then dominated by the Nubian Taharqa, king of
Kush in modern-day Sudan. Assyria's first attempted invasion in
673 resulted in a hasty retreat. But in 671, when the new Arab allies
were employed for an unexpected attack across the Sinai desert,
Egypt was conquered. Although reinforcing Assyrian supremacy
necessitated further campaigns (see Figure 11) in 667 BC and 664
BC, leading as far south as Thebes, the region was organized into a
unified Assyrian vassal state, first under the rule of Nekho of Sais
and then under his son Psammetikh.

All Assyrian rulers sought the sun god's advice, although due to the chances of preservation and recovery, the only queries surviving in the original are from the reigns of Esarhaddon and his successor Aššurbanipal. For the royal decision-making process, seeking divine council was crucial, as formulating the problem as a question and then interpreting the god's answer allowed a far more open discussion with officials and advisers than would otherwise have been possible in an absolute monarchy where no man was the almighty king's equal. The known queries cover a wide range of military and political matters such as appointments to key positions in state and court. But inquiries about possible betrayal survive only for Esarhaddon. His concern for security also shaped the way in which he had palaces in Nineveh and Kalhu redesigned: as impregnable fortresses.

## A king in grief

Esarhaddon's inscriptions portrayed him in the traditional style as the solitary hero who triumphs all by himself. From his private letters, too, the king emerges as a lonely man, but in an altogether different way. The correspondence with the scholars in his entourage allows us detailed insight into his mental and physical state and shows that, despite his political and military successes, Esarhaddon was not a happy man. In 673 he experienced traumatic bereavement when he first lost his wife, the queen Ešarra-hammat and, shortly afterwards, their infant son during whose birth she may have died. As we read in a letter from his personal exorcist Adad-šumu-uṣur, one of the experts charged with caring for the king's well-being:

> As to what the king, my lord, wrote to me: 'I am feeling very sad; how did we act that I have become so depressed for this little one of mine?' – had it been curable, you would have given away half of your kingdom to have it cured! But what can we do? O king, my lord, it is something that cannot be done.

Esarhaddon was often ill, suffering from spells of fever and dizziness, violent fits of vomiting, diarrhoea, nosebleeds, and painful earaches. A permanent skin rash disfigured parts of his body and especially his face. Depression and fear of death cast a shadow on his life and for days he withdrew to his sleeping quarters, refusing food, drink, and human company. In one of his letters, Adad-šumu-uṣur tried to reason with his royal patient:

> Why is the table not brought to the king, my lord, today already for the second day running? Who would stay in the dark much longer than (the sun god) Šamaš, the king of the gods, stays in the dark, a whole day and night, and again two days? The king, the lord of the world, is the very image of Šamaš. He should keep in the dark for half a day only! ... Eating bread and drinking wine will soon remove the illness of the king. Good advice is to be heeded: restlessness, not eating and not drinking disturb the mind and add to illness. In this matter the king should listen to his servant.

Modern audiences may feel sympathy with the suffering Esarhaddon. But in a society that saw disease as divine punishment, an ailing king could not expect much compassion. On the contrary, his subjects would see his affliction as an indication that the gods lacked goodwill towards their ruler. Therefore, the king's frailty needed to be concealed. Given the restrictions regulating direct interaction with the monarch, this could be achieved to some extent, but it was essential that Esarhaddon shouldered his manifold public duties as king.

The ancient ritual of the Substitute King was used repeatedly to allow Esarhaddon to escape from the burden of kingship. This ritual was meant to protect the king from mortal danger which was predicted by an eclipse. A substitute took his place for one hundred days. He wore the king's clothes, ate the king's meals, and slept in the king's bed while the true monarch, under the alias 'The Farmer', lived hidden from the public, which given Esarhaddon's desire to do just that was no hardship. Although he was not the only ruler to have the ritual performed, Esarhaddon did so at least four times, which is without parallel. Through references in the private correspondence we can date these instances. One ritual was performed in 671, just eleven days after the first decisive victory of the ongoing Egyptian campaign. While his army continued the war under the Chief Eunuch Aššur-naṣir's command (as an appointment query indicates), Esarhaddon went into hiding. In the following two years, the ritual was performed twice more, allowing Esarhaddon to withdraw for substantial periods. Politically, these absences were perhaps only possible as, in 672, Esarhaddon's son Aššurbanipal had been appointed crown prince of Assyria and subsequently shouldered a significant portion of his father's duties. But Esarhaddon's escape from the throne was not without victims. The ritual directed the predicted evil onto the Substitute King, but this was not left to chance: he was executed at the end of the hundred days. Although a simple mind was normally chosen who would not question his sudden rise to the throne, on at least one occasion Esarhaddon picked a political adversary as Substitute King, in a scheme designed to kill two birds with one stone.

One aspect of his royal duties Esarhaddon fulfilled very well: he fathered many children (at least eighteen). In 670, the first son of his heir Aššurbanipal was born, securing kingship for his descendants into the next two generations. But this same year, a prophecy spread like fire from Harran in northern Syria. A local woman had fallen into ecstasy, uttering a sensational divine message: 'This is the word of (the light god) Nusku: "Kingship belongs to Sasî. I shall destroy the name and the seed of Sennacherib!"' Today, Sasî remains an enigmatic figure whose origins are unknown, but, at the time, he quickly found supporters throughout the empire. The movement to dispose of Esarhaddon was halted promptly but at great cost for the state. According to Esarhaddon's chief physician, the insurrection 'made all other people hateful in the eyes of the king, smearing them like a tanner with the oil of fish', and the Babylonian Chronicles' entry for 670 reads: 'In Assyria, the king killed many of his great ones with the sword.' After the executions in the wake of Sennacherib's murder, this was the second mass culling among the Assyrian state officials that Esarhaddon had ordered within a decade. But the well-oiled machinery of Assyria's administration was the backbone of the empire and these executions caused permanent harm to the state, perhaps more than murdering a king. After all, it had been a testament to the empire's sound administrative structure that the state apparatus could largely absorb the damaging effects of Esarhaddon's frailty and periodic refusal to carry the burden of kingship, while even dramatically expanding the influence of the Assyrian Empire with the conquest of Egypt. In hindsight, the year 670 marks the time when the empire reached its zenith. The second series of executions among the officials greatly weakened the state and brought the expansion of Assyrian power to a grinding halt. Esarhaddon himself died only shortly after in 669, apparently without foul play.

## Two scholars of distinguished birth, with frustrated ambitions

The most prominent position for a man of learning was that of the king's principal scholar, called first Royal Scribe (see Chapter 5) and later Master Scholar (*ummānu*). Ever since Gabbu-ilani-ereš had been Master Scholar to kings Tukulti-Ninurta II and Aššurnasirpal II in the 9th century, his family was Assyria's pre-eminent learned clan. Gabbu-ilani-ereš moved with the court from Aššur to the new residence city Kalhu, where his family subsequently flourished. Many of his descendants enjoyed royal patronage as leading experts in the arts of exorcism or in celestial divination, using astrology to predict the future. His descendant Nabu-zuqup-kenu contributed numerous manuscripts of literary and scholarly works to the royal library (see Chapter 6), including a copy of the Gilgameš Epic, and two of his sons served Esarhaddon in very prominent positions. We have already encountered Adad-šumu-uṣur as the king's personal exorcist, trying to coax Esarhaddon out of bouts of depression. His brother Nabu-zeru-lešir was, like their illustrious ancestor, Master Scholar, and as Chief Scribe ultimately responsible for the composition of the king's inscriptions. His son Issar-šumu-ereš succeeded him in this position, continuing his service under King Aššurbanipal. But his other son Šumaya and his nephew Urdu-Gula, who were both trained as exorcists, failed to achieve permanent positions at court. They both wrote petitions to Aššurbanipal that contain detailed descriptions of their economic and social circumstances.

After his father's death had saddled Šumaya with inherited debts, he petitioned crown prince Aššurbanipal twice for financial support and to be assigned some of his father's previous roles. Šumaya used to work for the crown prince and reminded Aššurbanipal in his letters of the family's long association with the royal house, pleading that he should be recognized like his father and grandfather before him. He holds up King Esarhaddon as a role model who would not hesitate to do right by Šumaya—but his attachment, unfortunately, was to Aššurbanipal who was rather less keen to protect this scion of an ancient learned family.

Urdu-Gula, Šumaya's cousin and son of Adad-šumu-uṣur, also found himself excluded from court and cold-shouldered by Aššurbanipal, now king of Assyria. In his emotional petition, Urdu-Gula professed to be bitterly ashamed. With only a small agricultural estate and master of just eight slaves, reduced to wearing old clothes and having to walk ever since his two beasts of burden had died, he was the laughing stock of the scholars who continued to enjoy the king's favour, or so he imagined. He was certainly not a poor man, but his being accustomed to a more affluent situation had led him to incur debts of (at least) three times his former annual income at court. He also despaired over his lack of son and heir and worried who would care for him in old age. He sacrificed to the goddess Ištar of Kadmuri at Kalhu to bless his wife with the desired pregnancy. If this strategy continued to fail, Urdu-Gula would probably have adopted a boy, the usual Assyrian solution to childlessness.

Why did these two men, despite their education, their excellent pedigree, and their familiarity with the royal family, not enjoy a privileged position at court, with all the attached material benefits, that they so obviously thought to be theirs by right? During Esarhaddon's reign, numerous highly qualified scholars joined the king's scholarly entourage from all over the world. Esarhaddon had an Egyptian physician, charged a Babylonian expert with the reorganization of the Babylonian cults, and employed various native experts in specifically Egyptian and Anatolian disciplines of divination and ritual practice. Some of the Assyrian scholars who had grown up expecting to find easy acceptance at court found the competition for the king's favour fiercer than ever before and their ambitions frustrated.

## Very rich and friends with the king: a landowner from Dur-Katlimmu

Wealthy landowner Šulmu-šarri was another contemporary of Aššurbanipal. We know about him from the documents excavated in the ruins of his stately home at Dur-Katlimmu (see Chapter 2), the so-called 'Red House' (Figure 9). The archive consists of c.150 tablets in Assyrian cuneiform and some fifty triangular clay dockets in alphabetic Aramaic: legal texts that contain much information on the economic situation of Šulmu-šarri's household. That he was an officer in the army is likely, as most people acting as his witnesses in the documents held military titles: Dur-Katlimmu housed a garrison with a chariot corps and intelligence service. When he was at least 50 years of age, Šulmu-šarri was promoted to the distinguished position of a 'Friend' (ša qurbūte, literally 'He who is close') of Aššurbanipal, which allowed him to represent the king in confidential matters all over the empire.

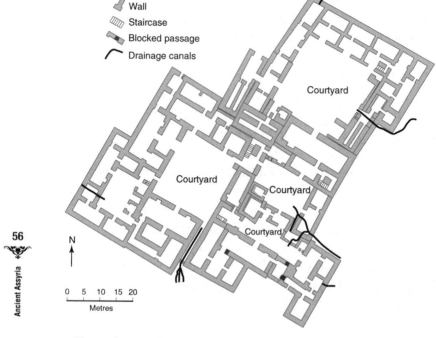

Wall
Staircase
Blocked passage
Drainage canals

Courtyard

Courtyard

Courtyard

Courtyard

N

0 5 10 15 20
Metres

**9. The Red House in Dur-Katlimmu.**

Like many who enjoyed the king's favour, Šulmu-šarri was a very rich man. His wealth was of an entirely different scale than of well-to-do scholars. The surviving purchase documents alone mention eight fields, three gardens, and three houses and agricultural buildings in and around Dur-Katlimmu, and he also owned an entire village in the region of Aqra in northern Iraq, as we know from a court record dealing with a crime committed there. We can be certain that he had additional estates beyond those mentioned in the documents, some perhaps granted by the king. The 'Red House' is testament to his wealth. With a living space of 5,400 m², this enormous building consists of three separate wings arranged around paved courtyards. The main entrance in the north led into the first part of the building with ample storage facilities, some refrigerated. A central reception hall provided and regulated access to the representative wing in the east and the private quarters in the west of the building. There were two wells, several kitchen areas, and four bathrooms, all connected to the complex sewage system. The building had a second floor, accessible by four staircases. Šulmu-šarri and his family shared this mansion with their many slaves. Within three decades, he bought more than fifty persons. Two-thirds were females, often mothers with young daughters, and the remains of horizontal looms along the walls of the courtyards of the 'Red House' suggest that they contributed to the household's textile production. The shepherds in Šulmu-šarri's employ who grazed their flocks in the steppe east of Dur-Katlimmu provided the necessary wool.

Three adult sons of Šulmu-šarri are attested in the family archive. We do not know anything about their mother, but it is possible that she was a relative, perhaps a sister or daughter, of Šulmu-šarri's close associate Rahimi-il, an officer in the chariot corps. Such a family connection would explain why some of Rahimi-il's legal documents were found in the family archive. The sons inherited their father's estate after he died sometime during the reign of Aššurbanipal's second successor Sin-šarru-iškun, certainly of old age. His grave is not known. Although underground tombs are attested elsewhere in Dur-Katlimmu, no such structure was found at the 'Red House'. Perhaps Šulmu-šarri was buried at another of his many estates.

## A wine merchant of Aššur and his customers

Duri-Aššur, head of a trading firm based at Aššur, was another contemporary of King Aššurbanipal. Unlike the scholars Šumaya and Urdu-Gula and the royal 'Friend' Šulmu-šarri, he is unlikely to have been personally acquainted with the king. He lived in the middle of Aššur in a house of c.150 m² living space. Compared with Šulmu-šarri's gigantic Dur-Katlimmu mansion, this may seem tiny, but in Aššur's densely built-up urban environment, this was a respectable size. The house served as the logistics centre of one of the many private trading companies operating out of Aššur. All its citizens were exempt from taxes, including 'harbour, crossing and gate fees on land or water' and this significantly reduced the cost of importing goods and made trading an attractive enterprise.

The letters and lists excavated in his archive in 1990, 2000, and 2001 during German excavations show that Duri-Aššur and three partners (called 'brothers') organized trade with the northern regions of the Assyrian Empire. He oversaw the logistics of the company in Aššur while his partners travelled to arrange their business activities. The firm employed four caravan leaders who each conducted three trips per year. They travelled upstream along the Tigris with donkeys laden with the silver needed to make the purchases and merchandise from Aššur: hats, shoes, and exclusive textiles, which also served as packing material for supplies and money. Their destination was Zamahu in Jebel Sinjar in the border region between Iraq and Syria, famous for its wines. Once the caravan arrived there, everything was sold, including the donkeys, and Duri-Aššur's agents bought wine with the proceeds, topped up with the silver funds. The wine was filled into animal skins (sheep, goat; rarely cattle). Incidentally, there is a modern link between Assyria and large wine containers, as the nine-litre bottles used for champagne and Burgundy are called 'Salmanazar' (after the French pronunciation of the Assyrian royal name Shalmaneser). The wineskins were bound together with logs to create rafts for the return journey to Aššur on the Tigris. This was good for the wine, as the river kept it cool and prevented it from spoiling. Back in Aššur, all components of the raft constituted valuable merchandise: the wineskins, of course, but also the logs which were much in demand as building timber in forestless Aššur. The wine was subsequently decanted into ceramic vessels similar to amphoras. When served, it was mixed with water. People had (roughly) a pint of wine, sipped from bowls with a volume of just over half a litre. These were balanced elegantly on the fingers of the right hand, which must have impeded overindulgence.

Wine drinking was common among the well-heeled inhabitants of Aššur in the 7th century BC. From the 9th century onwards, the integration of wine-producing regions along the southern flank of the Taurus range into the empire had allowed wine consumption to spread beyond the palace and the temples: wine had long been part of the ritual meals served to the Assyrian gods. For the private consumers in Aššur, wine had to be procured over considerable distances and was an expensive luxury. The solution was to invest in Duri-Aššur's firm, with guaranteed shares of the wine imports in return for silver paid up-front. The firm had a base of loyal customers with repeat investments, who presumably kept their wine cellars well-stocked in this way. Although some investors contributed substantial sums of money, most of the amounts invested were quite small, sometimes just a fraction of a shekel of silver. The investment lists in Duri-Aššur's archive allow a glimpse into the composition of Aššur's wine-loving population in the late 7th century BC: mostly craftsmen and administrative personnel in the service of the temple of Aššur, but also city officials and affiliates of the households of members of the royal family who maintained residences at Aššur. A large number of women invested in the wine firm, and most of them were identified as Egyptian. Egyptian men, too, were among the customers and their presence is not surprising, given that the house right next to Duri-Aššur belonged to an Egyptian family—one of many that settled in the city after the conquest of Memphis in 671 BC. But why did the firm have so many female Egyptian clients? In Egypt, women routinely conducted independent business, unlike in the Assyrian heartland where women could certainly do so, if necessary, but would usually be represented by a male relative. The evidence from Duri-Aššur's archive suggests that even decades after the relocation to Assyria, the Egyptian community still granted their women their traditional independence.

According to their archive, the wine firm was active from 651 until the Medes conquered the city of Aššur in 614 BC; some of Duri-Aššur's letters had not yet been opened when his house went up in flames. The ensuing wars not only terminated the firm's activities but interrupted trans-regional trade on a large scale while the spoils of the Assyrian Empire were divided up between the Babylonian, Median, and Egyptian armies.

# Chapter 4
# Assyrians abroad

Through the lens of a range of primary sources from different periods, we will capture snapshots of the lives of various Assyrians far away from the city of Aššur and the Assyrian heartland: some happy, some not.

## Family matters at the trading colony of Kaneš, c.1900 BC

The Assyrian traders active in Anatolia (see Chapter 2) were far from home, often and for long periods. Those who travelled on business from Aššur were away for at least three months if Kaneš was their destination, and considerably longer if they were on their way to the even more remote Anatolian trading posts such as Durhumit or Purušhaddum. But many lived permanently in Kaneš, or one of the other colonies, as the local representatives of their family firm, sometimes even for several decades. Their families back home in Aššur missed them, as letters excavated in the Assyrian quarter at Kaneš illustrate, especially those from female relatives.

This letter was sent by concerned sisters:

> Here (at Aššur), we have consulted female dream interpreters and diviners and the spirits of the dead: the god Aššur keeps on warning

you! You love money but you hate your life. Can you not satisfy Aššur (here) in the city? As soon as you read this letter, come here to see the eye of Aššur and (thus) save your life.

The records of the family firm show that when the brother returned to Aššur after many years abroad, it was with sadly depleted funds. Once in a while, female family members made the trip to Anatolia but a male relative needed to chaperon them. As a mother from Aššur wrote to her son in Kaneš:

> Come quickly (to Aššur) so that I can depart with you and watch over your father's and your house (i.e. the family firm) in Kaneš so that no one will make trouble for your father's house.

It would seem that the father was in a frail state of health and did not have long to live. Earlier in the same letter, the mother reminded the son of his obligations to his family:

> If not you, who else do we have over there (in Kaneš)? If not you, your father has nobody else over there! Act like a man, heed your father's instructions, keep your father's documents safe and ask all his outstanding claims to be paid. Sell your father's merchandise, then get ready and come here (to Aššur) so that you may see the eye of the god Aššur and of your father and thus please your father!

Some wives followed their merchant husbands through Anatolia— not necessarily a recipe for harmony and happiness, if one consults one wife's letter chronicling the stations of her life in Anatolia and the increasingly dysfunctional relationship with her husband who was most of the time in another place and treated her shabbily when they were together. The wife wrote the following, after she found herself once again abandoned, this time in the trading colony at Hahhum (near Samsat in Turkey):

> You left me in Purušhaddum and I really was wiped from my husband's mind. (Now) you do not take care of me when I have

come here (to Hahhum)! In Kaneš, you degraded me and for a whole year would not let me come to your bed. From Timilkiya you wrote to me: 'If you don't come here you are no longer my wife! I will make it even worse than in Purušhaddum.' Then you went from Timilkiya to Kaneš, saying: 'I will leave again (from Kaneš) within 15 days,' but instead of 15 days you stayed there for a year! You wrote to me from Kaneš: 'Come up to Hahhum.' So now I have been living in Hahhum for a year and you do not even mention my name in your business letters!

No wonder most wives stayed behind in Aššur.

During their residency in Kaneš, some Assyrian residents married local women and started another family there despite the fact that they already had wife and children back home. Such an arrangement was perfectly above board, as long as the two women did not live in the same city: only one was considered the 'wife' (*aššatum*), usually the one residing in Aššur, while the other was merely a consort and designated as *amtum:* this word elsewhere means 'slave woman' in Assyrian but in this specific context stands for secondary local wife. Bigamy was not otherwise practised in Kaneš and the records of local families indicate that the native inhabitants were monogamous. But an exception was made, and gladly, when the groom was a prosperous Assyrian trader and an attractive catch on the marriage market.

A few houses inhabited by local Anatolian families yielded archives of cuneiform tablets, mostly legal texts documenting debts and purchases. The extensive correspondence that is characteristic for the Assyrian archives is missing—unsurprising, given that there was no need to maintain long-distance relationships with family and business associates abroad. Interestingly, the inhabitants of Kaneš did not adapt the cuneiform script to Hittite, their spoken language: deliberately, it seems, as it would have been perfectly possible to do so, as the many loanwords and names in the Assyrian-language tablets demonstrate. Instead, they preferred to write in Assyrian even within their own community, and this is in line with the high regard in evidence for all things Assyrian.

Regardless of their social standing in Aššur, traders who married local girls generally seem to have had their pick from among the wealthiest local families, even though the Kaneš-born spouse had to accept being in a lopsided relationship that favoured the Assyrian husband. In a marriage between locals, on the other hand, husband and wife would have been equals and owned all property jointly. But perhaps this imbalance was offset by the fact that mixed marriage was not 'till death do us part'. Instead, such a relationship had an expiry date, the husband's permanent departure to Aššur, when a divorce contract was drawn up that typically left the woman with the house in Kaneš, a certain sum of money, and the freedom to remarry. While the Assyrian father might choose to take some of the children to Aššur, he had to provide for the upbringing of those who remained in Kaneš with their mother. The prospect of future financial gain clearly eclipsed any concerns that the local women's families might otherwise have entertained regarding the suitability of the arrangement.

## Envoys to Pharaoh Akhenaten's court, c.1340 BC

Pharaoh Thutmose III (15th century BC; 18th Dynasty) greatly expanded Egyptian power by leading military campaigns deep into Syria and even reached the Euphrates, to him 'that inverted water which goes downstream in going upstream'. He established a border with Mittani and on three occasions accepted gifts from the rulers under its authority, including the unnamed leader of Aššur. This was most likely Aššur-nadin-ahhe I who, if we can believe one of his successors, had at one point received twenty talents of gold from Egypt. The actual sum may have substantially increased in Assyrian memory in the intervening century or else Aššur-uballit I, who quoted this figure, may have deliberately inflated the amount in order to shame his correspondent Pharaoh Akhenaten into sending a similarly generous gift; after all, his former overlord, the king of Mittani (Hanigalbat to the Assyrians), also had received twenty talents. But however that may be, Egypt's gold certainly captured the Assyrian ruler's imagination and emerges from the sources as a key incentive for diplomatic contact with the faraway kingdom on the Nile.

Aššur-uballit I was the first Assyrian ruler to adopt the titles of a king and, during his rule of over three decades, he proved extremely successful in establishing his brand-new kingdom as a powerful state. Towards the end of his reign, he even marched on Babylon in order to install a king acceptable to him (see Chapter 5). The two letters found among the state correspondence of the pharaohs of the later 18th Dynasty of Egypt, dubbed the 'Amarna Letters' after their findspot, date from earlier in his reign. He appears to have not yet fully undergone the metamorphosis from local ruler to international statesman. The first of his letters was composed in Assyrian and is quite short, especially if one considers that it had to be transported over a vast distance to reach its recipient. From Aššur, the envoy carrying the letter had to cross all of Syria, and then travel down the Mediterranean Coast. Skirting the Sinai Peninsula along the coastal route, he would then have reached the Delta of the Nile and continued upstream to the capital of Akhetaten, modern Amarna. In total, this is a distance of 1,450 kilometres, as the crow flies, but overland of at least 1,800 kilometres.

Aššur-uballit's envoy brought with him a greeting gift, which would have been officially presented once he secured an audience with the pharaoh. In his first diplomatic overture, the Assyrian king sent a chariot and two horses as well as a lump of lapis lazuli, a highly prized precious stone of dark blue colour from faraway Afghanistan. Apart from initiating contact, the first letter of Aššur-uballit was mostly concerned with making sure that his envoy would return promptly:

Do not delay the envoy whom I sent to you for a visit. He should visit and then leave for here. He should see what you are like and what your country is like, and then leave for here.

The second letter is perhaps more polished in style but not very different in tone. It was not written in Assyrian but in Babylonian, the language of international politics. It was also much longer. Aššur-uballit and his chancellery had been researching past dealings with Egypt and, as we have seen, peppered the letter with facts and figures in a bid to secure a suitable gift in return for the Assyrian offering: a chariot with two white horses fit for a king, another chariot, and a lapis lazuli seal. The Assyrian king stated very clearly what he wanted as a return gift: gold, and ideally more than he had received before.

Gold in your country is dust; one simply gathers it up. Why are you so sparing of it? I am engaged with building a new palace. Send me as much gold as is needed for its adornment.

And the letter continued:

We are countries far apart. Are our messengers to be always on the march for such (poor) results?

For fledgling statesman Aššur-uballit, diplomatic contact with Egypt may have been mainly about the money, but he was truly pleased that Akhenaten had sent a delegation for a return visit to Aššur. Although he had insisted that his own envoy should be sent back immediately, he had no such intentions:

When I saw your envoys, I was very happy. Certainly your envoys shall reside with me, held in great esteem.

Showing off Egyptian diplomats to the Assyrian elite and to visiting dignitaries was bound to raise Aššur-uballit's prestige.

His own envoy remains anonymous in the available sources, but he was certainly a high-ranking individual, and perhaps a member of the royal family. The Hittite envoy Teli-Šarruma who was dispatched to the court of Tukulti-Ninurta I of Assyria in the 13th century, for example, was a prince. He is attested as one of a group of diplomats visiting Assyria in texts from Harbe (modern Tell Chuera in north-east Syria). Teli-Šarruma travelled with four teams of horses, three teams of mules and six donkeys, having delivered letters and gifts to the city of Aššur, as had the envoy of the Syrian state of Amurru who took the trip with ten donkeys. The Phoenician envoy from Sidon in Lebanon travelled much lighter, with just a chariot and three donkeys, but he had only letters to deliver, albeit important ones sent from the Egyptian pharaoh to the Assyrian king. All envoys, their staff and their animals were guaranteed board and lodging. The documents excavated at Harbe arranged for the delegations' provisioning at each stop on their way back home, as long as they were in Assyrian territory. For Aššur-uballit's envoy travelling from Aššur to Akhetaten a century earlier, the situation would have been similar.

## Banished to the mountains, c.1082 BC

Palaeoclimatologists explore past climatic conditions by analysing materials whose properties were influenced by the surrounding climate in order to recover proxy data. Two approaches work well for the ancient Middle East. The first method uses a very big drill to recover ancient sediments, preferably from the bottom of lakes ('lake cores'), and collect pollen and other climate indicators in order to measure temperature, oxygen content, and nutrient levels, as well as charcoal in order to date the layers through carbon dating. The other method uses a much smaller drill to cut into karst cave formations (speleothems) to recover sequences of the microscopic layers, added annually as water drips down and whose chemical properties differ each year. The resulting analyses show that around 1200 BC, a period of comparative cool with associated increased rainfalls came to an end, having lasted for about three centuries. Subsequently, climatic conditions warmed up and there was less rain: this more arid period lasted until *c.*900 BC. The drier climate was bad news for marginal farming regions because it made rain-fed agriculture, as traditionally practised in northern Mesopotamia, a hazardous gamble.

In 1987 climatologist Jehuda Neumann and assyriologist Simo Parpola had already proposed a connection between the climate shift and the mass migrations that destabilized much of the Middle East at the time. In particular, Parpola refined the understanding of a long-known but fragmentary Assyrian chronicle text, that gives the following entry for the year 1082 BC:

[In King Tiglath-pileser I's 32nd year, a famine occurred so severe that] people ate one another's flesh; [...] Aramean 'houses' plundered [the land], seized the roads, and conquered and took [many fortified cities] of Assyria. [The people of Assyria fled] to the mountains of Habriuri [to save their] lives. [The Arameans] took their [houses?], their money and their property.

The chronicle text uses the spectre of cannibalism to indicate that the food shortage was so bad that social order collapsed. The same image is used elsewhere, for example in the inscriptions of King Aššurbanipal in accounts about the consequences of the Babylonian insurrection led by his brother Šamaš-šumu-ukin from 652 to 648 BC. However, the 1082 BC famine did not happen in Assyria but elsewhere, triggering an Aramean invasion that was not simply a raid for food but an effort to claim land. The specific setting for the events recorded in the chronicle was the valley of the Upper Zab, as the region of Habriuri can be identified with the high plain of Herir, east of Arbela in the western flanks of the Zagros. This was where the Assyrians fled to from the Aramean invaders, its mountain location promising safety as well as relatively stable economic conditions. But subsequently,

Habriuri too was lost to Assyrian control. In the mid-10th century, King Aššur-dan II made efforts to regain the region and sacked several settlements there, as reported in his inscriptions. Also,

> I brought back the exhausted [people] of Assyria who had abandoned [their cities and houses because of] want, hunger, and famine and [had gone up] to other lands. [I settled] them in [suitable] cities and houses and they dwelt in peace.

Assyrian control of Habriuri was imposed for good when Aššurnasirpal II established an Assyrian province there in 883 BC.

Similar events to these took place elsewhere in the realm at the beginning and the end of the dry spell. A private legal document from Dunnu-ša-Uzibi (modern Giricano near Diyarbakir in south-eastern Turkey) dates to the year 1069 or 1068 BC and highlights the weakening of Assyrian control in the Upper Tigris region at a time when the Arameans were attacking the area according to a royal inscription of King Aššur-bel-kala. According to the legal document, a man had entered into a commercial partnership to finance a business trip. A unique clause not known from any other contract protected his partner's investment, should the man 'flee into the mountains': the partner could then claim his estate's next harvest. Again it was only Aššurnasirpal II who was able to reclaim the region for Assyria in 882. He relocated the people to the settlements that had been abandoned a few generations earlier for the highlands of Šubria, the mountainous region to the north of the Upper Tigris valley, quite similar in character to Habriuri. Using the same language as his great-grandfather Aššur-dan II for the Assyrians of Habriuri, his inscription reads:

> I brought back the exhausted people of Assyria who had gone up to other lands, to the mountains of Šubria, because of famine and hunger and I settled them in the city of Tušhan.

From these sources, it appears that the Assyrian territories on the
Upper Zab and on the Upper Tigris, as well as on the Khabur and
the Euphrates, were lost to the kingdom. It was not because the
more arid conditions failed the large-scale agriculture there; but
these economically relatively stable lowlands attracted hungry
Aramean clans, called 'houses' and typically named after a
founding father, such as Bit-Aduni, 'House of Aduni'. The
Arameans had previously settled in more marginal regions such as
Jebel Bishri in Central Syria where farming had been possible
during the colder, wetter period from *c.*1500 to 1200 BC. Now,
they sought out territories with a more secure economic basis and
settled there, each 'house' developing into a small regional state.
The local Assyrian population was forced to move to higher
altitudes. How keen they were to be brought 'back home' into the
realm from the mid-10th century onwards is open for discussion.
But from the point of view of the Assyrian government, the need
to rescue these enclave populations, routinely described as
'exhausted', provided a welcome reason for beginning a war of
liberation against the Aramean houses that had in the meantime
established themselves as small regional states.

## An unpopular ambassador, c.710 BC

By the late 8th century, the Assyrian Empire controlled regions
organized in around sixty-five provinces, run by governors who
were appointed by the king. In those regions that accepted Assyrian
authority but remained client states under the control of local
governments, ambassadors ('Trusted Ones' in Assyrian) represented
the empire's interests. Like the governors, they routinely
communicated with the king through letters and envoys.

One such client state was Kumme. Like many polities that were
allowed to keep their nominal independence, this small mountain
kingdom occupied a location that impeded direct Assyrian
control. Whereas the Phoenician states of Tyre and Arwad were
protected by their island location off the Mediterranean coast,

Kumme was located north of the Iraqi–Turkish border in the upper reaches of the Lesser Khabur, in the region of modern Beytüşşebap. Kumme was an ancient city-state with a temple dedicated to the storm god. Beytüşşebap boasts a hot thermal spring whose water is said to cure various ailments, and the spring alone would have recommended the site as a major sanctuary. Moreover, the dramatic mountain landscape provided the setting for myths about the storm god's battles against such foes as the rock monster Ullikummi; the avalanches and landslides that occur frequently in the region were seen as a manifestation of the god's power. His shrine had since the early second millennium BC attracted royal patronage from far away, including Mari in Syria, Hattuša in Central Anatolia, and also Assyria; King Adad-nerari II sacrificed at the shrine in 895. In 879 delegates from Kumme celebrated the inauguration of the imperial centre Kalhu as the guests of Aššurnasirpal II.

After Tiglath-pileser III had conquered the nearby kingdom of Ullubu in 739 BC, Kumme's territory bordered directly onto the newly established Assyrian province of Birtu. But at first the empire made no attempt to incorporate the tiny state. The correspondence of Sargon II provides us with much information on the relationship between Assyria and its client state, which remained under the control of its native ruler. At the time (c.710 BC) Ariye was city lord of Kumme. He was bound to the empire by treaty and in return for Assyria's protection had to accept certain obligations: to supply manpower, horses, and timber; and to provide intelligence on the region. For this purpose, Kumme was excellently positioned, as it was located on the direct, if difficult mountain route leading from Assyria's heartland to the centre of Urartu on Lake Van in eastern Turkey. Despite its links to Assyria, Kumme entertained close relations with Urartu, even providing it with men and information. This did not happen behind Assyria's back but with its encouragement and support, as it was considered a good way of gaining access to intelligence about the arch enemy.

A key strategy in ensuring Kumme's loyalty to Assyria was the permanent presence of an ambassador at Ariye's court. This position was held by Aššur-reṣuwa, whose letters to Sargon constitute the most extensive surviving dossier of any Assyrian ambassador. His messages frequently describe routine affairs such as timber transports. But they also concern Assyrian–Urartian espionage and counterespionage, thrilling to read even millennia after the events. Most exciting, perhaps, is to learn about the last-minute disclosure of an Urartian plan to abduct several Assyrian governors from Kumme's territory. Crown prince Sennacherib reports to his father, quoting Ariye's report on his neighbour, the ruler of Ukku, who was conspiring with Urartu:

> The ruler of Ukku has written to the Urartian king that the governors of the king of Assyria are building a fort in Kumme, and the Urartian king has given his governors the following order: 'Take your troops, go and capture the governors of the king of Assyria alive from the Kummeans, and bring them to me.' I do not have the full details yet; as soon as I have heard more, I shall write by express to the crown prince that they should rush troops to me.

For Kumme, this plot seems to have resulted in a significant tightening of Assyrian control. When sometime after 714 BC the new king of Urartu questioned the absence of Kummean delegates at his court, the answer from Kumme, according to the information conveyed back to Sargon, was this:

> Since we are subjects of Assyria, a cavalry foreman is our superior. Only the houses of Kumme are left to us; ... we cannot put our feet anywhere.

Kumme was now firmly under the thumb of the Assyrian military. While city lord Ariye and his son Arizâ, who are both mentioned in this letter, seem to have been loyal to Assyria, not everyone in Kumme shared their zeal. Aššur-reṣuwa, like all ambassadors serving in the Assyrian client states, had unlimited access to Kumme's ruler and influenced his decisions openly. The privileges of these officials are sketched in one of the few bilateral Assyrian treaties to survive in the original, the 676 BC agreement between Esarhaddon and the king of Tyre. A fragmentary passage outlines how the client ruler had to interact with the Assyrian ambassador:

[When] the elders of your country [convene to take] counsel the ambassador [must be] with them....[If...], do not listen to him, [do not...] without the ambassador. Nor must you open a letter that I send to you without the ambassador. If the ambassador is absent, wait for him and then open it.

Not surprisingly, many Kummeans perceived ambassador Aššur-reṣuwa's activities as oppressive and invasive. He in turn identified several people as dangerous to the Assyrian interests, writing to his king:

There are four men who should be removed. They must not walk free in my presence while I am here. They are inciting the country.

Aššur-reṣuwa became so unpopular that the people of Kumme petitioned Sargon and others to recall him from his post, protesting that while he was utterly loathsome they were still loyal to the empire. Hence in a letter to the king from another official,

The Kummeans who previously appealed to the king, my lord, have returned and come to me, saying: 'Kumme in its entirety cannot stand the ambassador. But we can and will bear the responsibility (towards the empire).'

Another letter, however, reveals that the city lord's standing had been affected by the hatred for the Assyrian ambassador:

Now then Kumme in its entirety has turned against Ariye; they [...] and speak of killing [the ambassador].

How this particular situation ended for the ambassador Aššur-reṣuwa personally is unknown. But crucially, a client ruler who had lost his ability to lead his country was worthless to the empire.

The available sources do not reveal whether these sentiments gave way to an attempt to oust Ariye but similar events happened repeatedly in the client states. Time and again, their own subjects unseated pro-Assyrian rulers and instead backed other pretenders who would not accept Assyria's supremacy. This usually led to a quick Assyrian intervention and quite frequently to the annexation of the state in question. Action against those representing Assyria, whether ambassador or native ruler, whether only planned or implemented, was enough to bring Kummean independence to an end, and not even the Assyrian appreciation for the famous temple of the storm-god would have changed that. The city-state disappears from the sources and we can assume that the tiny mountain realm became part of the Assyrian province of Birtu. The maintenance of a cordon of buffer states against Urartu was advantageous for the Assyrian Empire, but if the mechanisms of indirect control were not respected in the client states, the next best solution was to simply do away with local government altogether.

## Sibling rivalry: Šamaš-šumu-ukin, king of Babylon, 648 BC

In 672 Aššurbanipal was elevated to the rank of crown prince of Assyria, and at the same time, his older brother Šamaš-šumu-ukin was declared crown prince of Babylon. Their father Esarhaddon himself ruled as king of Assyria and Babylon but wanted to see the southern territory under separate government. As he put it in an inscription:

> I gave Šamaš-šumu-ukin, my son and offspring, as a present to the god Marduk and the goddess Zarpanitu.

The whole empire had to swear to respect and honour the king's decision to appoint his sons Aššurbanipal and Šamaš-šumu-ukin as his successors, with governors and client rulers taking an oath on behalf of their subjects. The text of the loyalty treaty was inscribed on large clay tablets that were sealed with the three sacred seals of the god Aššur. The first was created in the 19th century, the second in the 13th century, and the last *c.*700 BC. About 200 copies must have been written and distributed at the time, and 10 manuscripts have been found in Aššur (a fragment only), Kalhu (8 copies), and most recently Kullania (Tell Tayinat in the Hatay region of Turkey), where a Canadian team led by Tim Harrison unearthed the copy of the governor of Kullania inside the cella of a small shrine in 2008. It was apparently displayed there as a divine icon, following the treaty's instructions:

> You shall guard this covenant tablet which is sealed with the seal of the god Aššur, king of the gods, and set it up in your presence, like your own god.

Esarhaddon's new succession arrangements were disseminated throughout the empire, also expressed by visual means. Assyrian royal steles usually show only the king. But Esarhaddon had steles erected in Sam'al (Zinjirli, also located in the Hatay; see Figure 8) and Til-Barsip (Tell Ahmar in Syria) that depict himself on the front and, in smaller scale, the two crown princes on the left- and right-hand sides of the stele. Šamaš-šumu-ukin is shown wearing the traditional Babylonian royal garments. Also the image displayed on the royal seal was adapted to fit the new situation and to promote the succession arrangements. While the traditional depiction showed the king killing a lion the updated design repeated this subject three times (Figure 10). All this conveys that Esarhaddon and the princes were to govern the empire jointly, and contemporary letters indeed show both princes involved in matters of political and cultic importance.

**10. Impression of a stamp seal with three depictions of the
king fighting a rampant lion, the emblem of Assyrian kingship.
From Nineveh.**

When Esarhaddon died in 669, Aššurbanipal ascended to the
Assyrian throne, and Šamaš-šumu-ukin became king of Babylon, as
planned. But their relationship quickly soured as the Assyrian king
thought himself the overlord and his brother a mere client ruler.
A host of Babylonian officials reported directly to Aššurbanipal
who also controlled Babylonia's foreign affairs; there was no
separate army either. At some point, Aššurbanipal even claimed
publicly that it was he who had installed the king of Babylon.
Šamaš-šumu-ukin made a bid to break free of the embrace of
brother and empire in 652. We do not know what prompted him.
Had he gone native after nearly two decades in the south? But
it is clear that not everyone in Babylonia supported this bid for
independence. The country was deeply divided between Assyrian
loyalists and a Babylonian faction that, somewhat perversely,

followed an Assyrian. The Iranian kingdom of Elam and the leaders of the southern Aramean tribes supported Šamaš-šumu-ukin and provided badly needed military assistance. In turn, Aššurbanipal sent his army south.

Four years of bloody war followed, documented in a number of letters from the Assyrian state correspondence as well as Aššurbanipal's inscriptions. The conflict greatly destabilized Babylonia and led to severe famines, especially in those cities put under siege. People were forced to abandon their children, selling them for extremely little money at a time when prices for food were skyrocketing. Legal texts include clauses that specifically reference this in order to protect the buyer from future claims. The Assyrian side eventually emerged victorious but at great cost for Babylonia and for the entire empire. Šamaš-šumu-ukin's rebellion had severely damaged the credibility of Assyrian imperial sovereignty; other client states dared to push their luck and some, like Egypt, slipped out of the empire's hold.

Aššurbanipal and Šamaš-šumu-ukin had an older sister, Šerua-etirat, who had occupied a prominent position at her father's court, as documented in various letters. She tried to mediate in the conflict between her royal brothers. This is not known from contemporary sources but from a later literary composition about the conflict, recorded in Aramaic language and Demotic script on an Egyptian papyrus of the 4th century BC. In this story, Šerua-etirat appears firmly in Aššurbanipal's camp. She pleads with Šamaš-šumu-ukin to reconcile with the brother, but fails to convince him. She then suggests that he should kill himself together with his children and, interestingly, his scholars whom she blames for his unreasonableness. After all, they had filled his head with ideas about Babylonian kingship that were directly responsible for the present crisis. Says Šerua-etirat in the story:

> If you will not listen to my words and if you will not pay attention to my speech, leave the house of (god) Bel, go away from the house of

(god) Marduk. Let there be built for you a house of [...] construct a house of [...]. Throw down tar and pitch and sweet smelling perfumes. Bring in your sons and daughters and your scholars who have made you arrogant. When you see how (low) they have sunk to your detriment, let fire burn your fat with (that of) your sons and daughters and your scholars who have made you arrogant.

Šerua-etirat's suggestion for her brother to construct a funeral pyre and then burn himself, his children, and the scholars can be connected with Šamaš-šumu-ukin's death in a fire, as recorded in the inscriptions of Aššurbanipal.

This story, dubbed today The Tale of Two Brothers, is one of several Aramaic compositions that appraise 7th century Assyrian palace life. The Tale of the Sage Ahiqar is another example. It is known from a 5th century BC papyrus found in Elephantine in southern Egypt and deals with a scholar in Sennacherib's and Esarhaddon's service. Both tales draw on historical events and feature some accurate insider information, suggesting that they originated in the palace milieu. That such literature was composed in Aramaic highlights how widely spoken and used this language was even at court. That these stories are still transmitted centuries later, and in Egypt, demonstrates the lasting fascination of the cosmopolitan Assyrian imperial court culture.

# Chapter 5
# Foreigners in Assyria

This chapter looks at Assyrian interactions with the wider world
by focusing on foreigners in the city of Aššur and how they got
there. The first two cases explore Assyrian political and cultural
links to the Mesopotamian south in the second millennium BC.
The third case shows Assyrian diplomacy in action when an
Anatolian ruler was invited, like it or not, to visit Aššur. The last
two cases focus on inhabitants of the city of Aššur who had been
relocated there by force from Iran and serve to emphasize how
the Assyrian heartland was an increasingly multicultural,
cosmopolitan environment during its imperial phase.

## Role model: Samsi-Addu, conqueror of Aššur, 18th century BC

Although he did not originate from the city, King Samsi-Addu
ruled over Aššur for thirty-three years during the 18th century BC,
having subjugated it in the course of his extended wars of
conquest. So successful were his victories that he claimed the title
'King of the Universe'. While Aššur was a valuable addition to his
growing realm, he did not take up residence there but installed his
elder son as regent over the city; Išme-Dagan resided in nearby
Ekallate. The city and its god, however, were important enough to
Samsi-Addu to merit his special attention. He rebuilt the god

Aššur's sanctuary and added a monumental stepped tower in the southern Mesopotamian tradition to the temple complex. The remains of his building works were unearthed during Walter Andrae's excavations in Aššur, which also yielded copies of the inscription celebrating this effort.

The Assyrian kings Shalmaneser I in the 13th century BC and Esarhaddon in the 7th century prominently referenced him, as Šamši-Adad under the Assyrianized version of his West-Semitic name, when describing the building history of the Aššur temple prior to their own renovation projects. In doing so, they also honoured his request as expressed in the inscription:

> When the temple becomes dilapidated, may whoever among the kings, my sons, renovate the temple, anoint my clay and stone inscriptions with oil, make sacrifices and return them to their paces.

Assyrian rulers habitually looked for the foundation documents of their predecessors and deposited them with their own. This is the relevant passage in Esarhaddon's inscription from the Aššur temple:

> The earlier temple of the god Aššur, which Ušpia, my ancestor, regent of the god Aššur, had first built, became dilapidated and Erišum (I), son of Ilu-šuma, my ancestor, priest of the god Aššur, rebuilt it. 126 years passed and it became dilapidated again, and Šamši-Adad (I), son of Ilu-kabkabi, my ancestor, regent of the god Aššur, rebuilt it. 434 years passed and that temple was destroyed in a fire, (and) Shalmaneser (I), son of Adad-nerari (I), my ancestor, regent of the god Aššur, rebuilt it. 580 years passed and the inner cella, the residence of the god Aššur, my lord,…became dilapidated, aged, and antiquated. I was worried, afraid, and hesitant about renovating that temple. In the diviner's bowl, the gods Šamaš and Adad answered me with a firm 'yes' and they had (their response) concerning the rebuilding of that temple and the renovation of its chapel written on a liver.

The last passage refers to the sacrificial divination (see Chapter 3) undertaken to confirm that the gods indeed supported the intended building project.

In Samsi-Addu's inscription for the Aššur temple, the god is called Enlil, after the great southern Mesopotamian god. Aššur was seemingly taken to be but a facet of that deity as whose protégé Samsi-Addu described himself here and elsewhere. Šubat-Enlil 'Seat of Enlil' was the name that the king gave to the capital city that he created for his newly forged realm at Tell Leilan in the Khabur Triangle region of north-eastern Syria. In his own words of the Aššur temple inscription, he was the one 'who combined the land between Tigris and Euphrates'. The 18th century BC was in general a period marked by the formation of large trans-regional polities in the Middle East. At that time, for example, the rulers of Kaneš created a territorial state in central Anatolia that was the first incarnation of the so-called Hittite kingdom. The changed geopolitical situation was bad news for the merchant firms from Aššur as the additional costs enforced by the powerful new states cut deeply into their profit margins. Eventually, they abandoned their trading colonies in Anatolia altogether.

Towards the end of his long reign, Samsi-Addu expanded his power beyond the Tigris as far as the western flanks of the Zagros mountains and conquered regions that later constituted the Assyrian heartland. The extent of his realm therefore anticipated the borders of the kingdom of Assyria in the 13th century BC. But it was a fleeting creation that did not outlast its creator and quickly disintegrated after his death. The city of Aššur remained under the authority of his son Išme-Dagan, but he had to rely on allies in the south for his political survival and three times even fled to the city of Babylon. Soon after his death, Aššur reverted to local rule.

While the later rulers of the kingdom of Assyria habitually refer to Samsi-Addu as their ancestor, the immediate successors of his short-lived dynasty begged to differ. Thus we read in an inscription of Puzur-Sin:

> By the command of the god Aššur, my lord, I destroyed that improper thing which he had worked on: the wall and the palace of Šamši-Adad, his grandfather—a foreign plague, not of the flesh of the city of Aššur, who had destroyed the shrines of the city of Aššur.

Earlier in the inscription, the grandson is identified:

> When I, Puzur-Sin, regent of the god Aššur, son of Aššur-bel-šamê, destroyed the evil of Asinum, offspring of Šamši-[Adad],...and reinstituted proper rule for the city of Aššur.

The text creates an opposition between good and evil, between Assyrian and foreign, between Samsi-Addu's fortifications and palace and the city's temples. The conqueror, his heirs, and what they had created are rejected wholesale.

Samsi-Addu was indeed a foreigner whose rule over Aššur was not a birthright but the prize of conquest. Already the close relationship claimed with the god Enlil suggests his southern origin. Moreover, the list of his ancestors corresponds to the genealogy of another ruler who forged himself a large realm by conquest. Hammurabi, king of Babylon, is today best known for the monumental stele whose inscription includes a long list of legal rulings to demonstrate that he was the 'King of Justice': the so-called Code of Hammurabi. He and Samsi-Addu are likely to have been members of the same clan. The roots of the conqueror of Aššur are therefore today sought in the region of modern Baghdad where the Diyala flows into the Tigris.

Despite his non-Assyrian origins, Samsi-Addu was featured prominently in the so-called Assyrian King List, a document that records the rulers of Aššur and the length of their reigns. It incorporated not only Samsi-Addu and his son Išme-Dagan into the list of native rulers, but also their (and Hammurabi's) ancestors who had never even set foot into the city. Was this an attempt to legitimize Samsi-Addu's rule over Aššur by muddling his origins, or were the famous 'King of the Universe' and his ancestors claimed by the later Assyrian rulers as prestigious forefathers? Modern opinions are divided, and much depends on how the editorial history of the Assyrian King List is reconstructed. Neither Samsi-Addu's last heir, Asinum, nor Puzur-Sin, who ushered in a period of restoration after the end of Samsi-Addu's dynasty at Aššur, was included in the composition. This suggests that the text was compiled only at a later date when it was considered again more opportune to integrate Samsi-Addu smoothly into Assyrian history. However that may be, the resultant text was subsequently subject to periodic updating as entries for each Assyrian ruler were added. The text survives in several manuscripts, the latest written at the time of Shalmaneser V at the end of the 8th century BC. It is a key source for the reconstruction of the chronology of the entire ancient Middle East.

At the very least, by the 13th century BC, when King Shalmaneser I mentioned Samsi-Addu's renovation of the Aššur temple in his own building account, the conqueror was unreservedly understood as an Assyrian ruler and direct ancestor of the present king. At that time, no one desired to eradicate the memory or the physical traces of Samsi-Addu's rule over Aššur. As the previous master of a vast realm, the illustrious predecessor now served as a role model for the kings of Assyria and to mark this, they adopted his titles 'Appointee of the God Enlil' and the programmatic 'King of the Universe'.

## Marduk-nadin-ahhe, Royal Scribe from Babylon, c.1328 BC

Peace with Babylonia was important to Aššur-uballit I, the first king of Assyria in the 14th century BC. According to Babylonian chronicle texts, he secured good relations with the southern neighbour by marrying his daughter Muballitat-Šerua to Burnaburiaš

II, king of Babylon. Their son (Aššur-uballit's grandson) would inherit the Babylonian crown. However, when Burnaburiaš died in 1328 BC, the Babylonians turned against their new ruler Karahardaš, executed him and replaced him with Nazibugaš, the 'Son of a Nobody', that is, a person not related to the royal family. Why this happened is unknown, but as the slain king's royal grandfather Aššur-uballit immediately invaded Babylonia, it may have been precisely Karahardaš's Assyrian connections that had been the cause of his unpopularity. The Assyrian army made short work of the usurper, who was killed. Aššur-uballit claimed the throne for Kurigalzu II, another of his grandsons.

The loyalties of the Babylonians must have been divided between the rebels backing Nazibugaš and the supporters of the legitimate royal house. One man who may have been caught up in the conflict was the scribe Marduk-nadin-ahhe, a member of a distinguished family that had served the Babylonian rulers for several generations in high administrative and scholarly offices. This man chose to leave Babylonia and found a new home at the Assyrian capital of Aššur where he took up the distinguished position of Aššur-uballit's Royal Scribe. This office seems to correspond to the later title of Master Scholar (see Chapter 3) and presumably the incumbent fulfilled similar duties towards his kingly patron, composing royal inscriptions and other official texts, advising the monarch in scholarly matters, and perhaps even tutoring members of the royal family in scribal lore. Marduk-nadin-ahhe is the earliest Royal Scribe attested at the Assyrian court and presumably the office was created at that time. Aššur-uballit's mission was to confirm his kingdom of Assyria, until recently subordinate to Mittani, as a great realm. Establishing a highly visible role for a scholarly adviser to the king fits this objective very well, especially if the newly appointed Royal Scribe was descended from a family whose members had served the Babylonian crown in this fashion.

What we know about Marduk-nadin-ahhe derives from an inscription that he composed on the occasion of moving into his new house in Aššur. The text, known only from a later copy, concludes with appeals to the god Marduk, the lord of Babylon, for whom a shrine had been erected in the crowded temple quarter of Aššur during the reign of Aššur-uballit:

> May the god Marduk, my lord, inspect that house, and grant (it) to me for my troubles. May he allow (it) to endure in the future for my sons, my grandsons, my offspring, and the offspring of my offspring, so that we, I and my family, can revere Marduk, my lord, and Zarpanitu, my lady, forever, and perhaps, by the command of Marduk, someone can set straight my [relatives] and ancestral clan that have embraced treachery. May [Marduk], my lord, grant to Aššur-uballit, who loves me, king of the universe, my lord, long days with abundant prosperity.

From the unusual references to his troubles and to treacherous family members, it emerges quite clearly that Marduk-nadin-ahhe had been caught up in conflict in Babylonia prior to finding a new home under his patron and benefactor Aššur-uballit at Aššur, where he permanently hoped to establish himself and his family. He clearly did not contemplate that he or his descendants would ever return to his native Babylon.

The exile built his house from scratch next to the Marduk shrine, certainly with royal blessing, as living space in the cramped city of Aššur was at a premium and constructing a new house in the temple quarter would have required clearing away the existing buildings. The Divine Directory of Aššur (see Chapter 2) would seem to suggest that the Marduk shrine was part of the extended Aššur temple complex, and this would mean that Marduk-nadin-ahhe's house, 'erected in the shadow of the temple of Marduk', was built very close-by or perhaps even inside it. This would imply a priestly function for the Babylonian, most likely in the service of the cult of Marduk and his consort Zarpanitu.

Regardless of its location, with two wings, one accessible to the public, the other private living space with an underground tomb underneath the innermost room, the house conforms to the typical standards of an elite residence in Aššur, and even had its own well. The first part of the inscription reads:

> I, Marduk-nadin-ahhe, royal scribe, son of Marduk-uballit, son of Uššur-ana-Marduk, blessed by god and king, the humble, the obedient, the one who pleases his lord, took up residence in a distinguished manner in the house which I had erected in the shadow of the temple of Marduk, within which I had opened a well of cold water, which I had staked off by the exalted wisdom of the god Marduk, my lord. I had made the burnt brick rooms beneath it, about which no one knows, with wise understanding and the greatest care. I constructed and completed the entire house, its reception suites and residential quarters. I will not allow imbeciles to take possession (of it).

Does the last sentence betray chauvinism of this Babylonian luminary against his Assyrian neighbours?

## Royal hostages and an accidental tourist in Aššur, 1112 BC

In the first example of a new type of inscription that structured the narrative in chronological order (hence 'Assyrian Annals') and gave a summary of the king's deeds for each year of his reign up until the time that the text was composed, Tiglath-pileser I details how he led an expeditionary force deep into Anatolia in 1112 BC. On the plain of Manzikert to the north of Lake Van, best known as the battlefield where the Seljuq Sultan Alp Arslan annihilated the Byzantine army in AD 1071, the Assyrian king, too, celebrated a triumph. He defeated an alliance of twenty-three local rulers there. His account of the battle ends with this passage:

> I captured all the kings of Nairi (= Anatolia) alive. I had mercy on them and spared their lives. I released them from their bonds and

fetters before the sun god, my lord, and made them swear an oath of everlasting servitude by my great gods. I took their royal sons as hostages. I imposed on them a tribute of 1,200 horses and 2,000 cattle. I allowed them to return to their lands.

The defeated rulers had to accept Assyrian sovereignty and concluded a treaty with their new overlord. An oath and their children's placement as hostages protected the agreement which stipulated the regular delivery of cattle and horses, urgently needed in Assyria for the chariotry and, in later times from the 9th century onwards, for the cavalry (see Chapter 6). The Anatolian hostages were to be raised at the royal court of Assyria where their presence served a twofold purpose. While in Assyria, they were to guarantee their families', and countries', loyalty with their lives. And when they returned to their native land, ideally as its ruler or in another influential position, the time spent at the Assyrian court would have attuned them to Assyrian sensibilities and thus ensured their dependable conduct at home.

This is especially well attested in the early 7th century BC when several former hostages returned to rule their native country in line with Assyria's wishes: Bel-ibni, whom Sennacherib appointed as king of Babylon in 703 BC, 'had grown up like a puppy in my palace' (or, given the timing, rather his father Sargon's palace), while Tabua, whom Esarhaddon made queen of the Arabs, 'was raised in the palace of my father (Sennacherib)' according to the royal inscriptions. These royal hostages had been children when they were sent to the Assyrian court—an obvious advantage for the objective of pro-Assyrian indoctrination. But the distinction between hostage and protégé could be somewhat blurred. On occasion, foreign dynasts saw the Assyrian court as a safe haven for their children, especially in times of upheaval back home. Balassu, leader of the southern Babylonian tribe of Bit-Dakkuri, for example, sent his son and daughter to Sargon II for their protection when his enemy Merodach-baladan, of the rival Bit-Yakin tribe, proclaimed himself king of Babylon.

Tiglath-pileser I's inscription about the Anatolian campaign continued:

> I brought Seni, king of Daienu, who had not been submissive to the god Aššur, my lord, in bonds and fetters to my city Aššur. I had mercy on him and let him leave my city Aššur alive in order to proclaim the glory of the great gods.

One of the Anatolian kings, it would seem, needed to be taught a special lesson. Unlike his twenty-two allies, he was brought to Aššur. Does the reference to his not being submissive mean that he refused to swear the loyalty oath and was he therefore taken as a punishment? Or would this classification have equally applied to all the other Anatolian rulers and the visit to the Assyrian capital was a special distinction? However that may be, after Seni's sojourn to Aššur he was sent back home. There, he was to sing the praise of the gods and presumably of Assyria and its king, of whose power a visit to the capital would have given Seni a fair idea.

Such visits to central Assyria were a typical experience for rulers who had been made to accept Assyrian sovereignty. The imagery of the royal palaces from Aššurnasirpal II onwards was specifically designed to make an impact on them. Chaotic scenes of conquest and surrender on the one hand and orderly scenes of royal audiences and delivery of tribute on the other showed the two modes of interaction with Assyrian power, and it was the latter that was meant to appeal to the foreign visitors.

## An Iranian family in Aššur, 715–614 BC

We have already encountered in Chapter 3 members of the substantial Egyptian community living in Aššur, relocated there after the Assyrian conquest of Memphis in 671 BC. They were not the first foreigners from beyond the Semitic-speaking world of Mesopotamia and Syro-Palestina to be settled in the ancient city.

Already, forty years earlier, in the aftermath of the creation of two Assyrian provinces in the region of modern Hamadan in western Iran, people from these Median territories had been brought 500 kilometres westwards, across the Zagros mountains to Aššur in 715 BC.

The initial situation in the provinces of Harhar and Kišessim, which Sargon II had established in 716, was dangerously volatile, as the king's correspondence with his governors and vassals in the area illustrates. The Assyrian administration struggled with the harsh weather that slowed down the establishment of the necessary infrastructure, and snow in the Zagros cut the new provinces off from the Assyrian heartland for parts of the year. Already in 715 the new provinces rose in rebellion against the fledgling Assyrian government and the imperial army returned. The intervention was very bloody and, according to the inscriptions of Sargon II, 4,000 enemy warriors were beheaded. A further 4,820 persons were selected for relocation (see Chapter 6), and this brought some of them to the city of Aššur.

One extended family from Hundir, the hinterland of Kišessim, moved into houses within the monumental gateway leading into the north-western part of Aššur—erected in this somewhat awkward location because it had become increasingly difficult to find suitable accommodation elsewhere in the cramped city. Walter Andrae excavated these buildings in 1906 while investigating the city's fortifications. He found them well preserved, as the city wall, against which they leaned, had collapsed at some point after 614 BC and buried them. The houses and especially the documents found there give us insight into the Iranian clan living there. In the 620s the household consisted of the members of three generations and their twenty-one slaves, a total of at least thirty-five permanent residents. The family is known in detail because of two legal documents recording the division of the estate left by family head Mudammiq-Aššur to his six sons. This was a well-to-do family spread out over two sizeable houses. With the ground floors taking up areas of 240 m² and 320 m² respectively, they lived in considerably grander style than their contemporary, the wine merchant Duri-Aššur (see Chapter 3).

Since the arrival of the Medes at Aššur, the men of the family held positions at the Aššur temple (as did most of the city's notables), but as their professional title was 'Hundurean', after their place of origin, it is not clear what their actual occupation was. They worked with a certain type of textile that may have been a kind of rug. If this is correct then perhaps they introduced to central Assyria the art of hand-knotting carpets with a pile. The family was also involved in overland trade but unlike in the case of Duri-Aššur's wine firm, the destination of their caravans is not mentioned in the records. As caravan staff were given working contracts of seven–twelve months, which covered both legs of the trip, these were long-distance journeys. Given the family's origins, it seems most likely that they were trading with their Iranian homeland. After all, the Median centres Harhar and Kišessim had been renamed by their conqueror Sargon II: Kar-Šarrukin, 'Sargon's Harbour,' and Kar-Nergal, 'Harbour of the God Nergal' (using the conventional designation for trading posts; see Chapter 2) in appreciation of their role in the overland trade along an important stage of the Silk Route.

The distinct cultural heritage of the Egyptians, including names, deities, and material culture was still apparent decades after their arrival; but the Iranian clan, who of course had arrived at Aššur two generations before the Egyptian community, used—at least by the second half of the 7th century—only Assyrian names invoking Assyrian deities, and no recognizably Iranian material was found in the remains of their houses. Although such evidence would seem to suggest that the family embraced the Assyrian lifestyle, it is also clear that the Medes at Aššur preserved some part of their Iranian identity: they maintained their own distinct occupation (whatever its nature) and also traded with the old country.

The sources tell us nothing about their role in the Median assault on Aššur or their fate after the conquest in 614. It is tempting to link the swift success of the siege with the fact that Medes lived inside one of the city's principal gates and were therefore in a prime position to help the besiegers enter the city. After all, it is otherwise surprising that the Medes succeeded so swiftly when the Babylonian army had failed to take Aššur during its surprise attack in the previous year, especially as the city's fortifications and food reserves had been increased in anticipation of a further attack.

## Two female prisoners of war, sold as slaves, c.645 BC

By now, we have encountered a great many slaves who were ubiquitous throughout the cities of the Assyrian Empire. In Assyrian society, owning slaves was an indication of wealth and social status, and slave owners were generally members of the urban elite. In this section, we will focus on two of them, mother and daughter, and trace how they came to live in Aššur as slaves. Like many Assyrian slaves, they were of foreign extraction. But native free-born Assyrians, too, could be sold into slavery as a last resort in lieu of debt; they could be released if they, or someone else on their behalf, paid up. Most slaves that we encounter in the sources served as domestic staff and lived in their owner's house. A slave woman's child was born a slave, regardless of who the father was. Often, this would have been the owner. He could adopt the child if he wanted to acknowledge his offspring, and only in that case would the child have had the right to inherit. This happened rarely, usually if there were no legitimate sons, and the wife's consent was needed, as stipulations in marriage contracts indicate.

Between 664 and 648 BC, Assyrian forces repeatedly invaded and plundered the south-western Iranian kingdom of Elam. After a brief period of peace under Esarhaddon the two states were in a state of war during much of Aššurbanipal's early reign, documented in royal inscriptions, on the wall decorations of his palaces in Nineveh, and in letters of the state correspondence. A private legal text from Aššur documents the fate of one woman and her daughter who were caught up in the wars and taken away from Elam as captives. In the document recording their sale (for one mina (c.500 grams) of silver, an average price in the mid-7th century), they are described as 'booty from Elam whom the king had given to Libbali (i.e. the city of Aššur)'. Depictions on the palace wall decoration frequently show how after battle, administrators registered and distributed the spoils, including human captives. But the further fortunes of individual prisoners of war are hard to trace in the sources, and the case of the two Elamite captives is a rare example that highlights the effects of war on women.

The sale contract's date is lost but its context suggests that Nanaya-ila'i and her child were snatched during the sack of Susa in 646 BC when enormous amounts of booty were captured. When they reached Aššur as part of the booty contingent reserved for that city, our text documents that ten men owned them jointly and sold them to one man, Mannu-ki-Aššur. The sellers, identified by name and profession, were a group of various temple craftsmen, among them a baker, a cook, a weaver, a goldsmith, an ironsmith, and a shepherd. Although they were of course all serving the Aššur temple, they had otherwise little in common. However, as there are ten of them and because a military connection links them to the Elamite captives, we may assume that they constituted a work unit (*kiṣru*, literally 'knot') that fulfilled their work obligations to the state, including military service, as a group. As part of the contingent from Aššur, they may have participated in a military campaign against Elam (most likely as non-combatant maintenance staff; see Chapter 6) and received the Elamite captives as their reward from the battle spoils reserved for their city. As owning the slaves jointly was of limited practical use to the men, selling them and dividing the proceeds was the obvious solution and the sale took place as soon as the Elamite captives arrived at Aššur.

From then on, Nanaya-ila'i and her daughter spent their lives as domestic slaves in Mannu-ki-Aššur's household. Their fate was very different from, say, the Medes or Egyptians who had been settled in Aššur. The latter may have had little say in their relocation but once there, they were 'counted among the Assyrians' and had the same rights and duties as the other free inhabitants. They were not slaves, in contrast to war spoils like Nanaya-ila'i and her daughter. The woman's name means 'The goddess Nanaya is my deity'. It was certainly not her original one and Nanaya-ila'i would only have received it once she had come into Assyrian captivity. The name is a deliberate reference to Aššurbanipal's widely publicized repatriation of an ancient statue of the goddess Nanaya that had been abducted over a millennium ago to Elam. Her daughter's name was not given, which suggests that she was quite young and considered dependent on her mother. She was likely older than four years as she is neither identified as a baby ('Of the milk' or 'Of the breast') nor as a toddler ('Separated', referring to being weaned from the breast).

Just as Nanaya-ila'i was stripped of her name, she would have lost much that constituted her previous identity. We know nothing about her original social background in Elam. But at least she was not separated from her child. This was usual practice in Assyrian slave sales, certainly as long as the children were small. In this specific case it was sensible to keep mother and daughter together because it would have made integrating the foreigners easier into their new environment. Elamite is a language entirely unrelated to Semitic languages like Assyrian and Aramaic that were widely spoken in Aššur. This makes it unlikely that Nanaya-ila'i would have been able to communicate fluently in her new surroundings. Given her young age, her daughter would have picked up the local languages more easily and facilitated also her mother's integration.

In their new life, the two Elamites contributed to the everyday running of the household of their master Mannu-ki-Aššur.

Nothing else is known about this man but given that he was from Aššur, he probably lived in a house rather like the ones owned by the wine merchant Duri-Aššur (see Chapter 3) or the Median family already discussed. His family would have had a number of slaves but the Elamites were certainly not part of a household numbering scores of people, unlike the one inhabiting Šulmu-šarri's gigantic mansion in Dur-Katlimmu (see Chapter 3). Nanaya-ila'i and her daughter would have spent their time performing household chores: grinding flour, baking, cooking, and sweeping, and they may have added to the household's prosperity by spinning wool and weaving textiles that could be sold at a profit. We may imagine their existence as a quiet one, a relief after the trauma of their wartime experiences and their abduction to the Assyrian heartland. But unless she died early (for example during childbirth, as happened frequently), Nanaya-ila'i's daughter would have witnessed another invasion, the conquest of Aššur in 614 BC. She may well have been claimed as booty again, this time by the Median army who would have taken her back east into Iran.

# Chapter 6
# Assyrian world domination: pathfinder empire

The Assyrian Empire, as it was configured in the 9th century BC, was the pathfinder among the sequence of empires subsequently dominating the wider Mediterranean and Middle East, including the Persian and the Roman empires. Its ideological, infrastructural, and organizational innovations provided the basis and template for the successor states. Winning an empire is a challenge, but making it cohere is an even bigger one, and Assyria faced this task with aplomb. This final chapter is devoted to key aspects of governance and ideology that contributed to the fact that the Assyrian Empire managed to control its holdings for three centuries. Warfare is prominently reviewed in sources such as Assyrian palace art, royal inscriptions, and the Bible, and we will have a closer look at the empire's fabled army. The ideology of absolute kingship, the innovative long-distance relay postal service and the empire-wide resettlement programme provided powerful tools for the empire's cohesion. The final section deals with the royal library that the Assyrian kings assembled and maintained from the 14th century BC. Since its rediscovery in the mid-19th century by the indefatigable Austen Henry Layard, it has contributed much to our knowledge of Assyria's cultural history. If a love of books played any role at all in the library's creation then it was certainly not the only motivation.

# The 'hosts of Aššur'—an ancient army you'd rather not join?

When Assyria emerged as a territorial power in the 14th century BC, the bulk of its armed forces consisted of an infantry mustered from conscripted farmers and of a chariotry led by members of the leading families who fought with bow and arrow. The second member of the chariot crew, the driver, was apparently a dependant of the fighter. He was always mentioned in second place and, unlike the fighters who were so well known that they often needed no further qualification in archival documents, usually identified by military title. The chariotry of that age can be seen as semi-professional in that its members had to spend a good deal of time exercising their skill. But it remains unclear whether they were permanently stationed or, as seems more likely, only assembled when called up by the king. The conscripts drafted from the tax-paying population could provide military service only during the summer months when the agricultural calendar permitted the absence of farm workers. They were organized into units based on the decimal system (10, 50, 100), and the resultant social structures counterbalanced the importance of the family and were a forceful reminder of the impact of the state on each individual's life. The entire armed forces were structured in this way.

The mid-9th century BC saw the definitive shift from an army dominated by temporarily mobilized conscripts to one largely consisting of fighters maintained all year round. Shalmaneser III established standing armies that were permanently stationed in vulnerable border regions. In doing so, he also drew on captured specialized fighters who had been absorbed into the Assyrian army during a century of conquest. At the same time, the first Assyrian cavalry units were created. The integration of fighters from defeated regions into the permanent forces continued routinely and focused on chariotry and mounted troops, that is, those fighters with the most specialized training. Once the expansion begun under Tiglath-pileser III had resulted in doubling Assyria's former holdings, the standing armed forces were so numerous that the tax-paying population was no longer required for temporary military service and mostly used for civilian purposes, such as public building works. No longer dependent on personnel tied to the agricultural calendar, campaigning was now possible also outside of the summer months, enabling much longer military operations to much further destinations, such as Egypt.

The Assyrian army of the first millennium BC was really many armies, termed poetically the 'Hosts of the God Aššur' in the royal inscriptions. The different contingents were allowed to preserve and develop their own customs and idiosyncrasies. Rather than being forged into a unified army, its individual components found themselves in intense competition with each other for royal recognition and favour. This strategy aimed at neutralizing the armed forces' otherwise unbridled power vis-à-vis king and state: a useful and successful policy that significantly contributed to Assyria's internal stability and the longevity of its royal dynasty. The different bodies of the army were structured into smaller contingents led by officers, at least some of whom were promoted from the ordinary ranks. The basic command unit numbered fifty men. One can distinguish between the 'Royal Cohort' that the king himself commanded and the armies he placed under the authority of others. Although troops were stationed at forts set up in strategic border locations, the provinces were not permanently garrisoned and the provincial governors controlled troops only in the short term, either mobilized temporarily or brought in from elsewhere. An efficient defensive system concentrated the bulk of the standing army in four strategically located border marches established during the reign of Shalmaneser III.

Alongside the Assyrian contingents fought auxiliaries from adjoining regions and internal peripheries (steppes, deserts, mountains). These were of great importance and in the main assumed the role of the infantry that conscripted fighters had held previously. The empire cultivated long-standing relationships with certain auxiliary units. But the politics of the day and opportunity certainly influenced the use of auxiliaries as well. Hence, the forces mustered by Sennacherib during his war in Judah in 701 BC, as depicted in the siege of Lachish on the walls of his Southwest Palace in Nineveh, included auxiliary contingents of slingers, specialized infantry fighters using slingshots that were typical of that very region, as the Biblical story of David's victory over Goliath best illustrates. In the palace wall decorations, auxiliary troops can be easily distinguished from Assyrian troops by their dress. While the latter wear standardized uniforms together with the typical conical helmet, the auxiliaries are always shown wearing their own specific clothes. In Assyrian art, warfare is a matter for grown-ups: all warriors are shown as mature men in their physical prime, with full beards (unless they are eunuchs; see Chapter 2), and heavily muscled.

In terms of specialization, the imperial army consisted of the chariotry, the cavalry, and the infantry divided into ranged archers and close combat spearmen. The term for spearmen was 'Bearer of shield and spear', referencing the typical armoured shield and spear, but this was often abbreviated to 'Shield-bearer'. These fighters closely correspond to the Greek hoplites. The term for chariotry is simply the designation for chariot while the cavalry is called after the riding horse (literally, 'The one opening one's thighs'). All of these troops were professional fighters. Various textual sources suggest that a ratio of 1:10:200 for chariotry, cavalry, and infantry, with the latter divided 2:1 into archers and spearmen, was considered an ideal balance. However, the armed forces were mustered to suit specific objectives and an appropriate selection of troops was dispatched accordingly. When on the move, the Assyrian army lived in tents inside fortified camps that were temporarily constructed. Building the camp was one of the tasks of the non-combatant support staff, some recruited from conscripts, that constituted a very large part of the armed forces.

Every provincial capital maintained food and fodder storage facilities for the use of the army. Abroad, the troops and their animals lived off the land by foraging as bulky supplies were kept to a minimum while travelling.

Chariots manned by archers continued to be used in the Assyrian armed forces from the late second to the first millennium BC, without disruption and little change in equipment and tactical use. In the plains of Mesopotamia and Syria the chariot's twin advantages of speed and manoeuvrability continued to make it an excellent weapon of attack. The cavalry, on the other hand, was established as a regular component of the army only in the 9th century under Shalmaneser III. The light and brittle construction of a chariot and its lack of suspension made driving this expensive vehicle in mountainous landscapes impossible as the resultant damage to the wheels would immobilize it completely. Chariots had to be disassembled in order to be transported in such terrain, rendering them inconvenient ballast rather than dangerous weapons. The cavalry grew out of the attempt to develop a rough terrain chariot suitable for the rugged landscapes of the Taurus and Zagros regions—key arenas of conflict since the emergence of Urartu, Mannea, and the Medes in the 9th century BC. The earliest depictions of Assyrian cavalry on Shalmaneser III's bronze decoration of the temple gates at Balawat near Kalhu, show teams of two riders operating like a chariot would (one serving the role of the 'driver', one as the archer), but without the terrain limitations of the chariot's physical body.

The chariot troops retained their value in the plains, but by the mid-8th century the more economical and more mobile cavalry had replaced the light chariotry in the battlefield. Chariots were now armoured and manned by teams of three: the chariot driver, the fighter, and the so-called 'Third Man' who shielded the others. In the 7th century BC chariots were still maintained in the hundreds but now even more heavily armoured, drawn by four horses and with a fourth man on the chariot team providing additional protection. These tank-like constructions were much taller than previous models, with wheel diameters of close to two metres, and were used to shoot at enemy archers at close range, serving, moreover, very effectively the twin purposes of show-of-force and intimidation.

Chariot troops, cavalry, and the majority of the infantry fought with bow and arrow, using a traditional composite model with a triangular profile and a length of 110–125 cm. The bow was therefore the most important weapon of the Assyrian forces, and this fact should inform all considerations of their tactics in pitched battle. However, the biased nature of the sources makes any attempt to reconstruct particular battles inherently problematic.

Sea warfare played a relatively minor role. The first Assyrian fleet was constructed in 694 and deployed in the Persian Gulf. Ships built by Syrian craftsmen at Nineveh and manned with crews of Phoenicians and 'Ionians' (probably a general term for Greeks) were sailed down the Tigris to Babylonia, then transported overland to a side arm of the Euphrates and from there sailed to the Persian Gulf to mount a surprise attack on the coast of Elam in Iran. The ships were presumably biremes (galleys with two decks of oars), as routinely depicted on the palace wall decoration. In the Mediterranean, the empire relied on collaboration with its Phoenician clients, especially Tyre. Assyria did not maintain a Mediterranean navy of its own until Sidon was annexed in 677 and established as an Assyrian port, under the new name 'Esarhaddon's Harbour'. The hold over Sidon was used to provide rearguard for the land-led invasion of Egypt.

Siege warfare, on the other hand, was a key tactic of the Assyrian forces but even more so the threat of siege. Without catapults (widely used only from the early 4th century BC onwards) or any other kind of heavy artillery that could be deployed from a safe distance, the only option was to overcome or destroy the fortifications while operating within reach of the defenders.

11. Capture of a fortified Egyptian city on the Nile and its aftermath, the arrest of Nubian soldiers from Kush and the deportation of the civilian Egyptian population. From King Aššurbanipal's North Palace in Nineveh.

Depictions of sieges on the palace wall decorations (Figure 11) show an impressive arsenal of battering rams and manned siege engines, ladders, and mobile siege towers as well as sapping and tunnelling. These images were designed to create the impression that Assyrian conquest was inevitable. The popular view of the Assyrian Empire rarely goes beyond the impression gained from these images, resulting—absolutely in line with the intent of their creators—in the perception of a people hell-bent on conquest. This is, for example, the key message of *You Wouldn't Want to Be an Assyrian Soldier: An Ancient Army You'd Rather Not Join*, by Rupert Matthews and David Antram, a rare, and amusing, example of a children's book dealing with Assyria.

However, if a fortified city had to be taken entirely by force, without help from within, the cost would have been very high. Consequently, sieges were avoided whenever possible, as for example oracle queries (see Chapter 3) indicate. Various methods were used to persuade the besieged to surrender. Promises of amnesty were honoured if accepted; resettling the population was not considered punishment. If this did not yield results, the trees in the fruit orchards and palm tree plantations outside the city walls were put to the axe one by one. As these take many years to yield fruit, this lastingly damaged the livelihood of the besieged community. Finally, selected prisoners of war or hostages were executed in plain sight of the defenders. The method of choice was live impalement, but it is clear that most sieges ended before it came to this. If the besieged did not yield, as for example the cities of Babylon and Nippur over several years during the war between Aššurbanipal and his brother Šamaš-šumu-ukin for control over Babylonia, then famine and disease quickly made life in the enclosed cities harrowing and unremittingly bleak.

## The blessed king: absolute monarchy

When Aššurnasirpal II relocated the court from Aššur to Kalhu in 879 BC, the images decorating the throne room of his new palace were consciously designed to promote a crucial twofold ideological message. Firstly, that Aššurnasirpal II controlled all lands. We have already highlighted the opposition between the orderly, calm scenes of audiences and tribute delivery that show the king interacting with his dutiful clients and the chaotic, violent scenes of conquest and siege that illustrate how the king reacted to resistance. Secondly, the throne room was to emphasize that despite the move away from the temple of Aššur, the relationship between the god and the king, his chosen representative, was as close and strong as ever.

To this end, a remarkable scene was depicted twice in the throne room (Figure 12), once on the wall opposite the entrance along the longer side of the oblong hall and again at its far end, above the platform on which the royal throne rested. As visitors entered the room, their glance was therefore directed forcefully onto the heraldic, mirrored image that showed Aššurnasirpal (twice) with the god Aššur. The king, guarded by a winged protective spirit,

12. The king in communion with the god Aššur. From King Aššurnasirpal II's throne room in the Northwest Palace at Kalhu.

raises his right hand in the typical gesture of worship to the deity; this scene is shown twice on either side of the god. Aššur is shown in human yet disembodied form as the divine counterpart to the king in the guise of a bearded man wearing the distinctive fez-like headdress of the Assyrian ruler and holding the king's weapons of choice, the bow and arrow. A winged disc surrounds the figure, emphasizing the deity's ethereal otherworldliness, and hovers above an enigmatic emblem that is today called Sacred Tree or Tree of Life (although it does not really look like a tree at all). This imagery powerfully suggests that the king did not need the temple of Aššur in order to commune with the god. So strong was their link that the blessed king himself served as a conduit. With Aššur's blessing, his power was absolute.

But it did not need an audience with the king in Kalhu to come across this potent image. A carnelian cylinder seal (Figure 13) of the local ruler of Šadikanni (from Tell Ajaja on the Khabur in north-eastern Syria) demonstrates that the image was disseminated across the empire in the form of easily portable art. The seal bears the inscription in cuneiform script of Mušezib-Ninurta, son of Ninurta-ereš, grandson of Samanuha-šar-ilani, members of an

**13. Carnelian cylinder seal with a cuneiform inscription, showing a scene modelled on that from the throne room of Aššurnasirpal II.**

ancient dynasty that ruled over the city of Šadikanni. Samanuha-šar-ilani was a contemporary of Aššurnasirpal, attested as an Assyrian ally in the reconquest of the Khabur region in the account for the year 883 in the Assyrian king's inscriptions. His grandson was presumably a contemporary of Aššurnasirpal's long-lived successor Shalmaneser III. The inscription was engraved in the positive on the seal, meaning that it was impressed in mirror writing when the seal was used. This suggests that the text was not an original part of the seal design and it may have been added at a considerably later time. A likely scenario is that Aššurnasirpal bestowed the precious object as a gift on his ally, for the seal shows a scene modelled on the heraldic design displayed in the throne room of Aššurnasirpal's palace at Kalhu.

By (at least) the 7th century, royal ideology saw the king as a being quite separate from ordinary humans and superior to them. In a literary text about the creation of man, the gods fashioned the king in a separate act after having already created mankind:

Ea (god of wisdom) opened his mouth to speak, saying a word to Belet-ili (goddess of creation): 'You are Belet-ili, the sister of the great gods; it was you who created man, the human (*lullû amēlu*). Fashion now the king, the counsellor man (*šarru māliku amēlu*)! Gird the whole of his figure so pleasingly, make perfect his countenance and well formed his body!' And Belet-ili fashioned the king, the counsellor man.

The blessed royal family held a very special status in Assyrian society and only its male members were eligible for kingship. Although there were usurpations and succession wars, all Assyrian kings until the end of the empire are descended from this one family through the male line, making it one of the longest serving royal houses of all time.

## Long-distance express communication

A key strategy for ensuring cohesion across the vast Assyrian Empire was fast communication connecting the king with the governors in the provinces and the ambassadors at the client rulers' courts abroad. The imperial communication network was carefully planned and created in the 9th century BC and known as the 'King's Road'. The governors had to maintain road stations in strategic positions within their province that served as stages and intersections in the imperial communication system; whenever a new province was added to the realm, it was one of the key challenges of the new administration to connect it to the 'King's Road'. The road stations were either situated within existing settlements or constituted settlements of their own, with the necessary agricultural basis to provide for personnel, envoys, and transport animals. The caravanserais of the medieval Muslim world may serve as a convenient comparison, in that they, too, are purpose-built structures along long-distance routes providing short-term shelter and protection for travellers and their animals, but a crucial difference is that the Assyrian road stations served only the state and were not open to commercial travellers.

The circle of people allowed to make use of the resources of the 'King's Road' was therefore restricted and only available to those who had been formally appointed to a state office. The magnates of the empire all received a copy of a signet ring engraved with the universally recognized imperial emblem (showing the king killing a lion; see Figure 10) as a symbol of their office and as a tool to act in the king's stead. They used this ring to seal their letters, and this enabled all those playing a role in the transmission of their missives, such as the personnel of the road stations and the king's secretaries, to instantly identify them as letters of state importance, treating them with the required attention and urgency.

Messages were exchanged either by letter only, passed on from courier to courier, or by envoy (who might or might not carry a letter). Sending an envoy, who travelled the whole distance, was the preferred means of communication when the message was very sensitive or when it was important that a decision could be made on the spot. The king's 'Friends' (see Chapter 3) often served as his envoys. The first method was considerably faster, as each courier travelled only one stage of the distance from one past station to the next, where the letter was passed on to a new courier, enabling the message to travel without delay. The disassociation between letter and messenger was an Assyrian innovation of the 9th century BC, radical at the time. Until the advent of the telegraph, this relay system set the standard for communication speed for almost three millennia.

The couriers and envoys were mounted, travelling with pairs of mules in order to reduce the possibility that the rider was ever left stranded with a lame animal. The offspring of a horse mother and a donkey father, these infertile hybrids combine the body of a horse with the extremities of a donkey and often grow taller than the parents. Mules mature five years later than the parent animals but have a longer working life of up to twenty years. Infertile, slow to develop physically and in need of extensive yet sensitive training, mules were an expensive investment. For the Assyrian state, however, the expense was easily offset by the fact that mules are stronger and more resilient than horses, while sharing the donkey's sure-footedness and instinct for self-preservation; they are also good swimmers. The military use of these animals has continued into the present, for example, in the British and the US armies.

The king's correspondents used the expensive communication system only when they needed to involve the central administration in their decision-making or in order to pass on essential information. The magnates were appointed in order to exercise power locally on behalf of the crown and, in doing so, were meant to rely on their own judgement. Their main duty was to act on behalf of the king wherever and whenever he himself could not be present. Most of their letters therefore deal with the unexpected rather than with routine matters: opportunities arising and catastrophes unfolding, turns of events that galvanize or, on occasion, stupefy the wardens of the Assyrian Empire. Many of the letters therefore focus on problems, hiccups, and challenges.

About 2,000 letters from the state correspondence of the first millennium are presently known. These letters are rather unevenly distributed over two centuries, from the reign of Adad-nerari III in the early 8th century to the end of the empire. Most of the state letters, about 1,200 texts, date to the reign of Sargon II. Most of these were found as part of the royal archives at Nineveh, where they had been moved to under Sargon's successor Sennacherib, but a smaller part of his correspondence has been excavated at Kalhu. These texts are one of the best sources available for historians studying how an ancient empire was run.

## Counting them as Assyrians: the resettlement programme

All people of the empire, no matter their origin, were 'counted among the Assyrians', as the royal inscriptions put it. The Bible quotes a message that King Sennacherib supposedly communicated to the people of Jerusalem during the siege of 701 BC. After urging them to abandon his treacherous vassal, their king Hezekiah of Judah, he said:

> Make peace with me and come out to me. Then each of you will eat fruit from your own vine and fig tree and drink water from your own cistern, until I come and take you to a land like your own—a land of grain and new wine, a land of bread and vineyards, a land of olive trees and honey. Choose life and not death! (2 Kings 18: 31–2)

'Deportation', as the strategy of mass resettlement in the Assyrian Empire is usually called (a misnomer, given various inapplicable associations such as marginalization and extermination), could indeed be regarded as a privilege rather than a punishment. People moved together with their families and their possessions (see Figure 11); they were not snatched away in the heat of battle or conquest, but were chosen as the result of a deliberate selection process, often in the aftermath of a war that had very possibly reduced their original home to ruins; and when the Assyrian sources specify who was to be relocated, they name the urban elites, craftsmen, scholars, and military men. The resettlement policy divided communities into those who had to stay and those who had to leave, according to the needs of the empire. The specialists from newly subjugated areas were most frequently resettled in the Assyrian heartland to the economic and cultural benefit of the empire, to generate knowledge and wealth.

On the other hand, disgraced Assyrians, rather than being killed, were sent away from their home in order to redeem themselves as colonists in the state's service. In complex circular movements that were carefully planned and executed over several years, populations were relocated within the boundaries of the empire, replacing and being replaced by people who were themselves moved. For example, inhabitants of Samaria, conquered in 722 BC, were moved to the two provinces Harhar and Kiššesim created in Median territory in the Hamadan region in Iran in 716 BC. People from there were in turn settled in Aššur (see Chapter 5), from whence some people, pardoned after a failed insurrection in 720 BC, had been relocated to Hamath (modern Hama in Syria) which had rebelled at the same time and been destroyed as a result. Its inhabitants were moved to Samaria, closing this circuit. It is only one strand of vastly complex, simultaneous arrangements that included also regions in Babylonia and Anatolia. It has been calculated on the basis of references in the royal inscriptions that 4,400,000 ± 900,000 people were relocated from the mid-9th to the mid-7th century BC, of which 85 per cent were settled in central Assyria—a gigantic number, especially in a world whose population was a small fraction of today's. For all of these people, resettlement was meant to provide a better future while at the same time benefitting the empire. Of course, their relocation was at the same time an effective way of minimizing the risk of rebellion against the central authority.

The settlers, their labour, and their abilities were extremely valuable to the state. Their relocation was carefully planned and organized. They were to travel comfortably and safely in order to reach their destination in good physical shape. In the depictions decorating the palace walls, men, women, and children are shown travelling in groups, often riding on vehicles or animals, and never in bonds. The travel provisions for one group of settlers from western Syria were the subject of an 8th century letter from an official to King Tiglath-pileser III:

> As for the Arameans about whom the king my lord has written to me: 'Prepare them for their journey!' I shall give them their food

supplies, clothes, a waterskin, a pair of shoes and oil. I do not have my donkeys yet, but once they are available, I will dispatch my convoy.

That the state also supported the settlers once they had reached their destination is clear from another letter of the same correspondence:

As for the Arameans about whom the king my lord has said: 'They are to have wives!' we found numerous suitable women but their fathers refuse to give them in marriage, claiming: 'We will not consent unless they can pay the bride price.' Let them be paid so that the Arameans can get married.

This statement highlights how the state actively encouraged a mixing of the new neighbours. The ultimate goal of the Assyrian resettlement policy was to create a homogeneous population of 'Assyrians' with a shared culture and a common identity.

## Knowledge and power: the royal library

If the discovery of the palace sculpture made Assyria popular and resulted in best-selling books and crowded exhibitions in the mid-19th century AD, the recovery of the extensive archives and libraries from the royal palaces of Nineveh and their decipherment heralded the foundation of a new academic discipline dubbed Assyriology. While its core had been gradually assembled over centuries, the collection is today called the 'Library of Aššurbanipal', after the most avid among the royal collectors. The once substantial holdings of wax-boards (see Chapter 2) have been completely lost to the fires engulfing the palaces on Nineveh in 612 and the ravages of time. But about 20,000 library tablets have survived and are today kept in the British Museum as part of its 'Kuyunjik Collection' (named after the settlement mound housing the palaces of Nineveh). Although much has been published, the library is so vast that it is still impossible to give a fully informed overview of its contents. It is, however, certain that only a tiny minority of texts can be called literature, including the famous Epic of Gilgameš, whereas ritual instructions and the prognostic disciplines of astrology and sacrificial divination emerge as the key subject areas from the published part of the library. The collection's primary function was to provide the scholarly advisers of the king with materials to support royal decision-making and secure divine favour for king and state: texts containing detailed guidelines for the performance of rituals or huge reference collections of omens.

All Assyrian kings, at least in the 8th and 7th centuries BC, were cuneiform literate, as were the other men destined for a role in the running of the empire. However, Aššurbanipal's fascination with esoteric and arcane knowledge went far beyond basic literacy. In his inscriptions, he claimed to have undergone an extensive scholarly education. Moreover, in some of the wall decorations of his North Palace in Nineveh, he had himself depicted with a writing stylus tucked into his belt, instead of the more usual knife. But the beginnings of the Assyrian royal library likely reached back to the 14th century BC and King Aššur-uballit I, whose Royal Scribe Marduk-nadin-ahhe from Babylon (see Chapter 5) would have been well placed to initiate such a project. When Tukulti-Ninurta I sacked Babylon in the 13th century BC, he brought back library tablets to add to the holdings, and by the 7th century, the collection had grown into the biggest cuneiform library of all times.

For the most part, the royal library was the product of local Assyrian copying, editing, and composing. But Aššurbanipal also made focused use of the empire's control over Babylonia, and perhaps Egypt, to collect library texts. So organized was this effort that the king had search parties dispatched in order to locate rare scholarly works and appropriate them, by force if needed. Records listing 2,000 tablets and 300 writing-boards demonstrate that these were integrated into the royal library after the end of the

Babylonian insurrection from 652 to 648 BC (see Chapter 4) from private collections. In addition, Babylonians were drafted into the existing large-scale programme of copying tablets. Some were commissioned and paid to produce tablets, but others were forced to do so. One administrative text reveals that captive Babylonians 'in fetters' were made to copy tablets under duress, including the son of the governor of Nippur who had supported the rebellion. This sheds some light on the treatment of political prisoners at Nineveh and also illustrates that the members of the urban Babylonian elite were highly educated. Well-read gentleman scholar Aššurbanipal was certainly not a unique case.

By the beginning of the 7th century BC, the central Assyrian cities of Nineveh, Kalhu, and Aššur housed experts from all over the known world. Without them, some of the most enduring achievements of the Assyrian kings, such as constructing and furnishing the magnificent palaces and temples or assembling the contents of the fabled library of Aššurbanipal, would have been impossible. Regardless of whether he was motivated by a thirst for knowledge and the wish to control and utilize this knowledge in the interest of the empire, or whether he indulged in the wealthy collector's voraciousness, today the library is Aššurbanipal's and perhaps Assyria's most lasting monument.

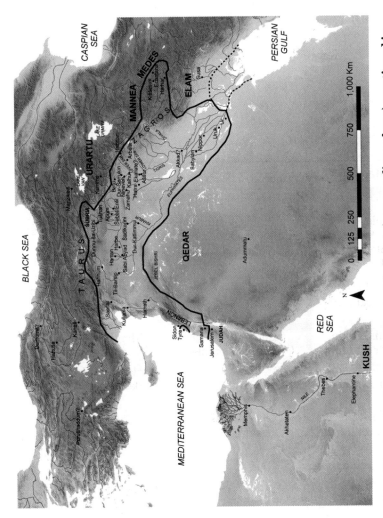

**Map.** The Assyrian Empire, *c.*670 BC, and all sites (some earlier or later) mentioned in this volume.

# Timeline

## Rulers of Aššur

...

| | | |
|---|---|---|
| Ušpia<br>late 3rd<br>millennium BC | Builds Aššur temple | |
| ... | | |
| Erišum I<br>19th century | Enlarges Aššur temple | Merchants in Kaneš:<br>level Ib |
| ... | | |
| Samsi-Addu<br>18th century | Conquers Aššur;<br>rebuilds temple | Merchants in Kaneš:<br>level II |
| Išme-Dagan<br>18th century | | Hammurabi, king of<br>Babylon |
| ... | | |
| Puzur-Sin<br>17th century | Liberates Aššur from<br>foreign rule | |
| ... | | |
| Aššur-nadin-ahhe I<br>15th century | | |
| ... | | |

## Kings of Assyria

| | | |
|---|---|---|
| Aššur-uballiṭ I<br>1356–1322 | First king of Assyria | Royal Scribe<br>Marduk-nadin-ahhe |
| ... | | |

| | | |
|---|---|---|
| Adad-nerari I 1300–1270 | | |
| Shalmaneser I 1269–1241 | Final defeat of Mittani | Ibašši-ili, first viceroy of Hanigalbat |
| Tukulti-Ninurta I 1240–1205 | Capture of Babylon | |
| ... | | |
| Aššur-nerari III 1200–1195 | Succession crisis | Ili-pada, last viceroy of Hanigalbat |
| ... | | |
| Ninurta-apil-Ekur 1189–1178 | | |
| ... | | |
| Tiglath-pileser I 1114–1076 | Famine starts causing migrations | |
| ... | | |
| Aššur-bel-kala 1073–1056 | | |
| ... | | |
| Aššur-dan II 935–912 | Conquest of lost territories begins | |
| Adad-nerari II 911–891 | | |
| Tukulti-Ninurta II 890–884 | | |
| Aššurnasirpal II 883–859 | 879: New capital Kalhu | Master Scholar Gabbu-ilani-ereš, Palace Overseer Nergal-apil-kumu'a |
| Shalmaneser III 858–824 | Ancient borders restored | |
| Šamši-Adad V 823–811 | | |
| Adad-nerari III 810–783 | | Governor Nergal-ereš |
| ... | | |
| Tiglath-pileser III 744–727 | Conquest of new territories begins | |

| | | |
|---|---|---|
| Shalmaneser V 726–722 | | |
| Sargon II 721–705 | 706: New capital Dur-Šarrukin | Ambassador Aššur-reṣuwa |
| Sennacherib 704–681 | c.700: New capital Nineveh | Hezekiah, king of Judah |
| Esarhaddon 680–669 | 672: Covenant with all subjects | 680–612: People of Chapter 3 |
| Aššurbanipal 668–630 | | Šamaš-šumu-ukin, king of Babylon |
| Aššur-etel-ilani 629–627 | | |
| Sin-šarru-iškun 626–612 | 614: Destruction of Aššur temple | Nabopolassar, king of Babylon |
| Aššur-uballit II 611–608 | 612: Fall of Nineveh | |

## Rulers of Aššur

| | | |
|---|---|---|
| Cyrus II of Persia 538–530 | Second Aššur temple ('Temple A') | Assyrian community in Uruk |
| ... | | |
| Ŕuth-Assor 1st century AD | Third Aššur temple ('Parthian') | Church of the East |
| ... | c. 240: Destruction of Aššur temple | Ardashir I, king of Sassanian Empire |
| | | Saint Matthew and Saint Behnam |

# References

## Chapter 1: Introducing Assyria

Irving Finkel, ed., *The Cyrus Cylinder: The King of Persia's Proclamation from Ancient Babylon* (London & New York: I.B. Tauris, 2013).

Mario Liverani, 'From city-state to empire: the case of Assyria', in *The Roman Empire in Context: Historical and Comparative Perspectives*, ed. Johann P. Arnason and Kurt A. Raaflaub, 251–69 (Oxford: Wiley-Blackwell, 2011).

Mirko Novák and Helen Younansardaroud, 'Mar Behnam, Sohn des Sanherib von Nimrud: Tradition und Rezeption assyrischer Gestalten im iraqischen Christentum und die Frage nach dem Fortleben der Assyrer', *Altorientalische Forschungen*, 29 (2002): 166–94.

Diana Pickworth, 'Excavations at Nineveh: the Halzi Gate', *Iraq*, 67 (2005): 295–316.

## Chapter 2: Assyrian places

### Aššur

Pauline O. Harper, Evelyn Klengel-Brandt, Joan Aruz, and Kim Benzel, eds., *Assyrian Origins: Discoveries at Ashur on the Tigris* (New York: Metropolitan Museum of Art, 1995).

Stefan M. Maul, 'Die tägliche Speisung des Assur (*ginā'u*) und deren politische Bedeutung', in *Time and History in the Ancient Near East*, ed. Luis Feliu, Jaume Llop, Adelina Millet Alba, and Joaquín Sanmartín, 561–74 (Winona Lake IN: Eisenbrauns, 2013).

Nicholas Postgate, *Bronze Age Bureaucracy: Writing and the Practice of Government in Assyria* (Cambridge: Cambridge University Press, 2014): chapter 4.

## Kaneš

Gojko Barjamovic, Thomas Hertel, and Mogens Trolle Larsen, *Ups and downs at Kanesh: Chronology, History and Society in the Old Assyrian Period* (Leiden: Nederlands Instituut voor het Nabije Oosten, 2012).

Tahsin Özgüç, *Kültepe Kaniš-Neša: The Earliest International Trade Center and the Oldest Capital City of the Hittites* (Istanbul: Middle Eastern Culture Center in Japan, 2003).

Sharon R. Steadman and Gregory McMahon, eds., *The Oxford Handbook of Ancient Anatolia* (Oxford & New York: Oxford University Press, 2011): chapter 13 (Cécile Michel), chapter 47 (Fikri Kulakoğlu).

## Kalhu

John E. Curtis, Henrietta McCall, Dominique Collon, and Lamia al-Gailani-Werr, eds., *New Light on Nimrud* (London: British Institute for the Study of Iraq, 2008)

Joan and David Oates, *Nimrud: An Assyrian Imperial City Revealed* (London: British School of Archaeology in Iraq, 2001).

Steven W. Holloway, 'Biblical Assyria and other anxieties in the British Empire', *Journal of Religion & Society*, 3 (2001): <http://moses.creighton.edu/jrs/2001/2001-12.pdf>

## Dur-Katlimmu

Hartmut Kühne, 'Tell Sheikh Hamad: the Assyrian-Aramean centre of Dur-Katlimmu/Magdalu', in *100 Jahre archäologische Feldforschungen in Nordost-Syrien: eine Bilanz*, ed. Dominik Bonatz and Lutz Martin, 235–58 (Wiesbaden: Harrassowitz, 2013).

Nicholas Postgate, *Bronze Age Bureaucracy: Writing and the Practice of Government in Assyria* (Cambridge: Cambridge University Press, 2014): chapter 5.5.

Frans A. M. Wiggermann, 'The seal of Ili-pada, Grand Vizier of the Middle Assyrian Empire', in *The Iconography of Cylinder Seals*, ed. Paul Taylor, 92–9 (London: Warburg Institute, 2006).

# Chapter 3: Assyrians at home

Karen Radner and Heather D. Baker, eds., *The Prosopography of the Neo-Assyrian Empire* (Helsinki: Neo-Assyrian Text Corpus Project, 1998–2011).

## King Esarhaddon

Mikko Luukko and Greta Van Buylaere, *The Political Correspondence of Esarhaddon* (Helsinki: Helsinki University Press, 2002): no. 59 (Sasî prophecy).

Simo Parpola, *Letters from Assyrian and Babylonian Scholars* (Helsinki: Helsinki University Press, 1993): nos. 187, 196, and 316.

Karen Radner, 'The trials of Esarhaddon: the conspiracy of 670 BC', in *Assur und sein Umland*, ed. Peter Miglus and Joaquín M. Cordoba, 165–84 (Madrid: Universidad Autónoma de Madrid, 2003).

Frances Reynolds, *The Babylonian Correspondence of Esarhaddon* (Helsinki: Helsinki University Press, 2003): no. 100 (Urdu-Mullissi's conspiracy).

Ivan Starr, *Queries to the Sungod: Divination and Politics in Sargonid Assyria* (Helsinki: Helsinki University Press, 1990): no. 139.

## Scholars

Mikko Luukko and Greta Van Buylaere, *The Political Correspondence of Esarhaddon* (Helsinki: Helsinki University Press, 2002): nos. 34 and 35.

Simo Parpola, *Letters from Assyrian and Babylonian Scholars* (Helsinki: Helsinki University Press, 1993): no. 294.

Karen Radner, 'The Assyrian king and his scholars: the Syro-Anatolian and the Egyptian schools', *Studia Orientalia*, 106 (2009): 221–38.

## Landowner

Karen Radner, *Die neuassyrischen Texte aus Tall Šēḫ Ḥamad* (Berlin: Reimer, 2002).

## Wine merchant

Peter Miglus, Karen Radner, and Franciszek M. Stępniowski, *Untersuchungen im Stadtgebiet von Assur: Wohnquartiere in der Weststadt* (Wiesbaden: Harrassowitz, forthcoming).

## Chapter 4: Assyrians abroad

### Family matters

Cécile Michel, 'The private archives from Kaniš belonging to Anatolians', *Altorientalische Forschungen*, 38 (2011): 94–115.

Cécile Michel, 'Akkadian texts: women in letters – Old Assyrian Kaniš', in *Women in the Ancient Near East*, ed. Mark W. Chavalas, 205–12 (London & New York: Routledge, 2013).

### Envoys

William L. Moran, *The Amarna Letters* (Baltimore & London: Johns Hopkins University Press, 1992): nos. 15 and 16.

Amanda H. Podany, *Brotherhood of Kings: How International Relations Shaped the Ancient Near East* (New York & Oxford: Oxford University Press, 2010).

Nicholas Postgate, *Bronze Age Bureaucracy: Writing and the Practice of Government in Assyria* (Cambridge: Cambridge University Press, 2014): chapter 5.3.

### Banished to the mountains

Albert Kirk Grayson, *Assyrian Rulers of the Early First Millennium BC*, vol. 1 (Toronto: University of Toronto Press, 1991): inscriptions of Aššur-bel-kala, Aššur-dan II and Aššurnasirpal II.

Wiebke Kirleis and Michael Herles, 'Climate change as a reason for Assyro-Aramaean conflicts? Pollen evidence for drought at the end of the 2nd millennium BC', *State Archives of Assyria Bulletin*, 16 (2007): 7–37.

Jehuda Neumann and Simo Parpola, 'Climatic change and the eleventh-tenth-century eclipse of Assyria and Babylonia', *Journal of Near Eastern Studies*, 46 (1987): 161–82 (translation of 1082 BC chronicle text: p. 178).

Karen Radner, *Das mittelassyrische Tontafelarchiv von Giricano/ Dunnu-ša-Uzibi* (Turnhout: Brepols, 2004).

### Unpopular ambassador

Giovanni B. Lanfranchi and S. Parpola, *The Correspondence of Sargon II, Part II: Letters from the Northern and Northeastern Provinces* (Helsinki: Helsinki University Press, 1990): chapter 6.

Simo Parpola, *The Correspondence of Sargon II*, Part I: *Letters from Assyria and the West* (Helsinki: Helsinki University Press, 1987): no. 29 (kidnapping plot).

Simo Parpola and K. Watanabe, *Neo-Assyrian Treaties and Loyalty Oaths* (Helsinki: Helsinki University Press, 1988): no. 5 (treaty with Tyre).

Karen Radner, 'Between a rock and a hard place: Musasir, Kumme, Ukku and Šubria – the buffer states between Assyria and Urartu', in *Biainili-Urartu*, ed. Stefan Kroll et al., 243–64 (Leuven: Peeters, 2012).

### Sibling rivalry

Frederick Mario Fales, 'After Ta'yinat: the new status of Esarhaddon's *adê* for Assyrian political history', *Revue d'Assyriologie*, 106 (2012): 133–58.

Grant Frame, 'Šamaš-šuma-ukīn', in *Reallexikon der Assyriologie und Vorderasiatischen Archäologie*, 11, ed. Michael P. Streck et al., 618–21 (Berlin & New York: de Gruyter, 2006–8).

Richard C. Steiner, 'The Aramaic text in demotic script', in *Context of Scripture 1: Canonical Compositions from the Biblical World*, ed. W. W. Hallo, 309–27 (Leiden & Boston: Brill, 1997).

## Chapter 5: Foreigners in Assyria

### Role model

Hannes Galter, 'Textanalyse assyrischer Königsinschriften: der Aufstand des Puzur-Sin', *State Archives of Assyria Bulletin*, 14 (2002–5): 1–21.

Albert Kirk Grayson, *Assyrian Rulers of the Third and Second Millennia BC* (Toronto: University of Toronto Press, 1987): inscriptions of Šamši-Adad and Puzur-Sin.

Erle Leichty, *The Royal Inscriptions of Esarhaddon, King of Assyria (680–669 BC)* (Winona Lake IN: Eisenbrauns, 2011).

Regine Pruzsinszky, *Mesopotamian Chronology of the 2nd Millennium BC: An Introduction to the Textual Evidence and Related Chronological Issues* (Vienna: Verlag der Österreichischen Akademie der Wissenschaften, 2009): chapter 9.

Nele Ziegler, 'Šamšī-Adad I.', in *Reallexikon der Assyriologie und Vorderasiatischen Archäologie*, 11, ed. Michael P. Streck et al., 632–5 (Berlin & New York: de Gruyter, 2006–8).

### Royal Scribe

Frans A. M. Wiggermann, 'A Babylonian scholar in Assur', in *Studies in Ancient Near Eastern World View and Society Presented to*

*Marten Stol*, ed. R. J. van der Spek, 203–34 (Bethesda MA: CDL Press, 2008).

### Royal hostages

Albert Kirk Grayson, *Assyrian Rulers of the Early First Millennium BC*, vol. 1 (Toronto: University of Toronto Press, 1991): inscription of Tiglath-pileser I.

Karen Radner, 'After Eltekeh: royal hostages from Egypt at the Assyrian court', in *Stories of Long Ago: Festschrift für Michael D. Roaf*, ed. Heather D. Baker, Kai Kaniuth, and Adelheid Otto, 471–9 (Münster: Ugarit Verlag, 2012).

### Iranian family

Kaisa Åkerman, 'The "Aussenhaken Area" in the city of Assur during the second half of the 7th century BC', *State Archives of Assyria Bulletin*, 13 (1999–2001): 217–72.

Andreas Fuchs and Simo Parpola, *The Correspondence of Sargon II, Part III: Letters from Babylonia and the Eastern Provinces* (Helsinki: Helsinki University Press, 2001): chapter 4.

Karen Radner, 'Assyria and the Medes', in *The Oxford Handbook of Ancient Iran*, ed. Daniel T. Potts, 442–56 (Oxford & New York: Oxford University Press, 2013).

### Prisoners of war

Betina Faist, 'An Elamite deportee', in *Homeland and Exile: Biblical and Ancient Near Eastern Studies in Honour of Bustenay Oded*, ed. G. Galil et al., 59–69 (Leiden & Boston: Brill, 2009).


## Chapter 6: Assyrian world domination: pathfinder empire

### Army

Robin Archer, 'Chariotry to cavalry: developments in the early first millennium', in *New Perspectives on Ancient Warfare*, ed. Garrett G. Fagan and Matthew Trundle, 57–80 (Leiden & Boston: Brill, 2010).

Andreas Fuchs, 'Assyria at war: strategy and conduct', in *The Oxford Handbook of Cuneiform Culture*, ed. Karen Radner and Eleanor Robson, 380–401 (Oxford: Oxford University Press, 2011).

Mario Liverani, 'Assyria in the ninth century: continuity or change?', in *From the Upper Sea to the Lower Sea: Studies on the History of*

*Assyria and Babylonia in Honour of A. K. Grayson*, ed. Grant Frame and Linda S. Wilding, 213–26 (Leiden: Nederlands Instituut voor het Nabije Oosten, 2004).

## Absolute monarchy

Dominique Collon, *Catalogue of the Western Asiatic Seals in the British Museum, Cylinder Seals 5: Neo-Assyrian and Neo-Babylonian Periods* (London: British Museum Press, 2001): no. 151.

Stephen Lumsden, 'Narrative art and empire: the throneroom of Aššurnasirpal II', in *Assyria and Beyond: Studies Presented to Mogens Trolle Larsen*, ed. Jan Gerrit Dercksen, 359–85 (Leiden: Nederlands Instituut voor het Nabije Oosten, 2004).

John Nicholas Postgate, 'The land of Assur and the yoke of Assur', *World Archaeology*, 23 (1992): 247–63.

Karen Radner, 'Assyrian and non-Assyrian kingship in the first millennium BC', in *Concepts of Kingship in Antiquity*, ed. Giovanni B. Lanfranchi and Robert Rollinger, 15–24 (Padova: Sargon srl, 2010).

Michael Roaf, 'The décor of the throne room of the palace of Ashurnasirpal', in *New Light on Nimrud*, ed. John E. Curtis, Henrietta McCall, Dominique Collon, and Lamia al-Gailani-Werr, 209–14 (London: British School of Archaeology in Iraq, 2008).

## Long-distance communication

Karen Radner, 'An imperial communication network: the state correspondence of the Neo-Assyrian Empire', in *State Correspondence in the Ancient World: From New Kingdom Egypt to the Roman Empire*, ed. Karen Radner, 64–93 (New York & Oxford: Oxford University Press, 2014).

## Resettlement programme

Mikko Luukko, *The Correspondence of Tiglath-pileser III and Sargon II from Calah/Nimrud* (Helsinki: Neo-Assyrian Text Corpus Project, 2012): nos. 17 and 18.

Peter Machinist, 'Assyrians on Assyria in the first millennium BC', in *Anfänge politischen Denkens in der Antike: die nahöstlichen Kulturen und die Griechen*, ed. Kurt Raaflaub, 77–104 (Munich: Oldenbourg, 1993).

Bustenay Oded, *Mass Deportations and Deportees in the Neo-Assyrian Empire* (Wiesbaden: Harrassowitz, 1979).

## Aššurbanipal's Library

Grant Frame and Andrew R. George, 'The royal libraries of Nineveh: new evidence for King Ashurbanipal's tablet collection', *Iraq*, 67 (2005): 265–84.

Eleanor Robson, 'Reading the libraries of Assyria and Babylonia', in *Ancient Libraries*, ed. Jason König, Katerina Oikonomopoulou and Greg Woolf, 38–56. (Cambridge: Cambridge University Press, 2013).

Ursula Seidl, 'Assurbanipals Griffel', *Zeitschrift für Assyriologie und Vorderasiatische Archäologie*, 97 (2007): 119–24.

# Further reading

Hartmut Kühne, 'State and empire of Assyria in northeast Syria', in **125**
  *Archéologie et Histoire de la Syrie 1: La Syrie de l'époque
  néolithique à l'âge du fer*, ed. Winfried Orthmann, Paolo Matthiae,
  and Michel al-Maqdissi, 473–98 (Wiesbaden: Harrassowitz, 2013).
Amélie Kuhrt, *The Ancient Near East, c. 3000–330 BC* (London &
  New York: Routledge, 1995).
Joachim Marzahn and Beate Salje, eds., *Wiedererstehendes Assur: 100
  Jahre deutsche Ausgrabungen in Assyrien* (Mainz: Zabern, 2003).
Karen Radner and Eleanor Robson, eds., *The Oxford Handbook of
  Cuneiform Culture* (Oxford: Oxford University Press, 2011).
Johannes Renger, ed., *Assur—Gott, Stadt und Land* (Wiesbaden:
  Harrassowitz, 2011).

## Second millennium BC

Brian Brown, 'The structure and decline of the Middle Assyrian state:
  the role of autonomous and nonstate actors', *Journal of Cuneiform
  Studies*, 65 (2013): 97–126.
Jan Gerrit Dercksen, *Old Assyrian Institutions* (Leiden: Nederlands
  Instituut voor het Nabije Oosten, 2004).
Jan Gerrit Dercksen, ed., *Anatolia and the Jazira during the Old
  Assyrian Period* (Leiden: Nederlands Instituut voor het Nabije
  Oosten, 2008).
Stefan Jakob, *Mittelassyrische Verwaltung und Sozialstruktur:
  Untersuchungen* (Leiden & Boston: Brill, 2003).
Mario Liverani, *The Ancient Near East: History, Society and Economy*
  (London & New York: Routledge, 2014): chapters 12, 20, 27.

Aline Tenu, *L'expansion médio-assyrienne: approche archéologique* (Oxford: Oxbow, 2009).

Klaas R. Veenhof and Jesper Eidem, *Mesopotamia: The Old Assyrian Period* (Fribourg: Academic Press; Göttingen: Vandenhoeck & Ruprecht, 2008).

## First millennium BC

Joan Aruz, Sarah B. Graff, and Yelena Rakic, eds., *Assyria to Iberia at the Dawn of the Classical Age* (New York: Metropolitan Museum of Art, 2014).

Hermann Born and Ursula Seidl, *Schutzwaffen aus Assyrien und Urartu* (Mainz: Zabern, 1995).

Ada Cohen and Steven E. Kangas, eds., *Assyrian Reliefs from the Palace of Ashurnasirpal II: A Cultural Biography* (Hanover & London: University Press of New England, 2010).

Paul Collins, *Assyrian Palace Sculptures* (London: British Museum Press, 2008).

John E. Curtis and Julian E. Reade, eds., *Art and Empire: Treasures from Assyria in the British Museum* (New York: Metropolitan Museum of Art, 1995).

David Damrosch, *The Buried Book: The Loss and Rediscovery of the Great Epic of Gilgamesh* (New York: Holt, 2007).

Tamás Dezső, *The Assyrian Army 1: The Structure of the Neo-Assyrian Army* (Budapest: Eötvös University Press, 2012).

Frederick Mario Fales, *Guerre et paix en Assyrie: religion et impérialisme* (Paris: Cerf, 2010).

Albert Kirk Grayson, *Assyrian Rulers of the Early First Millennium BC*, vol. 2 (Toronto: University of Toronto Press, 1996).

Isaac Kalimi and Seth Richardson, ed., *Sennacherib at the Gates of Jerusalem: Story, History and Historiography* (Leiden & Boston: Brill, 2014).

Mogens Trolle Larsen, *The Conquest of Assyria: Excavations in an Antique Land* (London & New York: Routledge, 1996).

Mario Liverani, *The Ancient Near East: History, Society and Economy* (London & New York: Routledge, 2014): chapters 28–31.

Stefan M. Maul, *Die Wahrsagekunst im Alten Orient: Zeichen des Himmels und der Erde* (Munich: Beck, 2013).

Simo Parpola and Robert Whiting, eds., *Assyria 1995* (Helsinki: Neo-Assyrian Text Corpus Project, 1997).

Karen Radner, 'The Neo-Assyrian Empire', in *Imperien und Reiche in der Weltgeschichte: Epochenübergreifende und globalhistorische Vergleiche*, ed. Michael Gehler and Robert Rollinger, 101–20 (Wiesbaden: Harrassowitz, 2014).

John Malcolm Russell, *Sennacherib's Palace Without Rival at Nineveh* (Chicago & London: University of Chicago Press, 1991).

John Malcolm Russell, *From Nineveh to New York: The Strange Story of the Assyrian Reliefs in the Metropolitan Museum and the Hidden Masterpiece at Cranford School* (New Haven & London: Yale University Press, 1997).

John Malcolm Russell, *The Writing on the Wall: Studies in the Architectural Context of Late Assyrian Palace Inscriptions* (Winona Lake IN: Eisenbrauns, 1999).

Irene J. Winter, *On Art in the Ancient Near East*, Volume I: *Of the First Millennium B.C.E.* (Leiden & Boston, Brill, 2010).

## Websites

*Assyrian Empire Builders*: <http://www.ucl.ac.uk/sargon/>

*Excavations at Tell Shech Hamad*: <http://www.schechhamad.de>

*Knowledge and Power in the Neo-Assyrian Empire*: <http://oracc.museum.upenn.edu/saao/knpp/>

*Kuyunjik Collection of the British Museum*: <http://cdli.ucla.edu/collections/bm/bm.html>

*Livius: Mesopotamia*: <http://www.livius.org/babylonia.html>

*Nimrud: Materialities of Assyrian Knowledge Production*: <http://oracc.museum.upenn.edu/nimrud>

*Royal Inscriptions of the Neo-Assyrian Period*: <http://oracc.museum.upenn.edu/rinap>

*State Archives of Assyria Online*: <http://oracc.museum.upenn.edu/saao>

# Index

Index

Ancient Assyria

Ancient Assyria

# 第一章

# 亚述简介

在公元前的几千年间，古代亚述只是中东地区众多繁荣昌盛的国家之一，但这个长寿的王国绝对是其中最具影响力的一个。回顾亚述历史，纵横千年，波澜壮阔，公元前 9 世纪，亚述成为了第一个世界帝国。帝国都城（今位于伊拉克北部）中作出的决定，影响着尼罗河到里海之间的芸芸众生。亚述在政治、行政管理和基础建设上留下的遗产，深刻地塑造了更广阔的中东地区与地中海地区的后世历史。

对于我们来说，亚述文化既熟悉又陌生。我们享受美酒的品位或许同亚述人一致，但可能不会把串在签子上的蝗虫当作零食。和我们一样，家里的淡水供应、室内洗手间和运作良好的排污系统对亚述人而言也很重要，但我们大概不需要一间直接通向起居室的地下墓室。我们会为亚述人能享受消费者保护和延长的保修期而感到高兴，但如果发现这些服务也适用于人的买卖，即被购买者在交易后的 100 天内不得癫痫发作或精神失常，我们可能会被吓一大跳。亚述人发明的可折叠遮阳伞非常实用，但撑着它却很危险——只有王室成员享有这项特权，私自使用就是犯下了叛国的罪行。和亚述人一样，我们也把信件装在信封里，只不过我们的信封不是黏土做的。

自 19 世纪中叶亚述再次被考古界发掘以来，其分布在伊拉克、叙利亚、土耳其、以色列，甚至更远处的伊朗、黎巴嫩和约旦的众多城址都被大面积地发掘出来，提供了重要的信息。由于亚述人最常用的书写材料是经久耐用的泥板，我们便可借此了解这一文化的特质和许多其他的细节。

## 亚述城邦

亚述的历史始于公元前 3 千纪初亚述城的建立。当时，亚述城很可能是一个贸易中心，为如今伊拉克南部的苏美尔城市提供来自北方的商品。自公元前 3 千纪中期起，文献史料记录了亚述城数次被南方的大国兼并的历史：这里曾是阿卡德国王们的领土，后归当地人治下，之后又听命于乌尔国多任国王的号令。在乌尔第三王朝期间，南方派遣官员扎里库姆（Zarriqum）管理亚述城，后来他官至埃兰地区（现伊朗境内）的总督，声望显赫。

乌尔王国在公元前 2000 年左右分崩离析之后，亚述城再度成为一个独立的城邦。这里的居民讲亚述语。和现代阿拉伯语、希伯来语一样，亚述语属于闪米特语族。尽管与亚述城以南地区使用的巴比伦语有着密不可分的关系，亚述语依然有其鲜明的特点。在古代，只有巴比伦语被称为阿卡德语，而如今，二者一般被视作阿卡德语的两种方言。这两种语言均用楔形文字符号记录，但二者所使用的符号截然不同，专家可以轻而易举地作出判别。

亚述城独立之后，世袭的本土统治者重新开始了对亚述城的统治，但与阿卡德和乌尔的统治者不同的是，他们并未以国王的身份自居，而是像公元前 2 千纪初一位亚述城统治者的铭文中所写的那样，认为"亚述神（Aššur）是国王，西鲁鲁（Silulu）是亚述神的代表"。亚述神与亚述城共享自己的名字，同时也是这座城市的神圣化身。亚述神被尊为至高无上的君主，人类统治者以它的名义进行统治。直到公元前 7 世纪，国王亚述巴尼拔（Aššurbanipal）于神的赞歌中仍在使用这样的说法："亚述神是国王，亚述神是国王，亚述巴尼拔是他的代表！"亚述城的统治者与城邦大会中的全体公民以及一位名年官（līmum）共享权力。名年官每年选举一次，当年便用当选者的名字来命名（比如说，公元前 1760 年是"恩纳姆亚述［Ennam-Aššur］为名年官之年"）。经证实，古代很多贯彻集体统治传统的地方都有这种做法（例如在雅典，公元前 594 年是"梭伦［Solon］为执政官之年"；而在罗马，公元前 59 年是"凯撒［Caesar］与比布鲁斯［Bibulus］为执政官之年"）。这种说法在公元前 19 世纪时最为常见，当时，植根于亚述城的家族商行在安纳托利亚地区建立了一个利润丰厚的贸易殖民点网络。在那时，"亚述的"一词仅仅指代亚述城和它的居民们。

## 亚述的诞生

从公元前 18 世纪开始，亚述城再次被更大的区域国家控制，但它守住了自身强大的文化身份。公元前 14 世纪，当亚述城最后的统治政权米坦尼（亚述人称之为"哈尼迦尔巴特"）衰落时，亚述城终于不再附属于更大的政治结构。亚述城的统治者利用这段权力真空期，把城市建成一个领土国家的中心，这个国家的领土范围包括现今伊拉克北部的大部分地区。此时，他们第一次采用了国王的称号。亚述凭借巧妙的外交手段谨慎处理与巴比伦、埃及等国之间的关系以达成自身目的，成为了美索不达米亚北部的主导力量。

亚述城、尼尼微和阿尔贝拉这三座城市构成的三角区域成为了国家的核心地域，这个国家后来统治了中东的大部分地区。每当有新的地区被兼并为行省时，原地区居民就被算作"亚述人"，他们通过参与祭祀亚述神的活动，使自己的亚述人身份在意识形态上得到认定。到了公元前13世纪末，亚述控制了米坦尼政权从前管制下的绝大部分领土，其西部国界直抵幼发拉底河河畔。他们在政治上和战场上同南方的巴比伦王国和西北方的赫梯王国对抗。

当这些国家衰弱的时候，它们疆域内的政治和社会结构就会发生巨大的变化。例如赫梯王国，它在青铜时代晚期的大迁徙浪潮中彻底瓦解。亚述也损失了一些领土，但其防备得当的核心地域依然维持在国家的直接控制之下，王权和国家结构也没有遭受重大威胁。据公元前11世纪的史料考证，迁徙族群之一的阿拉姆人在这一时期成为了极具破坏力的入侵者。在亚述的政治话语中，阿拉姆人非法攫夺的领土必须要回到亚述的手中，因为亚述才是这片土地的合法拥有者。

## 帝国的建立

与邻近的地区不同，亚述始终设有自己的战车部队，并且能够利用财政和社会力量一直维持这支特殊的武装力量。另外，亚述的疆域远远超过了邻国。这两方面因素使亚述在后来的征服战争中占据了优势地位。征服战争始于公元前10世纪，当时的亚述史料突出强调了收复失地、拯救那些被遗留在撤退边界以外的亚述人的责任。到了公元前9世纪中叶，亚述的领土面积重回巅峰，我们今天称其为"亚述帝国"。亚述帝国的政治架构发生了有利于国王的深刻变化：超大都市卡尔胡建立起来，成为了帝国的中心；一个更好地为国家利益服务的人口迁置计划也在大规模地持续进行。

经过长达 30 年的领土扩张，到公元前 700 年，从地中海沿岸到伊朗的哈马丹（古时称为埃克巴坦那）、从卡帕多西亚到波斯湾之间的辽阔疆域，都归亚述直接管辖。到了公元前 7 世纪末，亚述帝国成为了中东地区乃至更广大的东地中海地区无可匹敌的政治、经济与文化力量。

## 帝国的终结

然而，原亚述属国、新独立的巴比伦的国王那波珀拉萨尔（Nabopolassar）和一支由基亚克萨雷斯（Cyaxares）领导的米底军队随之发起了一场长达十年的战争。公元前 614 年，亚述城被攻陷，亚述神庙也被破坏。随后，在公元前 612 年，帝国都城尼尼微陷落，最后一位合法的亚述国王辛沙鲁伊什昆（Sin-šarru-iškun）在护城卫国时牺牲。以哈兰城为据点，亚述帝国在王储的领导下持续防守了几年。然而，由于王储再也无法在亚述神庙中加冕，这一神圣习俗此时不得不被忍痛舍弃。过去，加冕仪式意在认定国王为神的代表，又是帝王声索权力的意识形态支柱。亚述的最后一位统治者是亚述乌巴里特二世（Aššur-uballit II），他选名字时显然经过一番深思熟虑，祈求获得公元前 14 世纪第一位亚述国王的保佑。亚述乌巴里特二世在哈兰的月神庙举行了加冕仪式。月神是最伟大的亚述神之一，巴比伦的评注者认为这足以确立他的国王身份，不过在同时代的亚述史料中，他依然只被看作王储。由于没有了亚述神的庇护，这位末代国王的权威一定遭到了严重的削弱，即使是来自盟友埃及和伊朗的曼努亚王国的军事支援也没能拯救这个帝国。

亚述核心地域的大部分人口被重新安置在巴比伦，国王那波珀拉萨尔和他的继任者尼布甲尼撒（Nebuchadnezzar）将首都巴比伦城打造成了一个可以与亚述的卡尔胡、杜尔–沙鲁金和尼尼微相媲美的帝国中心。没有人接管这些亚述城市的维护工作，庞大的城市和众多的人口只能靠大范围的昂贵的区域灌溉系统来供应淡水，苟延残喘。在缺乏维护的状态下，运河和沟渠很快就残破不堪，再也无法使用。尼尼微哈勒兹城门的考古发现令人毛骨悚然：护城战中那些牺牲者的尸体从未被清理过。在卡尔胡，尸体被扔进为卫城提供饮用水的井里。这些行为证明入侵者只想摧毁和破坏，而非占用这一地区。

## 帝国没落之后的亚述历史

但是，亚述人的历史并未就此结束。一方面，他们继续流亡。公元前 6 世纪，在巴比伦的南部城市乌鲁克，一群亚述侨民供奉着一座小小的亚述神庙。直到很久之后的公元前 2 世纪，已成为塞琉西帝国一部分的乌鲁克依然保留着典型的亚述宗教与学术传统。另一方面，公元前 539 年之后，亚述城的亚述神庙得以重建，不过规模要小得多。据居鲁士圆柱铭文记载，征服了巴比伦的波斯国王居鲁士大帝许可了这一做法：

> 我将他们从巴比伦送回他们原来居住的地方，送到底格里斯河对岸那些神庙早已破败的圣所，众神曾居住之地——亚述、苏萨、阿卡德、埃什努那、扎姆班、麦图兰、得尔，直到古提的边界（扎格罗斯山区）。我为他们建立了永久的圣所。我把诸神的子民聚集在一起，将他们送回他们的家园。

这座小神庙汇集了从公元前 2 千纪初到公元前 614 年神庙被毁之间所有关于亚述神及其圣所的文献，展现了对这座城市光辉往昔的充分认识和由衷欣赏。公元 1 世纪，亚述城作为哈特拉王国的贸易中心，财库充盈，地位显赫，亚述神庙再次开展了宏伟庞大的重建工作。

根据巴尔戴伊赞（Bardaisan）在《诸国律法之书》第四十六章中的记载，当时的哈特拉已经拥有了一个完善的基督教社区，亚述城可能也有人开始信仰基督教。总之，约公元 240 年，萨珊人征服哈特拉王国，亚述城的新神庙和信仰都沦为了受害者，随后东方教会蓬勃发展，本土的基督教传统重新塑造了亚述历史中的杰出人物和重要地点，与《圣经》中记载的信息大为不同。因此，亚述城和亚述国王辛那赫里布（Sennacherib）出现在了公元 4 世纪的殉道者圣贝赫纳姆（Saint Behnam）的传说中。在当地圣人圣马太（Saint Matthew，阿拉姆语叫做马尔马泰［Mar Mattai］）奇迹般地治愈了他的妹妹后，圣贝赫纳姆皈依了基督教。在这个传说中，辛那赫里布变成了贝赫纳姆的父王，处决了自己改信基督教的儿子。结果，国王患病，只有他同意在亚述城接受圣马太的洗礼才能把病治好。辛那赫里布感激不尽，在摩苏尔附近建立了马尔马泰修道院，这里后来成为了东方教会的中心之一（即幼发拉底河以东的叙利亚正教会）。如今，原亚述核心地域的东方教会的叙利亚基督教团体（聂斯托利派和雅各派）认为自己是"亚述人"。这一观点的起源仍然存在争议，不过，相比于 19 世纪中叶的那次叹为观止、让亚述举世闻名的考古发现，它们出现的时间更早。

# 第二章

# 亚述各地

在本章，我们将首先介绍亚述的发祥地——亚述城，以及这个帝国在公元前 1 千纪勃发的起点——卡尔胡，这两座古城是如今伊拉克最重要的考古遗址。大致了解现位于土耳其中部的贸易殖民点卡奈什，有助于我们研究公元前 2 千纪初亚述人在外的历史；而现位于叙利亚的重要行省中心杜尔-卡特里穆则能够充分展示自公元前 13 世纪起亚述扩张的影响。从这些重要遗址的发掘故事中，我们能够深入了解 19 世纪中叶以来亚述考古再发现的成果。

## 亚述城：神与他的神圣之城

亚述城（图 1）位于亚述王国核心地域的南部边缘。核心地域是最重要的三座城市——亚述城、北部的尼尼微、东部的阿尔贝拉——构成的一个三角形地带，面积约为 4000 平方公里，与美国的罗得岛州（4000 平方公里）[1] 或英国的萨福克郡（3800 平方公里）相当。在这个三角形区域的北端，就是现伊

---

[1] 此处疑为作者之误。美国罗得岛州的面积应为 3144 平方公里。——译注，下同

拉克北部最大的城市摩苏尔，在其四处扩张的城区之下，埋藏着自 1842 年以来断断续续被发掘出来的尼尼微遗址。尼尼微俯瞰着一片横跨底格里斯河的重要浅滩，这里是依着托罗斯山脉南麓前往地中海沿岸地区，进入安纳托利亚的陆路的自然终点。三角形区域的东端是阿尔贝拉，它至今一直没有更名。如今作为伊拉克库尔德斯坦自治区的首府，阿尔贝拉还有另一个名字，叫埃尔比勒。阿尔贝拉遗址的考古工作 2006 年才开始进行。阿尔贝拉位于扎格罗斯山脉的西部边缘，控制着穿越群山前往伊朗的多条路线。和尼尼微一样，亚述城也坐落在底格里斯河的一处重要浅滩上，不过是在河的西岸。亚述城位于河流弯道上方的露岩处，战略位置极佳，是一座天然的堡垒。占据此处，便控制了向西穿过草原，进入哈布尔河和幼发拉底河

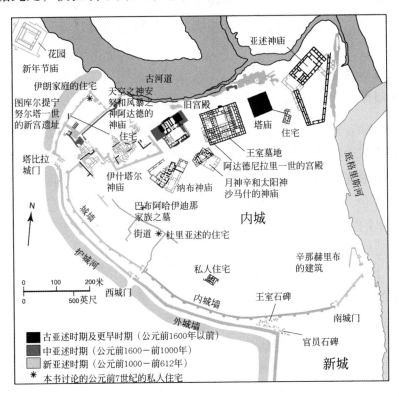

图 1. 亚述城

河谷，再从那里进入叙利亚西部，或穿过托罗斯山脉进入安纳托利亚的陆路。

亚述的核心地域占据了陆上金属贸易网络的重要节点。金属是中东经济不可或缺的一部分。锡和铜是制造二元铜合金青铜的基本材料，从公元前4千纪到前1千纪，这种合金都是铸造工具和武器的首选。锡矿石产自中亚地区，即现今阿富汗、乌兹别克斯坦和塔吉克斯坦等地的矿山中，途经伊朗运抵现在的伊拉克，距亚述核心三角区不过咫尺之遥。银是古代中东最受欢迎的货币，产自安纳托利亚的矿床，也就是传说中的"银山"。亚述核心地域的北部和东部紧邻托罗斯山脉和扎格罗斯山脉，盛产铁矿石、木材、石材，也是放牛牧马的好地方。从亚述核心地域向西，是杰济拉草原（幼发拉底河与底格里斯河之间的"岛屿"），放羊的好牧场。亚述核心地域以南是幼发拉底河与底格里斯河形成的冲积平原，巴比伦的所在地。巴比伦之所以能够繁荣昌盛，离不开其通过沟渠网络维持大规模劳动密集型的人工灌溉，继而维持这一地区政治结构的能力。

除亚述城这一特例之外，亚述的核心地域都位于底格里斯河的东岸。地处地中海气候区，这里的农业依赖降水灌溉，与巴比伦完全依赖人工灌溉的农作方式截然不同。该地区是天然的粮仓，土地肥沃，地势平坦，非常适合大规模的农业耕作。这里的主要农作物是大麦和小麦，每年的秋季迎来丰收。亚述城则处在地理和生态系统的边界线上，干旱的草原气候取代了适合农业生产的地中海气候。作为唯一一座位于底格里斯河西岸的亚述中心城市，亚述城是与草原上的牧羊人们交接的关键地点，这样的地理位置也促使它成为了一个贸易中心。公元前2千纪初的文献最能清楚地证明，亚述城作为重要的商业中心开始闻名于世。亚述城出土的史料相对有限，但好在有卡奈什城——亚述当时在安纳托利亚的贸易殖民点之一——出土的极为丰富的文献史料作为补充。

## 亚述神

从公元前 14 世纪开始,亚述开始自称"亚述之地"(*māt Aššur*)。我们沿用希腊语的说法,称它为"亚述"。"亚述"这个名字模糊了原名所表达的一些细微差别。它原先既指亚述国家最早的中心和王朝的起源地——亚述城,又指同名的亚述神,亚述神庙高耸于亚述全城之上。亚述神与亚述城是不可分割的,因为亚述神是底格里斯河湾一侧那面高耸的岩壁[1]的化身。在阿拉伯语中,这面岩壁被称作卡拉特-舍尔卡特。岩壁轮廓像船首,近似于三角形,高出河谷 40 米。至少从公元前 3 千纪中期开始,这里就开始为在此定居的人们提供居所和生存机遇。随着城市的发展,峭壁和下方的底格里斯河在北侧和东侧形成的天然屏障与一道新月形的防护墙相接,形成了一片大约 65 公顷的封闭区域。

常见的亚述名字表明,亚述神可以被看作一个非常具体的地理空间。例如,亚述杜里(Aššur-duri),意为"亚述神是我的堡垒";杜尔马基亚述(Dur-makî-Aššur),意为"弱者的堡垒就是亚述神";亚述奈美迪(Aššur-nemedi),意为"亚述神是我的基地";或者亚述沙迪伊里(Aššur-šaddî-ili),意为"亚述神是一座神山"。公元前 2 千纪初的一块石浮雕(图 2)便是这样描绘亚述神的形象的:运用亚述艺术中用来表现高山的设计,将亚述神化作一座山峰,一具蓄着胡须的男性的躯干从山峰上升起,旁边还有两座神化的喷泉和萌芽的植物养育着两只山羊——亚述神的象征动物。

---

1　即亚述城所在地。

图 2. 描绘亚述神与两座神化的喷泉的石浮雕。出土于亚述城

　　屹立在岩壁顶部的亚述神的神庙，是整座城市，以及后来整个亚述的中心。亚述神庙有好几个名字：公元前 2 千纪初叫做埃阿姆库尔库拉，意为"四方野牛之屋"；公元前 2 千纪末叫做埃胡尔萨格库尔库拉，意为"四方山峰之屋"；公元前 1 千纪又叫做埃沙拉，意为"宇宙之屋"。这些都是苏美尔语名字，

公元前 3 千纪，也就是亚述城诞生之际，苏美尔语在伊拉克南部使用广泛，后来继续用于仪式和学术领域。

作为唯一一座亚述神庙的所在地，亚述城是亚述神统治领域的核心，数千年来，亚述城的居民们一直供奉着神庙，直到公元 240 年左右最后重建的神庙被毁。公元前 12 世纪的时候，人们认为是据说生活在距此一千年前的一位统治者乌什皮亚（Ušpia）建造了最早的巨型神庙建筑群，这些建筑当时已经占据了岩壁顶端。亚述统治者被视为亚述神在人间的代理人，承载着神的恩典进行统治，与此同时，他还是亚述神的首席祭司，享有亚述神赠予的政治和宗教权威。乌什皮亚和他的继任者们有权利和义务维护亚述神的神庙。在神庙里发现的大量铭文歌颂了建造神庙的功绩。

## 发掘亚述城

亚述城的神庙是由瓦尔特·安德烈（Walter Andrae）领导的德国考古队在 1903 至 1914 年期间考古发现的。安德烈在这里生活和工作了十余年，在几名助手和数百名当地工人的帮助下考察了亚述城和附近的一些遗址。和安德烈一样，助手通常都是受过训练的建筑师。在伊拉克，专业的考古发掘者被称为"舍卡提"，因为这一职业发端于安德烈在卡拉特-舍尔卡特雇佣的工人们。出土的文物由发掘工作的资助方德国东方学会和当时控制伊拉克的奥斯曼当局各占一部分，因此现在大部分文物藏于柏林的西亚博物馆和伊斯坦布尔的古代东方博物馆。除了德国的考古发掘之外，自 1978 年以来，伊拉克考古队也时不时地对亚述城进行探索。不过，正是安德烈多年来在该遗址连续不断地开展发掘工作，才为我们详细了解这座城市奠定了基础。在亚述城遗址的北部，安德烈发现了亚述神的神庙建筑群，其中包括巨大的塔庙，还有周边围绕的其他圣所和王宫。作为一名受过训练的建筑师，安德烈的主要目标是复原这些雄伟建筑的平面图并重构其建筑历史，但他也希望能整体地了解这座城市。因此，他井然有序地在整个遗址内挖掘了间距100米、宽10米的探沟，由此发现了亚述帝国晚期的部分私人住宅区。公元前614年，当亚述城被米底国王基亚克萨雷斯的军队攻占时，很多私宅都被付之一炬，而高堂庙宇则是在被洗劫一空之后才遭到焚毁。因此，私人住宅区的发掘收获满满，其中包括经大火焙烤后完整保存下来的泥板。泥板上的文献主要是法律文件、信件，还有大量的学术著作和文学作品。这些材料为我们了解公元前7世纪亚述城居民的生活提供了独特的视角。我们将在第三章和第五章探讨其中的一些内容。

私人住宅建有地下墓室，家庭成员死后就埋葬在这里。地下墓室通常建在保存家庭档案的最靠里的房间下面。即使房屋重建或被夷为平地，地下墓室依然能安然无恙。安德烈发现了好几个可以追溯到公元前2千纪的地下墓室，其中包括1908年发现的45号巴布阿哈伊迪那（Babu-aha-iddina）家族之墓，该墓的随葬品相当丰厚。他们的部分档案是在通向地下墓室的竖井入口附近发现的。巴布阿哈伊迪那是公元前13世纪的一位国家高级官员，曾服务过多位国王。这些信件和行政文件记录了他的私人商业活动，并提及了这个家庭广泛经营的专业制造业，主要包括昂贵的成品，如香水、战车、复合弓、奢侈的皮革和纺织品等，均用从外地采购的珍稀材料制成。精美的随葬品和两具遗体——据信是巴布阿哈伊迪那夫妇——安放在之前家族墓葬的遗迹之上，其中包括黄金和宝石做成的精美首饰、精雕细琢的象牙梳子、别针、容器，还有装饰华丽的石制器皿，生动地展现了亚述王国成为中东领先的政治力量时，亚述精英所享受的奢华生活。

## 亚述神唯一的神庙

瓦尔特·安德烈发掘的主要目标之一是探索亚述神的神庙。但他的研究几乎没有触及神庙的早期遗存，因为这一部分被后来建的大型建筑覆盖了，这些建筑用的是中东传统的建筑材料——泥砖。安德烈所能发掘的与神庙相关的建筑最早可以追溯到公元前 2 千纪初。那时，安纳托利亚繁荣的贸易殖民点的收入充实了亚述城的金库。已发现的神庙中年代最久远的建筑铭文可以追溯到建立殖民点的古亚述时期，以埃里舒姆一世（Erišum I）的名义写成。铭文记载了这位统治者是如何为亚述神献上一个新的宝座，以及为了扩大神庙的占地面积，他又是如何拆除私人住宅的。关于亚述神的神庙，埃里舒姆一世写道：

> 那神庙叫做"野牛"，门叫做"守护女神"，锁叫做"强壮！"，门槛叫做"警惕！"。

人们认为神庙及其组成部分都有生命，甚至有知觉。神庙建筑和其中使用的所有物品都由专业工匠修建、制造和维护。专业工匠包括建筑工人、木匠、铁匠、金匠、书吏，等等。他们还负责制作并（通过一种叫做"开口"的仪式）唤醒亚述神和城中供奉的其他神的雕像。有些神拥有单独的神庙，比如说性爱与战争女神伊什塔尔（Ištar），她的神庙经过了多次重建。安德烈的考古队成功发掘了公元前 3 千纪初的女神神庙内殿。在内殿里，伊什塔尔女神的崇拜者的雕像沿着墙排成一行。风暴之神阿达德（Adad）和天空之神安努（Anu）共用一座神庙，月神辛（Sin）和太阳神沙马什（Šamaš）共用一座神庙。不过，大多数神祇还是在宏伟宽敞的亚述神庙建筑群中接受朝拜。

随着时间的推移，亚述的领土不断扩张，越来越多的神"住"进了亚述神庙。部分原因在于亚述人胜利之后会夺取敌方的神像，并将它们重新安放在亚述神的神庙中。公元前1千纪时，由于神庙居住者的名单实在是太长，有人甚至编撰了一份学术文档——现被称为"亚述神祇目录"——来描绘神庙复杂的布局。人们将神像视作神祇的显现，而这些神像以客人或人质的身份住在亚述神的家中，不言而喻，这些神便服从了亚述神的最高权威。例如，在公元前700年左右，国王辛那赫里布从阿杜马图绿洲（今沙特阿拉伯的杜玛占达）夺得了阿拉伯诸神的雕像，包括阿塔尔–沙马因（Attar-šamayin）、德伊（Day）、努海伊（Nuhay）、鲁道（Rudaw）、阿比尔–伊鲁（Abir-ilu）和阿塔尔–库鲁玛（Attar-qurumâ），并将它们安置在亚述神庙中。这一举措立即对阿拉伯部落产生了政治影响，他们认为自己的神遗弃了他们，而且众神似乎将亚述神视为主人和最高统治者。这种"绑架神祇"的策略旨在说服敌人或不情愿的盟友跟随他们的神的领导，从而接受亚述的统治。同这个例子一样，这一招屡试不爽。

定期供奉，即每日设宴祭祀亚述神，是亚述神的仆人的权利和义务。羊、牛、家禽和餐食所用的其他食材，即大麦、小麦、二粒小麦（脱壳小麦）、芝麻、蜂蜜，以及苹果和无花果等时令水果，定期从亚述神统治的地区运送到神庙中。这些原料并不罕见，很容易通过其他方式获得。但是，必须定期由亚述领土内的各个地区提供这些数量相对很少的食材，有时候长途跋涉也在所不惜。这样的一种安排可能在后勤上让人想不通，但在思想上具有至高无上的重要性——亚述的所有臣民必须共同参与到供奉亚述神的行动中来。只有交纳贡品，这些地方才能被定义为亚述神朝拜者的社区。相反，拒绝为亚述神提供贡品自然会被认为是叛国行为。

这些食材被送到亚述城后，神庙里的屠夫、面包师、酿酒师和榨油师——全都是男性——立即开始加工食材，备好菜肴献给亚述神。烹饪的大厨们可能算不上通俗意义上的祭司。不过，神庙祭祀的核心任务是为仪式做准备和主持每日供奉以纪念神祇，在这样的背景下，大厨自然也位于祭司之列。和负责神庙建筑和仪式用品的工匠一样，所有的后厨人员必须保持仪式上的洁净，才能与神祇密切互动。神庙里所有的工作人员都要剃净须发，看起来面容洁净。其他亚述男子通常留着及肩的长发和络腮胡（宦官除外，从公元前 9 世纪开始，他们在亚述帝国内扮演关键角色）。但是，神庙的工作人员必须剃光头，面部也不能留有毛发。只有到了公元前 7 世纪时，这些规矩才放宽了些，亚述神庙的一些后厨人员"蓄了好几年"才刮胡子。

1911 年，安德烈在亚述神庙建筑群的一栋建筑里发现了650 多块泥板，这些泥板存放在十个大陶瓷容器中，其中记载了连续四任神庙管理员的部分记录。这几位神庙管理员在公元前 12 世纪和前 11 世纪初负责组织亚述神的祭祀活动。时过境迁，在改造建筑结构时，这些沉甸甸的陶罐留在了原地，埋在新建筑之下。陶罐中的文件记录了亚述王国全部 27 个行省交付贡品的情况，有助于详细地再现亚述的政治组织形式。当时，亚述王国的领土从幼发拉底河一直延伸到小扎卜河。后来，在亚述帝国时期，宫廷暨政治权力和政府中心从亚述城迁走——公元前 879 年迁至卡尔胡，公元前 706 年迁至杜尔-沙鲁金，最后于公元前 700 年左右迁至尼尼微，几番周转，但供奉亚述神的传统一直延续了下来，所有的省份（到公元前 7 世纪 70年代左右大约有 75 个行省）按照既定的方式提供神宴所需的材料。正如尼尼微王宫中的行政文献所示，准备亚述神的宴席仍然是国家的重要事务。

人们认为众神通过"嗅"的方式享用宴席，因此，那些从供桌上撤下的菜肴，也就是亚述神的"剩菜"，可以再次分发出去。关于哪部分剩菜归谁所有，有严格的礼仪来规定，分到肉的人的地位是最显赫的。亚述的统治者作为亚述神在人间的代表，自然位于接受者名单之首，剩下的人还包括神庙工作人员和各省总督等达官显贵。为了将剩菜送到这些人手里，和之前准备食材时一样，菜肴必须千里迢迢运至各地。不过，饭菜不新鲜并不重要，因为吃神宴的剩菜是接受神的保佑，并不是为了享受美食。正如公元前 7 世纪的一位王室官员所说："吃剩菜的人都会活着。"通过这种方式享用亚述神的食物是一种极大的特权，它将亚述官员和亚述神联系在了一起，无论他们距离神庙多远。即使从公元前 879 年开始，亚述城不再是帝国的政治中心，但它从未失去自己在基本意识形态上的重要地位。

## 帝国覆灭后的亚述城

亚述城的神庙区被称为利巴里，意为"城市之心"。这个说法最早出现在公元前 13 世纪的文献之中，但实际上很可能比这个时间更早。后来，大概是为了避免同神名和国名混在一起，这个名字被用作整个城市的代名词。公元 2 世纪，在亚历山大城的托勒密（Ptolemy）的《地理志》中，这里被称作拉巴那。公元 6 世纪，拜占庭的斯蒂芬（Stephen）则将它记为利巴那。公元 1200 年，以罗马地图为原本绘制的波伊廷格地图可能将它误写成了萨宾。根据以上信息推测，在历史上晚得多的罗马帝国时期，亚述城归哈特拉王国统治时，此地依旧被称作利巴里。当时，尽管附着了时代的色彩，但亚述神（当时被称为阿索尔［Assor］）的膜拜仪式依旧按照千年来的古老传统和节日历法继续进行。神庙是按新近的帕提亚式建筑风格重建的，市民祈祷时，用的是神的阿拉伯语名字而不是亚述语名字。但是，这类仪式只受当地人重视，维护神庙的是城市的领主们，而非附近哈特拉的国王，他们坚定地按照过去亚述国王的传统行事，通向阿索尔神庙的通道上竖立的铭文石碑就是最好的证明。这些石碑具有亚述王室石碑（见图8）的典型特征——顶部呈半圆形；石碑上的城市领主们，如鲁特–阿索尔（R'uth-Assor，名字意为"亚述神的喜悦"），祈祷时的手势也和纪念碑上的亚述国王一样，只不过他们穿的是帕提亚风格的裤装，而不是传统的亚述披肩；另外，石碑上刻的是阿拉姆语字母，而不是亚述的楔形文字。（图3）

自公元240年开始，萨珊王朝的国王阿达希尔一世（Ardashir I）和沙普尔一世（Shapur I）入侵哈特拉王国，阿索尔神庙及整座城市被毁，居民流散。后来，由于战略位置优越，高耸的岩壁自然常被用作军事堡垒，最近一次是在奥斯曼时代。但是，神庙和亚述神的崇拜仪式再也没有恢复过，尽管亚述神庙里那些塔庙的荒凉残骸至今仍让人难以忘怀：曾经，这座雄伟的神庙是一个从地中海海岸延伸到伊朗中部的庞大帝国的宗教中心。

## 卡奈什：土耳其中部的"港口"

早在托罗斯山脉以外的地区向亚述神交纳的贡赋抵达亚述城之前，就有人以神的名义宣誓条约，保护亚述城和城中居民的利益。根据这些条约，亚述神并不是至高无上的宇宙之主。相反，他和那些引导并保护其他人的神处于平等的地位。"其他人"指的是公元前2千纪初安纳托利亚各国的统治者。根据条约的约定以及誓言的保证，当地的领导人允许亚述商人自由通行，有的地方还可以通过缴纳一部分利润换取在贸易殖民点的居住权。

图 3. 拉巴那（阿索尔）之主鲁特–阿索尔的石碑

亚述城最重要的合作伙伴之一是卡奈什的统治者。卡奈什是目前土耳其中部发掘最充分的考古遗址。它距离现代城市开塞利约 20 公里，位于肥沃的平原地区，好几条连接安纳托利亚西部和北部与叙利亚的长途路线汇聚于此。该遗址如今叫做居尔特佩，意为"灰烬之丘"，因为在公元前 3000 年左右到罗马帝国前期的这段漫长的时间里，这一古老的定居点多次被大火摧毁，留下厚厚的灰烬。正如通常这种情况所表明的那样，它有利于泥板——公元前 2 千纪初城市居民的书写材料——的保存，因为泥板就是经过焙烤保存下来的。1881 年，居尔特佩出土的第一批楔形文字文献吸引了学者们的注意，他们将其命名为"卡帕多西亚泥板"（卡帕多西亚是安纳托利亚中部高原在古典时代的旧称），因为这是他们唯一掌握的起源信息。泥板是用古亚述方言写成的，使用了一种特殊的楔形文字，不到 200 个字符，书写的内容表明它们和亚述城有关。学者们认识到，来自伊拉克北部的商人在距离他们的城市约 1000 公里的地方建立了殖民点，这条信息引起了学者们对泥板及其起源之谜的极大兴趣。

但 40 多年间，时不时从居尔特佩（图 4）挖出泥板并卖给古董商的当地人想方设法地隐藏泥板的来源。尽管有几个考古团队调查了这个遗址，然而他们总是将注意力放在高丘上。当地人在挖掘古代泥砖——中东地区传统的肥料和建筑材料——时发现了泥板，这令考古学家非常沮丧，因为这种挖掘行为对泥板造成了严重的破坏。约 2500 块泥板出土后被欧美各大博物馆和私人收藏家收购。直到 1925 年，当地一位马车夫酒后失言，才解开了"卡帕多西亚泥板"的起源之谜。他受雇于贝德里希·赫罗兹尼（Bedřich Hrozný）。这位捷克的东方学家因解读赫梯语而闻名，他将赫梯语界定为一种印欧语言。赫罗兹尼开始在居尔特佩进行发掘的时间不久，车夫不小心透露这些泥板并非出自高丘而是低城区的一个地方后，赫罗兹尼的团队

图 4. 居尔特佩的卫星照片，展示了考古发掘的现场：卡奈什的宫殿和神庙位于圆形高丘之上，高丘东北侧连接着低城区的商人聚居区

随即在后来被确认为古亚述商人区的遗址中找到了 1000 多块泥板。1948 年以来，在土耳其历史协会的赞助下，高丘和低城区每年都开展了考古调查。土耳其历史协会成立于 1930 年，由凯末尔（Mustafa Kemal Atatürk）建立，旨在推动土耳其历史研究。探索居尔特佩是该组织最重要的活动之一，从 1948 到 2005 年，安卡拉的考古学家夫妇塔赫辛·奥兹古奇与尼梅特·奥兹古奇（Tahsin and Nimet Özgüç）一直在此地开展挖掘，他们的毕生奉献对居尔特佩的考古工作产生了深刻影响。安卡拉的安纳托利亚文明博物馆收藏了该遗址出土的文物，其中重要展品在专为居尔特佩设置的展馆展出。

这些古亚述泥板使我们确认居尔特佩就是卡奈什城。城里的圆形高丘面积超过 20 公顷，高度约为 20 米，是安纳托利亚中部最大的高丘之一。低城区筑起围墙，占据了一片 100 多公顷的新月形区域，从北部、东部和南部围绕着高丘。如此看来，这个定居点比亚述城大得多。发现古亚述泥板的区域面积狭小，不足 9 公顷，从这一点便可判断广阔的低城区主要住着当地人，来自亚述城的商人则居住在其中的一块特定区域。泥板上的文本将亚述人居住区称作卡奈什的"港口"（*kārum*），亚述语中常用这个词指贸易点。在中东，"港口"一般建在水边，但卡奈什不属于这种情况。与有 3000 年历史的高丘不同，低城区只在公元前 2 千纪的上半期使用了大约三个世纪，并且重建了好几次。亚述商人的房屋最早可追溯至低城区定居点的 II 地层，低城区经历了一场大火之后，它们又出现在 Ib 地层。在这些建筑物中发现的泥板组成了卡奈什的亚述贸易商行的档案。安纳托利亚中部的其他几个遗址也出土了同一时期的亚述文献，但包括残片在内，总共只有大约 150 块泥板。而迄今为止，卡奈什出土了 23,500 块泥板，与这一惊人的数量相比，其他遗址出土的泥板数量的确微不足道。大多数文献的年代出自公元前 19 世纪的约 50 年间。目前为止，已对外公开的泥板仅有 4500 块，而且其中大部分是早期发现。另外还有 5000 块土耳其出土的泥板正在等待公布初版内容。要做的事情还有许多。

## 亚述人在安纳托利亚的贸易

卡奈什的亚述商人的档案有助于细致入微地再现他们的商业和私人活动。档案记录了居住在卡奈什的商人们的生活，尤其是他们商行的组织形式，同时也提及了同时代的亚述城。亚述城这一时期的考古发现非常有限，因为后来有大量的居住层覆盖了相关的考古地层。因此，我们对这一时期亚述城的政治和社会环境的了解大多来自卡奈什的史料。幸运的是，旅居国外的亚述人密切关注着家乡的消息，并与亚述城的家人和商业伙伴保持着频繁的通信往来。他们直接叫亚述城为"那座城市"

（ālum）。卡奈什出土的已知文件中，大多数是信件。信件通常包括一块刻有文字的泥板，外面包着一层薄薄的黏土作信封。信封上刻了字，用来确认发件人和收件人，并且盖有发件人的印章，还能保护信件内容不被泄露。这种设计在古亚述信件中很常见，之后在公元前2千纪和前1千纪的楔形文字信件中也能看到。

亚述商人在当地住了约两个世纪，在这期间，卡奈什是一个区域国家的首都，统治者是亚述人口中的"王子"（ruba'um），他住在防卫森严的高丘上的宫殿里。低城区由开阔的广场和铺了砖的街道构成，底下是排污的下水道。六到八栋双层楼房背靠背建在一起，组成低城区的居住区。目前为止，发掘最充分的是亚述人的居住区，他们的房屋按当地风格建造。私人住宅包括了一个含有起居室和厨房的居住部分，和一个较小的可上锁的部分，后者用来保存亚述人用楔形文字书写的文件等贵重物品。这些文件根据内容归档之后，存放在架子上或容器内（罐子、木箱或袋子里）。逝者通常和他们的随葬品一起被埋葬在房屋下的棺材或石棺墓（像一个石制的箱子）中。亚述人的房子下面也是如此，尽管文献指出他们通常更希望在亚述城寿终正寝。

亚述商人专营锡的进口生意，他们在亚述城采购从远处运来的锡，还有城里和外地的家庭制作的豪华纺织品。驴队走陆路运送货物，每只驴可以携带大约65公斤（等于130明那）的锡。这些体积小、分量重的锡铸块外面裹上布料，小心、均衡地放在驴子的背上和两侧，以免使驴子感到不适，也避免主人花钱更换受伤的牲畜。如果道路状况良好，亚述商人就会用能承重300到1500公斤的四轮牛车来送货。一到卡奈什，商人们就会把商品存放在宽敞的仓库里。仓库位于城堡上的宫殿中，文献指出它们被当作中央储藏库使用。私宅里的保险库主要用来保管金银——这是他们用买卖的收益换来的，准备运回亚述城。不过，他们大部分的经济活动是在没有现金的情况下，完全依靠信贷运作的，这远远早于近现代商业银行采用的核心策略。

卡奈什的统治者和亚述商人合作密切。亚述商人的一切盈利所得，卡奈什的统治者都会从中分一杯羹。作为回报，他在自己的领土内为亚述商人以及商队提供居住权和保护。亚述商人不是卡奈什统治者的臣民，因为该商业区在政治和法律上都被视为亚述城邦的域外之地。即便当地爆发战争冲突，商队也可以平安通过——当时的亚述人几乎没有军事力量（在安纳托利亚完全没有），所以他们热衷于维护自己的中立立场。反过来，按照条约规定，卡奈什统治者有权对进口的锡征收约3%的税（即对每头驴征4明那的锡），对纺织品征收5%的税，还可以选择以市价额外购买10%的布料。卡奈什统治者的签约方是"亚述城、亚述城的居民和'港口'"，后者不仅仅指卡奈什的亚述贸易区，也指在这里经商的全体亚述商人。

我们不仅可以通过参考各种文献来恢复卡奈什的统治者与亚述商人之间的协议，而且在2000年，亚述商人区第二居住阶段（Ib地层）的一座房子里出土了一块原始条约泥板，上面也记录了协议的详细内容。除卡奈什外，商人们还与沿途路过的其他王国——例如阿普姆（现叙利亚东北部的卡米什利地区）和哈胡姆（现土耳其的萨姆萨特市地区）——的统治者签订了条约。哈胡姆是另一个亚述"港口"的所在地，而且它确实位于水边，靠近幼发拉底河的一处重要的浅滩。和卡奈什条约泥板一起出土的还有另一块原始条约泥板，其中关于自由通行和保护的规定着实有趣，居然包括了保证不蓄意破坏渡船、不沉没商品——这表明河盗行为可能时有发生。哈胡姆的高官们没有直接征税，但他们有权以折扣价从亚述的商队里购买一定数量的锡和布料。

卡奈什在陆路网络中的有利位置使其成为了亚述人的商业活动中心，并从此地发散出一个小型的经销网络。商队需要五到六个星期才能从亚述城走到卡奈什，两地相距约 1200 公里。但实际上，亚述商人的贸易范围不止于此，他们还在安纳托利亚其他十几个国家的都城经营着类似的商业活动中心。其中最重要的城市"港口"包括杜尔胡米特，该城位于卡奈什以北250 公里的梅尔济丰平原上，很可能靠近大型铜矿和黑海，还有普鲁什哈杜姆，位于卡奈什以西 385 公里，据信相当于现在博尔瓦丁附近的于其休于克。运输成本和税收决定了哪里可以发财致富，时间和距离则与此无关。如果价格合适的话，亚述商人愿意到很远的地方做生意。然而，幅员辽阔的领土国家出现，剥夺了商人的法律和政治基础——这是他们通过长途贸易赚钱的根本，因此，亚述城终止了在安纳托利亚的贸易活动。

## 卡尔胡：与帝国相称的首都

公元前 879 年，国王亚述纳西尔帕二世（Aššurnasirpal II）将宫廷迁到新址，亚述城自此便不再是政治权力和国家行政的中心。亚述纳西尔帕二世选择了卡尔胡（图 5），这座古城在他和儿子暨继承人沙尔曼纳瑟尔三世（Shalmaneser III）的统治之下，成为了一个至高无上的帝国中心。

虽然亚述在公元前 9 世纪的疆域和公元前 12 世纪相差不多，但在青铜时代末期的大迁徙以前，它在更广阔的地域范围内所扮演的角色与此前完全不同。这时的亚述已是一个强大的帝国，周围不再是规模和人力与之相当的国家，而是比它小得多的公国。亚述重新夺回西部和北部的失地后，在领土面积和人力方面远远超过了邻国。重征的成功让亚述国王成为了邻国

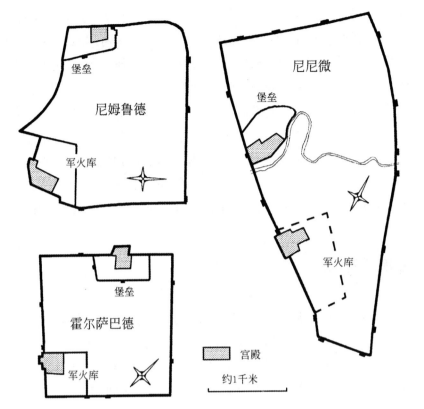

图 5.　亚述都城：卡尔胡（尼姆鲁德）、杜尔–沙鲁金（霍尔萨巴德）和尼尼微

之中的新霸主。卡尔胡被打造成为新帝国的首都，城里的建筑也经过一番设计，为的就是震慑四方。

　　卡尔胡位于亚述核心地域内独一无二的中心位置。它处在亚述中部三个最重要的城市——南部的亚述城、北部的尼尼微和东部的阿尔贝拉——形成的三角区域中间，位置优越，而且与这三座城市往来便利。卡尔胡位于底格里斯河东岸，控制着底格里斯河与大扎卜河交汇处以北的浅滩。因此，它掌管着该地区的两条主要水道，以及通向底格里斯河西岸的渡口。同在底格里斯河河畔，卡尔胡处在尼尼微和亚述城之间，再加上有一条运河连接大扎卜河，卡尔胡也可以通过水路直达阿尔贝拉。卡尔胡到亚述城的直线距离约为 70 公里，到阿尔贝拉约为 60 公里，到尼尼微约为 35 公里，去往其中任何一城的往返旅程快则只需一天，慢则最多两天，实际速度取决于行进的方向和方式。但无论如何，这都相当于这三座城市相互往来所需时间的一半。除此之外，卡尔胡在陆路和水路的长途交通网络中均占有重要地位。它是底格里斯河沿岸南北通道的一处站点，而且控制着一条关键的路线。沿着这条向东的路线，可以途经阿尔贝拉前往扎格罗斯山脉，再沿着山脉西麓向南进入巴比伦。

## 发掘卡尔胡

今天，卡尔胡的废墟被称为尼姆鲁德，当地的传统认为这处遗址与《圣经》人物宁录（Nimrod）有关联，遂取此名。宁录是挪亚（Noah）的孙子，他是第一个称王的人，被尊为亚述的奠基者。尼姆鲁德是伊拉克最重要的考古遗址之一。

自 1845 年 11 月起，英国探险家奥斯汀·亨利·莱亚德（Austen Henry Layard）开始对该遗址进行调查。他后续出版的图书记录了自己的旅行和考古经历，这些书大受欢迎，至今依然是可读性极强的中东游记。先驱者法国人保罗·埃米尔·博塔（Paul-Émile Botta）发现了萨尔贡二世（Sargon II）时期的首都杜尔–沙鲁金。受此启发和指引，莱亚德第一次在尼姆鲁德的卫城土丘上刮面时就发现了刻有铭文的石浮雕，后来这里被确认为国王亚述纳西尔帕二世的宫殿。尽管莱亚德的活动资金并不多，但他借用了采矿的方法，通过挖掘地道探查了该建筑的大部分区域。这种工作方式全然不同于安德烈约 60 年后在亚述城首次采用的审慎方法，但却迅速产生了惊人的效果，尤其是发现了雕刻繁复的墙壁浮雕和其他石雕。起初，莱亚德错误地认为自己在尼姆鲁德发现的是尼尼微，但他后来又在库云吉克土丘挖掘出真正的尼尼微城遗址。为了找到尽可能多的古物运回英国，他一直挖掘到 1851 年。

在 19 世纪的数十年间，亚述牢牢抓住了西方读者的想象力。源源不断的报纸文章即时报道莱亚德和同伴霍姆兹德·拉萨姆（Hormuzd Rassam）以及其他在亚述遗址工作的开拓者们的新发现。1847 年，亚述文物在巴黎的卢浮宫首次公开展出。随后，1852 年，大英博物馆展示了莱亚德的考古发现。这两次展览都吸引了大量观众。后来，尼姆鲁德出土的石雕在大英博物馆的亚述展廊以及世界各地永久展出，剩余的发现物则被运往欧洲和美国的其他博物馆中收藏。第一批古代亚述手工艺品到达欧洲时引发了人们的狂热，从而刺激了各种亚述风格的奢侈品的大量生产，如珠宝、银质餐具和壁炉装饰品等。

人们对亚述的一切充满了好奇心，尼姆鲁德等地出土的亚述铭文又得以迅速出版，这都使解读楔形文字成为了语言学界最热门的挑战。再加上人们发现亚述语同希伯来语和阿拉伯语一样属于闪语，解读工作更是热火朝天。1857 年，伦敦的皇家亚洲学会组织了一场竞赛，公开展示了亚述语的破译情况。自如火如荼的"亚述热"盛行以来，以英国和伊拉克考古学家为主的团队在尼姆鲁德断断续续地开展挖掘工作。他们主要把精力集中在卫城土丘，同时也在阿扎尔丘——第二座卫城土丘——和低城区进行了挖掘。

继莱亚德之后，尼姆鲁德最著名的发掘者并不是一位专业的考古学家，而是侦探小说家阿加莎·克里斯蒂（Agatha Christie），她的丈夫马克斯·马洛温（Max Mallowan）在 1949 至 1957 年间负责英国团队在当地的挖掘工作。克里斯蒂拍摄并记录了当时的考古发现，而且还巧用昂贵的润肤水清洁、加固那些脆弱的象牙雕刻，这些象牙雕刻曾经装饰过精美的宫殿家具和奢侈品。在遗址现场，克里斯蒂写下了像《他们来到巴格达》这样的谋杀小说。她也像莱亚德一样，以尼姆鲁德的工作为灵感，写下了大受欢迎的畅销书。可能是因为未经焚烧的泥板没有被考古学家认出，整个19世纪只出土了一块楔文泥板。而在马洛温挖掘尼姆鲁德期间以及之后一段时间里，卡尔胡发现了很多重要的文本，其中格外瞩目的当属1952年出土的"尼姆鲁德信件"——约300封国王提格拉特皮勒赛尔三世（Tiglath-pileser III）和萨尔贡二世的国务信件，还有国王埃萨尔哈东（Esarhaddon）在公元前672年加诸臣民的契约的多份抄本，后者于1955年出土。

在伊拉克文物局采取的常规保护措施之下，尼姆鲁德出土了最令人叹为观止的考古发现，即1988年和1989年，在亚述纳西尔帕二世的王宫之下意外发现的三座完好无损的王室墓葬。这里埋葬了公元前9世纪和前8世纪的几位亚述王后。她们的随葬品非常奢华，其中包括50多公斤精雕细琢的黄金首饰，以及由黄金和水晶制成的豪华器皿，多数物品上都刻有铭文。在挖掘过程中，遗体和服装的保存状态相对较好，人类学分析和纤维分析也迅速开展。这一伟大发现理应得到细致的科学研究，然而，1990年爆发的海湾战争以及随后的贸易制裁却中断了研究进程。目前为止，这些珍贵的文物只是间或非常短时间地拿出来公开展示。大部分时间里，它们都被锁在银行保险库中。不过，它们因祸得福，在近年来伊拉克的动荡历史中幸免于难。有朝一日，如果巴格达的伊拉克博物馆能够永久展出这些藏品，它们有望得到应有的关注。

到目前为止，尼姆鲁德的大部分考古发现都集中在公元前1千纪，偶尔才会出土更早期的史料。虽然该定居点的建立时间据信可以追溯到公元前6千纪，但是，在卫城土丘开展的小规模挖掘中出土的陶器和燧石只能追溯到公元前3千纪初。直到公元前 2 千纪初，即沙姆什阿杜（Samsi-Addu）统治时期，这座城市才彰显出跨地区影响力。当时，尼姆鲁德被称作卡瓦胡姆，据叙利亚马里的王宫档案记载（沙姆什阿杜曾任命他年龄较小的儿子为叙利亚的总督），这里是底格里斯河上的一个重要港口。1854 年，卫城土丘发掘出一座石墓，丰厚的随葬品中有一把青铜战斧，也可以追溯到卡瓦胡姆时期。公元前 14 世纪，亚述王国建立后，这里就成了行省的首府，一直持续到公元前 7 世纪末亚述帝国灭亡。

## 国王之城与国王之民

公元前 879 至前 706 年，卡尔胡是帝国的政治中心，这是它地位最为显耀的时期。卡尔胡的晋升不仅牺牲了亚述城——前者取代它成为了国王的主要居住地，也牺牲了尼尼微和阿尔贝拉。由于亚述城位于亚述相对边缘的位置，尼尼微和阿尔贝拉本身也是经济和政治中心，其重要性几乎不亚于亚述城，而且，就拿尼尼微来说，这座城市也建有王宫。亚述神的祭祀仪式需要国王定期关注和出席，尼尼微和阿尔贝拉举行的伊什塔尔女神的祭祀仪式对于国家而言同样具有特殊意义，也要求国王花大量时间待在这些城市，参加这些节日活动。卡尔胡上升为新的帝国中心，大大削弱了另外三个城市及其居民在国内的影响力。

不难想到，新帝国中心的建立背后有一个更庞大的战略，目的在于牺牲老一代城市精英的利益来巩固国王的地位。虽然他们曾经在亚述的政治生活中扮演重要角色，但从现在开始，行政和军事管理的最高官职留给了新一批公职骨干队伍，也就是宦官（ša rēši，意为"有头脑的人"，即国王的"私人随从"；与之相对的是 ša ziqni，意为"有胡子的人"，指未被阉割的官员）。男孩成为宦官需要具备哪些品质或条件，或者，最终决定将男孩变为宦官的人是谁，这两个问题至今仍是未解之谜。我们也不了解宦官的原生家庭背景，但是，我们没有理由认为成为宦官是一种悲惨的命运，也不能认定选择这条路都是被迫的。实际上，宦官很有可能也出身于官僚世家，因为排行较小无法继承到太多家产。王室宦官不仅有很高的社会地位，而且在国王的家庭中终生占有一席之地。但是，宦官们牺牲了生育孩子的能力，也因此永远放弃了家庭生活。他们没有结婚，所以能够一心一意为国家和国王服务，任凭差遣——他们是完美的员工。作为回报，王室为宦官承担了应尽的家庭义务，其中包括处理葬礼事宜，提供保证身后福祉所需要的供品。尽管宦官如此接近王权，但他们永远不可能成为国王。掌握亚述王权者必须是完人，因此，身体有残缺的宦官绝对被排除在外。

新帝国中心的居民由一位王室宦官，即王宫总管内伽尔阿皮库姆阿（Nergal-apil-kumu'a），亲自挑选。亚述纳西尔帕二世敕令他监督迁都卡尔胡一事。卡尔胡的发展不仅改变了亚述核心地域的定居模式，也改变了整个帝国的定居模式，因为定居新都的合适人选是从所有行省中挑选的。可以想见，只有那些拥戴国王、拥护他的宏图大略的人才能被选中。因此，公元前879年创造的不仅仅是一个新的政治中心，还是一个居民都是国王和帝国的忠实支持者的中心。通过在新的地点、新的社会结构下，创建新的权力和效忠模式，亚述纳西尔帕二世成功改变了亚述帝国中央地区之前的权力结构。迁都卡尔胡巩固并确保了国王和国家行政管理的支配地位，为新亚述帝国提供了一个至高无上的中心，一个受忠实支持者们保障的权力基础。

在建筑方面，卡尔胡古城经历了一番彻底的改造。为了解决超级新都的供水问题，这里新建了一个区域沟渠系统。古城大兴土木，不惜成本，只为向世界炫耀亚述的财富。由于长期有人居住，古老的定居土丘已经垒得相当高，于是被改造成了一座堡垒，里面建着王宫和神庙。不过，尽管土丘面积不小，但相比宽广的卡尔胡城区，它也只占据了城西南角的一小部分。亚述纳西尔帕二世时期的卡尔胡占地面积约为 360 公顷，周围还环绕着 7.5 公里长的城墙，比亚述城大了好几倍。在城东南角的第二个卫城土丘上建有军火库，是存储军备设施、集结军队的地方。此后的亚述首都也沿用了这种基本规划。卡尔胡的神庙是用来祭祀亚述最重要的神祇的，比如伊什塔尔（但以卡德姆里之女［Lady of Kadmuri］的形象出现，从而与她在尼尼微和阿尔贝拉的形象区分开来）、宁努尔塔（Ninurta）和纳布（Nabu）。但这里没有亚述神的神庙，亚述神唯一的圣所依旧位于亚述城。卡尔胡歌颂的帝国核心是国王，而不是亚述神。

在亚述纳西尔帕二世时期，卡尔胡令人印象最深刻的建筑一定是国王的新王宫，按照它在卫城所处的方位，王宫现在被称作西北宫。这座宏伟的建筑长 200 米，宽 130 米，俯视着周遭的一切，连相邻的神庙都相形见绌，这与亚述城的地势完全不同。巨型人首双翼公牛守护着参天大门，它们或许是亚述帝国最具标志性的建筑形象（图 6）。莱亚德试图将其中一些运回伦敦时，它们带来了不小的挑战。从黎巴嫩运来的雪松树干长达 30 米，成为了当时世界上最长的房梁，搭建起规模超前的大厅。整座王宫环三个庭院而建，分为国务部门、行政管理侧厅和王室私人住宅。前面提到的亚述王后地下墓葬就是从王室私人住宅区出土的。这种建筑布局成为了整个亚述帝国代表性建筑的模板，例如，舒尔木沙里（Šulmu-šarri）位于杜尔-卡特里穆的豪宅（见第三章）就是这种格局。巨大的雪花石板上雕刻着人物形象和赞美国王丰功伟绩的铭文，成排地镶嵌在国务部门的墙上（见图 12）。亚述纳西尔帕二世在王座厅接受国内外达官显贵的朝见，这里的装饰尤其夺目：描绘的有英勇征战和凯旋的场景，还有战利品、贡品、臣服的对手送来的礼物。

图 6. 国王亚述纳西尔帕二世时期的巨型人首双翼公牛，出土于卡尔胡西北宫，发掘者为 A. H. 莱亚德

宫殿中竖了一块石碑，据上面的铭文记载，有 69,574 人参加了新都的落成庆典，其中包括卡尔胡的居民、帝国各地的代表，以及邻近国家的 5000 名尊贵宾客。在这场持续了十天的盛宴上，亚述纳西尔帕二世摆酒设宴盛情款待客人们，菜单还保存在石碑上：17,000 头牛羊，34,000 只鸭、鹅和鸽子。这意味着每一位赴宴者都可以吃到半只禽和一块相当大的牛羊肉。除了这些主菜，盛宴还包括鹿肉、鱼肉和（不大合我们口味的）鼠肉，大量的蔬菜、水果、香料以及丰富的乳制品，另外有 10,000 桶啤酒和 10,000 囊葡萄酒供宾客畅饮。

公元前 706 年，萨尔贡二世将宫廷迁到他的新帝都杜尔-沙鲁金（意为"萨尔贡的堡垒"）。在此之前，卡尔胡一直是所有亚述君王的主要居住地。亚述纳西尔帕二世的几位后继者在西北宫之外建立了自己的宫殿，西北宫则继续作为行省总督的宅邸使用。直到 1993 年，伊拉克考古学家们才发掘出阿达德尼拉里三世（Adad-nerari III）的宫殿。提格拉特皮勒塞尔三世的宫殿如今则被称作中央宫殿，但这个平淡无奇的名字并没有反映出其旧称的含义："承载荣华、保佑使此殿长存之君王的欢乐之宫"。宫殿大门的名字则充满仪式感，该名称清楚地表明，卡尔胡不仅被看作亚述的中心，也被看作整个世界的中心：

> 对四方世界的统治者作出公正的评判，提供来自群山和海洋的贡品，将人们生产的东西带到他们的主、国王的面前的"正义之门"。

埃萨尔哈东在卡尔胡度过了很长一段时间。公元前 7 世纪，为了给他的新宫殿提供建筑材料，原来的这些宫殿的石材被拆除一空。他的宫殿一直没有完工，但殿中别具一格的柱廊大厅凸显了公元前 671 年征服战争后埃及文化的影响。

## 杜尔–卡特里穆：西部行省的生活

亚述人生活的杜尔–卡特里穆城，就是如今位于叙利亚东北部哈布尔河东岸的谢赫哈马德丘。从公元前 13 世纪开始，杜尔–卡特里穆就成了亚述王国一个重要的行省中心。公元前 7 世纪，富有的高官舒尔木沙里（见第三章）在此定居时，杜尔–卡特里穆还有一个阿拉姆语名字，叫马格达拉（意为"塔"）。这也反映了在公元前 1 千纪时，亚述帝国使用最广泛的口语并非亚述语，而是阿拉姆语。这种西部闪语族语言与希伯来语和腓尼基语密切相关，和亚述语属于同一语族。因此，任何说亚述语的人都能很好地理解阿拉姆语——虽然未必能够掌握语法的细微差别——反之亦然。在亚述的核心地域之外，阿拉姆语很可能也是最常用的书面语言。但是，不同于用楔形文字记录在泥板上的亚述语文本，阿拉姆语使用的是字母，写在类似纸张的材料上（如皮革或莎草纸）。这些材料只有在非常干燥的环境中才能保存下来，例如出土绝大多数早期阿拉姆语文献（但是年代很晚）的犹地亚沙漠里的洞穴，否则就会分解。

至少从公元前 9 世纪开始，亚述的官方语言同时采用了亚述语和阿拉姆语，这是与口头广泛使用阿拉姆语的西部各省进行融合的直接结果。据记载，自沙尔曼纳瑟尔三世即位以来，亚述的核心地域便也开始使用阿拉姆语：在首都卡尔胡的王宫里，釉面砖上绘有阿拉姆语字母，这很可能是装配工匠的标记。除此之外，宫殿浮雕和宫门装饰上通常绘有成对的书吏，一个用笔在卷轴上书写，另一个用尖笔在泥板或涂着多层蜡的木制写字板上压记楔文。这些书写工具通常也经受不住时间的考验。亚述城和卡尔胡出土了一些由象牙制成的高档书写工具，但是蜡层已经消失，文字也不复存在了。这种蜡板与在哈德良长城

图 7. 杜尔-卡特里穆出土的财产买卖合同，用亚述楔形文字
　　　书写，上方刻有两行阿拉姆语字母的概述，下方为两枚
　　　封印的印记

发现的著名的文德兰达木牍有些相似。文德兰达木牍可以追溯到公元1到2世纪，是英国现存最古老的手写文件；而楔形文字的书吏自公元前3千纪以来就惯常使用这类书写工具。

亚述帝国将阿拉姆语广泛用作书面语言有两个极为重要的标志。第一，在记录财产转移的泥板上，经常出现刻写或用墨水书写的字母注释。这些简短的注释总结了楔形文字合同的内容，显然是为了帮助那些能够阅读阿拉姆语，但不熟悉亚述楔形文字的人（图7）。第二，有一种特殊的泥板只刻写了阿拉姆语文本。这些债务票据有非常明显的三角形轮廓，被串在一条打了结的绳子上。目前尚不清楚绳子的另一端系着什么，但最有可能系的是写在阿拉姆语卷轴上的同一债务票据的副本。这样假设的理由在于，另一种更常见的债务票据有两个组成部分：放在内里的泥板，和包在外面带有封印的黏土信封，两者的文字内容是一致的。这些刻上了阿拉姆语的三角形泥板也有封印，因此可假设内里配有卷轴，泥板的作用就相当于信封。无论它们具体功能如何，杜尔–卡特里穆和亚述西部行省的其他地方都出土了很多这样的泥板，以及刻有阿拉姆语注释的合同。在亚述的核心地域，这类泥板出现的频率要低得多，这可能说明这里的人更熟悉楔形文字。虽然在杜尔–卡特里穆书写私人法律文件的书吏也能写出形状漂亮、字迹优雅的泥板，但他们一定不是以亚述语为母语的人——他们频繁出现典型的语法错误，这表明他们习惯使用的是西部闪语族语言，而且最有可能是阿拉姆语。

## 将西部融入亚述王国

1977年，哈特穆特·屈内（Hartmut Kühne）领导的一支德国考古队在绘制哈布尔河谷多处遗址的地图时，得知当地人发现了一组泥板。于是，从 1978 年开始，他们每年定期对谢赫哈马德丘进行考古发掘。当时，当地人在一座定居土丘上建水库时，不经意发现了一个建筑群里的几间房。在公元前 2 千纪末，这座建筑群管理着这座城市和整个地区。这里一共出土了约 400 块泥板，是公元前 13 世纪和前 12 世纪初的行政档案，涉及维持行省政府运行的农地管理事务。大火烧毁建筑时焙烤了这些泥板。因为离火太近，有些泥板上的文字被烤煳了，难以辨认，还有些最早发现的泥板被丢进了河里——泥板面平，又只有手掌大小，当地的小孩"机智地"用它们打水漂去了。幸存下来的文本中还引用了木制写字板的内容，当然，后者肯定已经被焚为灰烬了。

现存文本大多是行政文书，从中可以洞见杜尔–卡特里穆的经济情况。这里位于地中海气候和草原气候之间的"风险地带"。当地的灌溉渠系支撑着旱农生产，促进了大麦、小麦和芝麻，以及蔬菜、草药的丰收。"王宫农民"包揽农活，行省政府负责管理。他们养了两群驴作驮畜，共 150 头。牛养在河边牧场，被成对地赶去犁地播种，同时供应奶和肉。牧羊人则将成群的绵羊和山羊赶到草原放牧：（制成毛毡的）羊毛是当地纺织业的支柱。

杜尔–卡特里穆的文件和其中记载的农业活动，与当时的首都亚述城以及其他行省各地相差无几，例如附近的哈尔贝城（现叙利亚楚埃拉丘），和现位于吉里加诺（古代称之为杜努沙乌兹比；靠近土耳其迪亚巴克尔市）或萨比–阿比亚德（在叙利亚的巴利克河谷）的被称为"杜努"（dunnu）的小型设防定居点。这就反映了不断扩张的亚述王国已将生活方式带到新并入地区。总督和下属从中央被派到各个行省，在地方用亚述语言和文字推行行政章程以及各种文件的常规标准格式，为行省政府构建经济基础。每个行省中心必须向首都上交定额税收，其中包括呈献每天祭祀亚述神所需的食材——这在意识形态层面具有重要意义。

　　在公元前 2 千纪末的亚述王国，杜尔–卡特里穆具有特殊地位。那时，它不仅是行省中心，还是亚述王国西半部分的显赫名城。亚述王国一人之下、万人之上的官员，即亚述的首辅大臣（*sukallu rabiu*），就定居在该城。他被尊称为"哈尼迦尔巴特之王"，这也是亚述人对其从前的统治者米坦尼国王的称呼。第一个获得此称号的人是伊巴什伊里（Ibašši-ili），他是国王阿达德尼拉里一世（Adad-nerari I）年龄较小的儿子，也是王位的继任者沙尔曼纳瑟尔一世（Shalmaneser I）的弟弟。这两位国王先后向米坦尼发起战争，并占领了米坦尼的领土。当时，亚述并没有重新利用米坦尼过去的中心城市，而是把杜尔–卡特里穆设为西部的政府中心。这座古城与亚述城之间有一条直达的路线（后来成为了"国王之路"网络的一部分；见第六章），这也是从首都到哈布尔河谷的新领地的最短路线。因此，杜尔–卡特里穆的地位在沙尔曼纳瑟尔一世统治期间得以提升，他在这里为沙尔曼努神（Salmanu）建了一座神庙。沙尔曼努神与亚述王室家族关系密切，沙尔曼纳瑟尔一世就取了这个名字，以表达对该神的敬意。在亚述语中，他的名字表述为"沙尔曼努–阿沙莱德"（Salmanu-ašared），即"沙尔曼努神卓尔不群"。沙尔曼努的名字意为"善良之徒"，可能他只是亚述神的一种神化面目。因为亚述城与亚述神紧紧联系在一起，以亚述神的名义在别处修建神庙显得很不合适，所以便造出了沙尔努曼这个神。1879 年，奥斯汀·亨利·莱亚德的同伴霍姆兹德·拉萨姆在谢赫哈马德丘发现了公元前 8 世纪初的一块石碑的第一块残片，上面记载着国王阿达德尼拉里三世和当地总督内伽尔埃利什（Nergal-ereš）用出征地中海时从黎巴嫩获得的雪松原木修复这座神庙的过程：

沙尔曼纳瑟尔（一世），我的祖先（字面意思为"我的父亲"），建造的古老神庙已经破落不堪，我灵机一动，从地基到护墙，完完整整重建了这座神庙。我将来自黎巴嫩山的雪松顶梁放在上面。

沙尔曼纳瑟尔一世的弟弟伊巴什伊里将"哈尼迦尔巴特之王"这一手握重权的新职传给了他的后代。公元前1183年，亚述王室传承的主线中断了。在此之前，在位37年的老国王图库尔提宁努尔塔一世（Tukulti-Ninurta I）被儿子们暗杀。随后，他的儿子们卷入了血雨腥风的王位争夺战之中。最终，伊巴什伊里的玄孙宁努尔塔阿皮埃库尔（Ninurta-apil-Ekur）成为了亚述国王。新王的父亲伊里帕达（Ili-pada）曾是权倾一时的人物，以至于巴比伦国王在一封信中戏谑地将他和当时真正的国王——图库尔提宁努尔塔一世短命的儿子亚述尼拉里三世（Aššur-nerari III）——并称为"亚述的国王们"。显然，巴比伦国王是在嘲弄老国王被弑之后亚述的赢弱：

亚述尼拉里和伊里帕达，因为（你们）不负责任，酗酒成性，优柔寡断，所以亚述神把你们变成了疯子。你们当中没有一个人是清醒的。

在巴比伦的干预下，伊里帕达死后，他的儿子登上了亚述王位，此后所有的亚述国王都是他的后代，直到帝国终结。在杜尔-卡特里穆出土的石碑上，公元前8世纪的亚述统治者阿达德尼拉里三世称沙尔曼纳瑟尔一世为"他的父亲"——亚述国王对从前历代国王的通称，实际上叫错了，因为他其实是沙尔曼纳瑟尔一世的弟弟伊巴什伊里的后代。

公元前10世纪，亚述重新占领了西部失地，杜尔-卡特里穆作为亚述的飞地发挥了至关重要的战略作用。公元前9世纪，杜尔-卡特里穆纳入了一块较大的建有防御设施的低城区，从一个相对较小的城镇变成了一座占地 60 公顷的大城。它的城墙差不多有 4 公里长，还有一条 9 米宽的运河横穿城区——与当时占地 360 公顷的卡尔胡相比，杜尔–卡特里穆不算大，但它显然已经是哈布尔河河谷地区最大的定居点。1978 年以来，大部分考古工作都集中在低城区，人们在这里发现了以卡尔胡的王室宫殿为蓝本的大宅邸。其中最著名当属所谓的"红房子"（见图 9），这所宅子建于公元前 7 世纪，是军官和富裕的地主舒尔木沙里的住所。即使在亚述帝国瓦解期间和瓦解之后，舒尔木沙里的后代们的活动也被记录在册，这些记录反映了当时杜尔–卡特里穆的政治局势。亚述帝国战败之初，也就是在公元前 612 年之后，人们依然忠于亚述王权，但地方权力掌握在"城市领主"，而不是以前的城市管理机构手中。十年之后，杜尔–卡特里穆接受了巴比伦的统治：有四份完全符合亚述传统的私人法律文件，签署日期采用的方式却是巴比伦国王尼布甲尼撒二世（Nebuchadnezzar II）的纪年。其中两份文件提到了沙尔曼努神的祭司，这就证明神庙当时还在运转。

# 第三章
# 国内的亚述人

本章内容展现了亚述帝国境内各式各样的生活状况和人的经历。这批史料有两个共同点：一是它们都可以追溯到公元前7世纪，这是原始文献最丰富多样的时期；二是它们都来自城里。这并非巧合，因为目前找到的所有文献都来自城市，而且较为关注城市生活里的事务。本章所举的例子包括一位国王、出身于同一个书香门第的两位学者、一位富有的地主、一位葡萄酒商人，以及他们的家庭和亲族。

## 宇宙之主：国王埃萨尔哈东

在亚述所有国王中，埃萨尔哈东（图8）是现有史料里个性最突出的一位。我们对大多数亚述统治者的了解主要来源于他们的王室铭文。铭文以国王的名义写成，用来纪念国王的功绩，它们要么被刻在纪念碑（雕像、石碑和石浮雕）上，要么被刻在神庙、宫殿和城墙等建筑物上，或是被刻在墙和门上，显而易见，或是依照仪式被埋在地基里。在亚述语中，王室铭文的意思是"被写下的名字"，创作的目的是为了让国王超越物质存在而永垂不朽。这些铭文的作者是"首席书吏"领导下的王室学者，他们大大方方地关注着国王和他的一举一动，关注着统治者背负的期望，以及他取悦神明的方式——建造和维护神庙、宫殿和城市，保卫和扩张领土。这些作品写于国王生前，并且获得了国王的授权，它们讲述了国王的生平及其所处的时代，让人心生怜悯，那些不值得歌颂和纪念的东西往往略而不谈。王室铭文是我们了解大部亚述历史的最主要的史料，

古代亚述简史

图8. 亚述国王埃萨尔哈东的石碑，他面前站着臣服的提尔和库什的统治者，旁边站着两个儿子，分别是亚述王储亚述巴尼拔和巴比伦王储沙马什舒姆乌金

但它们往往又很片面。不过，公元前 8 世纪和前 7 世纪的情况并非如此。这一期间的信件和行政文献在卡尔胡和尼尼微的宫殿以及其他一些地方留存了下来。在公元前 7 世纪 70 年代国王埃萨尔哈东统治时期，文献史料尤其丰富。

埃萨尔哈东的名字意为"亚述神赐予了一个兄弟（给现有的兄弟姐妹）"，正如他的名字所示，他是国王辛那赫里布年龄较小的儿子。公元前 681 年，埃萨尔哈东成为亚述国王，尽管事实上他并非最初选定的王储——由国王选择，经诸神确认，并在公开场合得到任命的王位继承人。公元前 683 年，辛那赫里布立埃萨尔哈东为王储时，首先得放弃之前的选择，即已经做了十多年王储的乌尔都穆里西（Urdu-Mullissi）。之后，乌尔都穆里西仍然留在宫里，并没有完全失宠，但辛那赫里布易储的动机依然无人知晓。老国王没有意识到，这一决定将危及他的生命。被废黜后，乌尔都穆里西开始召集支持者发动政变（*coup d'état*）。然而，一名密谋者没能拉拢的官员请求觐见国王，阴谋差点被揭穿，但他们人多势众，乌尔都穆里西的亲信成功地拦住了这名官员。后来，一封寄给埃萨尔哈东的信中这样写道：

> 他们问他："你要向国王报告什么？"他回答说："是关于乌尔都穆里西的事情。"他们用他的斗篷蒙住了他的脸（这是觐见国王的礼节），并让他站在乌尔都穆里西本人面前，说："看！国王允许了你的请求，讲出来吧！"他说："你的儿子乌尔都穆里西将会杀了你。"

密谋者迅速除掉了他，他们的阴谋最终成功了：公元前 681 年，乌尔都穆里西和一位兄弟刺死了父亲辛那赫里布。但在弑君之后，密谋者之间发生了矛盾，乌尔都穆里西的加冕礼被推迟了。行刺时，埃萨尔哈东不在首都。在他赶回尼尼微的途中，整个城市一片混乱。在父亲遇刺两个月之后，埃萨尔哈东成功赶走了凶手并登上了王位。这一事件轰动了整个古代世界，《圣经》中关于弑君的王子们逃往乌拉尔图的记载（列王纪下 19:37；以赛亚书 37:38）就是最好的例子。

　　一个多世纪中，亚述帝国一直受困于与北方的竞争对手之间的冲突。现在，乌拉尔图庇护这些自称手握王权的觊觎者，因而对亚述政局产生了重大影响。在位期间，埃萨尔哈东无力触及发动政变的领导者们，所以尽量避开乌拉尔图。而在国内，他不遗余力地确保自己的兄弟没有留下强大的盟友以备他们日后结束流亡，卷土重来。举国上下，涉嫌同情敌人的官员，无论官职大小，一律下台。例如，尼尼微和卡尔胡的档案记录显示，整个王宫的保卫人员都被遣散。我们可以想见，他们并非提前退休，而是被处决了。埃萨尔哈东追求权力时的血腥作为深刻地塑造了新王的形象，他不信任周围的一切。为了确认是否有人希望他生病，他每三个月都要向无所不见的太阳神、正义与预言之神沙马什问卜。但问题是，头号嫌疑人物正是那些本该支持他执政的人：国家官员、王室大家族的成员、军队、宫殿内侍以及为帝国军队提供辅助部队的亚述盟友。下文是埃萨尔哈东统治晚期多次问卜的其中一个问题，和祭祀的羊肝的检验报告归在一起，据称羊肝能够揭示神谕：

　　　　是否有任何宦官或留胡子的官员、国王的朝臣、年长或年幼的王室成员、国王的其他任何亲属、军官、招募官、指挥官、王室护卫、私人守卫或国王的车夫、内门或外门的看守人、马厩的随从、用人、厨师、糖果师、面包师、工匠，或……（各种外国的）辅助部队，或是他们的兄弟、儿子或侄子，或是他们的朋友（意为"盐和面包的主人"）或任何与他们相识的人，无论他们是宦官还是留胡子的官员，或是任何敌人，他们是否在白天或黑夜，是否在城市或乡村，是否在（埃萨尔哈东）坐在王座或战车或轿子上、走路、外出或回宫、吃或喝、穿衣或脱衣或洗澡的时候，是否通过欺骗或诡计或其他办法，对亚述国王埃萨尔哈东发动起义和造反？……我请问您，伟大的主沙马什，从今天12月6日到来年的3月5日，他们是否会起义和造反？他们是否对他十分不满或者要杀死他？

问卜中所列的外国盟友之多，说明亚述帝国的实力达到了巅峰。通过诉诸武力或签订条约（通常二者皆有），亚述帝国获得了新的伙伴，并将自身的影响力扩展到了里海和苏丹，深入到阿拉伯半岛。本文列举了伊朗的埃兰和辛梅里亚游牧民族，包括库什王国在内的尼罗河沿岸的政权，还有基达等阿拉伯部族，它们都和亚述捆绑在一起。公元前674年，亚述和长期竞争对手——地处伊朗的埃兰——签订和平条约，这一巧妙的政治策略确保了帝国东部边境的安全，并为亚述第一次入侵埃及提供了机会。当时的埃及在政治上四分五裂，统治者是努比亚法老塔哈尔卡（Taharqa），库什（今位于苏丹）的国王。公元前673年，亚述首次入侵埃及便匆忙撤退。但在公元前671年，亚述指使新结交的阿拉伯盟友穿过西奈沙漠对埃及进行突袭，最终征服了埃及。为了巩固帝国的霸权，亚述在公元前667年和前664年进一步对埃及发动战争（见图11），大军远至南部的底比斯。随后，埃及成为了一个完整统一的亚述附庸国，先是被塞易斯王朝的尼科（Nekho）统治，后来由他的儿子普萨美提克（Psammetikh）统治。

所有的亚述统治者都会寻求太阳神的建议。不过，由于文献的保存和复原都需要运气，现存有关问询占卜的原始史料都来自埃萨尔哈东和他的继任者亚述巴尼拔统治时期。在王室决策的过程中，问询神谕是至关重要的，因为在问询中提出问题，然后再解读神谕，可以让官员和顾问们进行更公开的讨论，不然就只能由至高无上的君主作决定。目前发现的问询涉及广泛的军事和政治事务，例如任命政府和宫廷中的关键职位等。不过，关于潜在叛乱的问询只出现在埃萨尔哈东统治时期。出于对自身安全的十足重视，他还将尼尼微和卡尔胡的宫殿重新设计成了坚不可摧的堡垒。

## 一位悲伤的国王

埃萨尔哈东的铭文同以往一样，将他描绘成了一个独自战胜一切的孤胆英雄。他的私人信件也是如此，不过呈现出一副完全不同的模样。埃萨尔哈东与随行学者的信件详细地向我们讲述了他的精神和身体状况，而且从中可以看出，尽管埃萨尔哈东在政治和军事上很成功，但他一直郁郁寡欢。公元前673年，王后埃莎拉哈玛特（Ešarra-hammat）逝世，或死于难产，不久之后，男婴也夭折了，他经历了失去至亲的切肤之痛。国王的健康管理专家，即他的私人驱邪师阿达德舒姆乌苏尔（Adad-šumu-uṣur），在一封信中写道：

> 国王、我的主，写信给我："我感到非常难过。我因为这个小家伙变得如此沮丧，我们应该怎么做？"——如果能治好他的话，您会放弃您的半个国家来救他！但是我们能做些什么呢？王啊，我的主，这是不可能完成的事情。

埃萨尔哈东经常生病，不时地发烧、头晕，一阵阵地猛吐、腹泻、流鼻血，还要遭受折磨人的耳痛。久治不愈的皮疹毁损了他身上的部分皮肤，尤其是面部皮肤。抑郁以及对死亡的恐惧给他的生活蒙上了阴影。他会在卧室独处好几天，不吃不喝，拒绝有人陪伴。阿达德舒姆乌苏尔写了一封信，试图规劝这位王室病人：

> 为什么已经连续两天没有把餐食呈给国王、我的主

了？谁会在黑暗中独处一天一夜，又两天两夜，比众神之王（太阳神）沙马什留在黑暗中的时间还长？国王，世界之主，是沙马什的显现。他应该只在黑暗中待半天！……吃面包、饮酒很快就会消除国王的病痛。这些好建议您应当注意：坐立不安、不吃不喝会扰乱心智，加重病情。在这件事上，国王应该听从仆人的建议。

如今的读者可能会对倍受痛苦的埃萨尔哈东心生同情。但在一个将疾病视为神的惩罚的社会里，一位生病的国王是不可能期待太多同情的。相反，臣民会将他的痛苦视为神对他们的统治者缺乏善意的表现。因此，国王需要隐藏自己的脆弱。鉴于限制与君主直接接触的种种规定，这件事在一定程度上可以办到，但作为国王，埃萨尔哈东必须履行他的多重公职。

为了让埃萨尔哈东短暂地逃离国王身份的重负，"替身国王"这种古老的仪式被反复使用。这种仪式是为了保护国王免受日食预兆的致命危险。"替身国王"需要扮演国王的角色100天。他穿着国王的衣服，吃着国王的饭菜，睡在国王的床上，而真正的国王则化身"农民"，从大众视野中退隐，这对于埃萨尔哈东来说简直易如反掌。虽然他不是唯一一个举行过这种仪式的统治者，但他举行了不下四次，居众王之首。参考私人信件的内容，我们可以推定这些仪式发生的时间。公元前671年，入侵埃及的战争取得首次决定性胜利后仅过去11天，国王便举行了一次仪式。当他的军队（根据任命问卜结果的指示）在首席宦官亚述纳西尔（Aššur-naṣir）的指挥下继续作战时，埃萨尔哈东藏了起来。在接下来的两年里，仪式又举行了两次，埃萨尔哈东因此隐退了相当长的时间。从政治层面来讲，国王的缺席是完全有可能实现的，因为在公元前672年，埃萨尔哈东任命自己的儿子亚述巴尼拔为亚述王储，随后，王储承担了父王的部分重要职责。然而，埃萨尔哈东逃离王位的举动并非没有受害者。仪式将预言中的邪恶指向了"替身国王",而他们没有任何机会逃脱——"替身国王"在100天的仪式结束后会被处决。虽然埃萨尔哈东通常选择那些不会怀疑自己为何突然飞升王位的傻瓜当替身,不过,埃萨尔哈东至少有一次采用了一个一石二鸟的计划,选择了一个政治对手当"替身国王"。

埃萨尔哈东有一项王室任务完成得相当出色:他有很多孩子(至少有18个)。公元前670年,他的继任者亚述巴尼拔的第一个儿子出生,确保了他有两代后人可以继承王权。但在同一年,一则预言如星火燎原,从叙利亚北部的哈兰向四处传播。当地有一位妇女发了疯,讲了一条耸人听闻的神谕:"(光明之神)努斯库(Nusku)说:'王权属于萨西(Sasî)。我将摧毁辛那赫里布的名字和他的后代!'"到如今,萨西仍然是一位来路不明的神秘人物,但在当时,帝国境内纷纷出现了他的支持者。虽然废除埃萨尔哈东的行动很快就停止了,但是国家却因此付出了巨大的代价。根据埃萨尔哈东的主任医师的说法,叛乱"让国王觉得其他所有人都可憎,他怒斥他们就像沾了鱼油的皮匠一样"。"巴比伦编年史"在公元前670年的条目中写道:"在亚述,国王拿着剑杀死了很多忠仆"。辛那赫里布遇害之后一大批人被处死,这次则是埃萨尔哈东在十年之内下令对亚述官员进行的第二次大屠杀。运作良好的行政机制是亚述帝国的支柱,而这次处决对国家造成了永久的伤害,甚至可能比谋杀国王还要严重。毕竟,国家机关可以在很大程度上弥补埃萨尔哈东因身体虚弱和定期逃避国王职责造成的破坏性影响,甚至在征服埃及后,还显著地扩大了帝国的影响力,这的确证明了亚述帝国的行政结构稳固。事后看来,公元前670年是亚述帝国的鼎盛时刻。第二次处决大大削弱了国家力量,并使亚述的扩张戛然而止。不久之后,公元前669年,埃萨尔哈东去世,显然不是死于非命。

## 两位出身名门的失意学者

对于一个学者来说，最显要的职位是国王的首席学者。这一职位最初叫做"王室书吏"（见第五章），后来被称为"大学者"（ummānu）。自从加布伊拉尼埃利什（Gabbu-ilani-ereš）在公元前 9 世纪成为国王图库尔提宁努尔塔二世（Tukulti-Ninurta II）和亚述纳西尔帕二世的大学者后，他的家族成为了亚述杰出的学术世家。加布伊拉尼埃利什和王室一起从亚述城搬到了新都卡尔胡，此后，他的家族在卡尔胡发展壮大。他的很多后代成为了一流的驱邪师或占星师，用占星术预测未来，受王室青睐。加布伊拉尼埃利什的后代纳布祖库普克努（Nabu-zuqup-kenu）为王室图书馆（见第六章）贡献了大量文学手稿和学术手稿，其中包括一份《吉尔伽美什》的抄本。纳布祖库普克努的两个儿子也都在埃萨尔哈东统治期间担任重要职位。在前文中，我们看到阿达德舒姆乌苏尔作为国王的私人驱邪师，曾试图劝说埃萨尔哈东摆脱抑郁情绪；他的兄弟纳布泽鲁莱什尔（Nabu-zeru-lešir）则和他们声名赫赫的祖先一样，也曾担任大学者一职，并作为首席书吏总管国王的铭文的撰写。后来，纳布泽鲁莱什尔的儿子伊萨尔舒姆埃利什（Issar-šumu-ereš）接替了他的职位，继续为国王亚述巴尼拔服务。不过，他的另一个儿子舒马亚（Šumaya）和侄子乌尔都古拉（Urdu-Gula）也都经过训练成为了专业的驱邪师，却没能在宫廷中获得终身职位。他们俩都向亚述巴尼拔写了请愿书，详细讲述了他们的经济条件和社会地位。

父亲去世后，遗留的债务压在了舒马亚肩上，他两次请求王储亚述巴尼拔提供资助，并希望给他分配一些父亲曾担任的职务。舒马亚曾经为王储工作过，在信中，他试图提醒亚述巴尼拔自己的家族与王室是世交，恳求像父亲和祖父一样获得认可。他把国王埃萨尔哈东树为榜样，因为老国王会毫不犹豫地帮助舒马亚——但不幸的是，他依附的是亚述巴尼拔，这位国王可不会这么好心肠地去保护这个书香门第的子孙。

乌尔都古拉是舒马亚的堂兄（弟）、阿达德舒姆乌苏尔的儿子，他也觉得自己遭到宫廷的排斥和现任国王亚述巴尼拔的冷落。他情绪激动地写了一封请愿书，称自己感到非常丢脸。他只有一座小农庄和八个奴隶，只能穿旧衣服，在两头牲口死了之后，只能走路出行，那些仍受国王青睐的学者们都笑话他——这或许是他个人的臆想。当然，乌尔都古拉肯定没有到一贫如洗的地步，但他过惯了比这更有钱的日子，因而背上了（至少）三倍于他原先年俸的债务。另外，他没有儿子和继承人，没有人给他养老，因此感到非常绝望。他供奉着卡尔胡的卡德姆里之女伊什塔尔女神，希望女神能保佑妻子如愿怀孕。如果这一计还是不管用的话，乌尔都古拉可能会收养一个男孩——没有子女的亚述人通常都会这么做。

为什么这两个人既受过良好的教育，又出身名门，与王室相熟，却没能获得他们认为理应属于自己的好处：朝廷中的特权地位，以及随之而来的所有物质利益？在埃萨尔哈东统治期间，很多来自世界各地的高素质学者加入了国王的学术团队。埃萨尔哈东招聘了一名埃及医生，任命了一位巴比伦专家重新组织巴比伦的崇拜仪式，聘请了很多精通埃及和安纳托利亚的占卜和仪式的当地专家。一些亚述学者长大后期望轻轻松松就能获得朝堂认可，但事实上，他们发现获取国王垂青的竞争史无前例地激烈，他们的野心也常因此受挫。

## 国王的富豪朋友：来自杜尔–卡特里穆的地主

富裕的地主舒尔木沙里是另一个与亚述巴尼拔同时代的

人。他在杜尔–卡特里穆有一处豪华宅邸（见第二章），人称"红房子"（图9），我们便是从这栋房子的废墟里发掘出的文献了解到他的相关信息。这些文献包括约150块亚述楔文泥板以及大约50个写有阿拉姆语字母的三角形黏土标签，它们均为法律文本，大幅记载了舒尔木沙里的家庭经济状况。舒尔木沙里很可能是军队中的军官，因为他的证人大都持有军衔：杜尔–卡特里穆当时驻扎着一支卫戍部队，其中包括战车部队和情报部门。在舒尔木沙里至少50岁时，他被提拔为亚述巴尼拔的"朋友"（*ša qurbūte*，意为"他所亲近的人"），地位显赫，因此，他在全国范围内的机密事务上能够代表国王。

和许多受国王青睐的人一样，舒尔木沙里非常富有。那些有钱的学者完全无法和他相提并论。仅现存的购买文件就表明，在杜尔–卡特里穆及其附近地区，他有八处田地、三座花园、三处房产以及农用建筑。根据伊拉克北部阿格拉地区一份犯罪活动的法庭记录，我们得知舒尔木沙里在当地还拥有一整座村庄。我们可以肯定，除了上述文件提到的资产之外，舒尔木沙里还有其他资产，其中一部分可能是国王授予的。"红房子"就是他家财万贯的印证。这座恢宏的建筑有5400平方米的生活空间，涵盖三栋独立的楼房，各自围绕着铺了砖的庭院。北面的主入口通向宅子的第一部分，这里有宽敞的储藏间，部分带有冷藏功能。位于中心的待客大厅通向东部主楼和西部私人住宅区。"红房子"有两口井、四个浴室和数个厨房，全都连着复杂的排污系统。宅子的二楼有四个楼梯口。舒尔木沙里和他的家人以及数名奴隶都住在宅子里。30年内，他购买了50多人，其中三分之二是女性，而且通常是母亲和年幼的女儿。庭院的墙边留下了卧式织机的残骸，说明这些奴隶曾给家里织布。舒尔木沙里雇的牧羊人在杜尔–卡特里穆以东的草原上放牧，提供了纺织所需的羊毛。

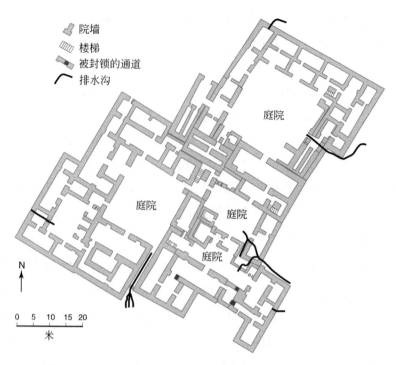

图例:
- 院墙
- 楼梯
- 被封锁的通道
- 排水沟

庭院

庭院

庭院

庭院

N

0　5　10　15　20
米

图 9.　位于杜尔–卡特里穆的红房子

　　家庭档案可以证实舒尔木沙里有三个已成年的儿子。我们完全不了解他们的母亲，不过，她有可能是舒尔木沙里的亲密伙伴、战车部队的军官拉西米伊尔（Rahimi-il）的亲人，或许是他的姐妹或女儿。如此一来便能解释，为什么我们在舒尔木沙里的家庭档案中找到了拉西米伊尔的一些法律文件。在亚述巴尼拔的第二个继任者辛沙鲁伊什昆统治期间，年迈的舒尔木沙里去世，三个儿子继承了他的财产。他的坟墓无人知晓。虽然据考察杜尔–卡特里穆的其他地方都有地下墓葬，但在"红房子"底下没有发现这样的结构。舒尔木沙里或许葬在他别处的庄园里。

# 一位亚述城的葡萄酒商和他的客户们

杜里亚述（Duri-Aššur），亚述城一家商行的负责人，是另一位与国王亚述巴尼拔同时代的人。与学者舒马亚和乌尔都古拉，以及国王的"朋友"舒尔木沙里不同，杜里亚述不可能与国王相熟。他住在亚述城中心一座约 150 平方米的房子里。同舒尔木沙里在杜尔–卡特里穆的豪宅相比，这座宅子可能看起来很小，但在拥挤的亚述城里，这个面积已经非常可观了。这幢房子是一家在亚述城外经商的私人商行的物流中心。由于所有公民都免交税赋，包括"陆路与水路的停留、过境和出入的费用"，进口货物的成本大幅降低，吸引了不少人经商。

德国考察队在 1990 年、2000 年和 2001 年发掘到了杜里亚述的档案中的信件和清单，这些文件显示，杜里亚述和三位合作伙伴（称作"兄弟"）与亚述帝国北部地区开展贸易活动。杜里亚述在亚述城里监督商行的物流，合伙人则前往外地处理生意。这家商行聘用了四名商队领队，每人每年出行三次。他们沿着底格里斯河向上游行进，同行的驴子驮着采购商品所需的银子和从亚述城采买的帽子、鞋子和高级纺织品等，纺织品里包着物资和钱。他们的目的地是位于伊拉克和叙利亚边境辛贾尔山区的扎马胡，这里产的葡萄酒闻名遐迩。商队到达那里后，便卖掉从亚述城带来的所有东西，包括驴子。杜里亚述的代理人会用卖货所得的收益和从亚述城带来的银子购买当地的葡萄酒。他们把葡萄酒装入兽皮酒囊中（用绵羊或山羊皮制成，很少用牛皮）。顺便提一句，如今，亚述和大葡萄酒瓶之间还有关联：用来装香槟和勃艮第葡萄酒的九升容量酒瓶被称作"亚述王瓶"（Salmanazar，按亚述王名沙尔曼纳瑟尔的法语读法命名）。他们将葡萄酒囊和原木绑在一起做成木筏，顺着底格里斯河返回亚述城。这种运输方法非常适合储藏葡萄酒，因为河水可以使其保持凉爽，防止腐坏。回到亚述城以后，木筏的所有部件都变成了贵重商品：葡萄酒囊自然不在话下，而作为建筑木材的原木在没有森林资源的亚述城里也有很大的需求。接下来，葡萄酒被倒入类似于双耳瓶的陶器中。葡萄酒要掺着水喝。人们把葡萄酒倒在容量半升多点儿的碗里，小口小口地啜饮。喝酒时，他们得用右手的手指优雅地端稳酒杯，这样定能有效防止酗酒。

公元前 7 世纪，饮酒在亚述城的富裕居民当中十分普遍。从公元前 9 世纪开始，分布在托罗斯山脉南侧的葡萄酒产区被兼并到帝国的版图之中，葡萄酒的享用便不再限于宫廷和神庙里。很长时间以来葡萄酒都是祭祀亚述众神的供品之一。对于亚述城的私人消费者来说，葡萄酒是一种昂贵的奢侈品，只有在很远的地方才能买得到。他们便想了个办法：投资杜里亚述的商行，提前支付银子，作为回报，商行保证投资者占有进口葡萄酒的一定份额。该商行有一个忠实可靠的客户基础，他们多次投资，可能是想通过这种方式来保证酒窖的藏酒量。虽然有的投资者贡献了大笔资金，但大多数人投资的金额非常小，有时都不到一舍克勒银子。通过杜里亚述的档案中的投资清单，我们可以了解到公元前 7 世纪末亚述城中有哪些人爱喝酒：大部分是为亚述神庙服务的工匠和管理人员，也有城市官员和住在亚述城的王室成员家里的相关人员。很多女性也投资了葡萄酒商行，经考证，其中大多数是埃及人。埃及男性也是商行的客户，这一点不足为奇，因为杜里亚述的邻居就是一户埃及人家，他们是公元前 671 年孟菲斯被征服后定居在此的众多埃及家庭之一。但为什么商行里会有这么多埃及女性客户呢？在埃及，妇女经常独立经营生意；而在亚述核心地域，如果有必要的话，妇女当然也可以这么做，但通常她们还是由男性亲属代表自己经商。杜里亚述的档案证明，即使在迁移到亚述几十年后，埃及团体仍然依照传统赋予妇女独立地位。

据这些档案记载，这家葡萄酒商行从公元前 651 年开始，一直经营到公元前 614 年，那一年，米底人征服了亚述城。杜里亚述的房子被付诸一炬时，他还有一些尚未打开的信件。随之而来的战争不仅终止了商行的活动，也打断了大规模的跨区域贸易，从亚述帝国掠夺的战利品也被巴比伦、米底和埃及军队瓜分了。

# 第四章
# 国外的亚述人

透过一系列不同时期的原始史料，我们将捕捉到那些远离亚述城和亚述核心地域的亚述人的生活瞬间：有人欢喜，有人愁。

## 卡奈什贸易殖民点里的家务事，约公元前 1900 年

活跃于安纳托利亚的亚述商人（见第二章）经常背井离乡，长期在外漂泊。如果目的地是卡奈什，那么那些从亚述城出发的生意人至少要离家三个月。如果他们要去安纳托利亚更远的贸易点，例如杜尔胡米特或普鲁什哈杜姆，那么他们离家的时间会更久。作为家族商行在当地的代理人，很多亚述人会定居在卡奈什或者其他贸易殖民点，有时甚至好几十年都居住在外地。正如在卡奈什的亚述人居住区里发现的信件，尤其是那些来自女性亲属的信件所示，远在亚述城的家人想念他们。

这封信是忧心的姊妹们写的：

在这里（亚述城），我们咨询了女解梦者、占卜师，以及往生者的灵魂：亚述神一直在警告你！你好财，但是

你不珍惜自己的性命。你能不能顺应（这里的）亚述神的心意？若读到这封信，就回来看着亚述神的眼睛，（从而）拯救你的性命。

这个家族商行的文献记录表明，当在国外工作多年的兄弟回到亚述城时，他已经一贫如洗。女性家庭成员偶尔也会在男性亲属的陪同下前往安纳托利亚。一位身在亚述城的母亲给远在卡奈什的儿子写道：

快回来（亚述城），这样我就可以和你一起离开，照看你父亲和你在卡奈什的房子（即家族商行），这样就没人会给你父亲的房子添麻烦了。

父亲的健康状态似乎不容乐观，或许来日无多。在这封信的前文，这位母亲提醒儿子履行对家人应尽的义务：

除了你，我们还有谁在那里（在卡奈什）？除了你，你父亲在那里就没有其他人了！做事要像个男人一样，听从你父亲的指示，保管好他的文件，要回所有的债。卖掉他的商品，然后准备好回到这里（亚述城），你就能看着亚述神和你父亲的眼睛，让你父亲高兴！

一些妻子会跟随商人丈夫游历安纳托利亚。如果你翻阅一位妻子写的信，你就会明白这并不是维持夫妻关系和谐幸福的良方：她在信中按时间顺序先后记录了在安纳托利亚生活过的地方，以及和丈夫日益紧张的关系。她的丈夫大部分时间都待在别处，而两人相聚时又待她不好。发现自己再次被遗弃之后，她在信中写了如下内容，这一次她被留在了哈胡姆贸易殖民点（现位于土耳其萨姆萨特附近）：

你把我留在普鲁什哈杜姆，我被自己的丈夫彻底地从心里抹去了。（现在）我来到了这里（哈胡姆），你也不照顾我！在卡奈什，你羞辱我，一整年都不让我上你的床。在提米基亚，你又写信给我："如果你不来这里，你就不再是我的妻子！我会使情况比在普鲁什哈杜姆更糟糕。"然后，你从提米基亚去了卡奈什，说："我将在 15 天内离开（卡奈什）。"但你在那儿待了一年！你在卡奈什写信给我："到哈胡姆去。"如今我已经在哈胡姆住了一年，但是你甚至都不肯在商函中提我的名字！

难怪大部分妻子都留在亚述城。

在卡奈什期间，一些亚述居民尽管已经在老家娶妻生子，却又同当地女人结婚，组建了新的家庭。只要两位女性没有生活在同一个城市，此番安排就完全光明正大。不过，只有一位女性是正妻（aššatum）——通常是指居住在亚述城的那位；另一位只是配偶（amtum），这个词在亚述语的其他语境中指"女奴"，但在这一特定语境中，指当地的侧妻。卡奈什并没有实行重婚制。当地家庭的记录表明，本地居民实行一夫一妻制。但如果新郎是一位成功的亚述商人，而且在婚姻市场中颇具吸引力，有人会乐于打破这种制度。

安纳托利亚当地的一些家庭中也有楔文泥板档案，主要是记录债务和买卖的法律文件。亚述人的档案中常有大量的信件，但在当地家庭的档案中却很少见——这一点并不奇怪，因为他们不需要与国外的家人和商业伙伴保持远程联系。有意思的是，卡奈什居民并没有对楔形文字进行改造以适应他们的口语赫梯语，这似乎是故意为之，因为他们完全可以这么做，就像亚述语泥板上那些频繁出现的外来词和名字一样。相反，他们甚至在自己的社区里更愿意用亚述语书写，这一点明显体现出当地人对一切亚述事物一贯的高度尊重。

无论亚述商人在本国的社会地位如何，他们总会从当地最富有的家庭中挑选女孩结婚，甚至那些出生于卡奈什的配偶也要接受这种偏袒亚述丈夫的不平等关系。不过，在当地人的婚姻中，夫妻双方是平等的，并且共同拥有一切财产。但是，异族通婚的不平等关系或许能够得到补偿，因为这并非"至死不渝"的婚姻。相反，这种婚姻关系是有有效期的，丈夫回到亚述永远不再回来，两人的婚姻便失效。此时，双方会制订一份离婚协议，男方通常会给女方留下卡奈什的房子、一笔钱，以及再婚的自由。亚述父亲可能会选择带几个孩子回亚述城，同时他也需要为留在卡奈什的孩子和母亲提供抚养费。相比日后可观的财产收入，当地的女方家庭对于婚事是否门当户对的顾虑显然不值一提。

## 前往法老埃赫那吞王宫的使者，约公元前 1340 年

公元前 15 世纪，在埃及第 18 王朝的法老图特摩斯三世统治期间，埃及的力量大大增强。图特摩斯三世率军远征，深入叙利亚直至幼发拉底河。在他看来，幼发拉底河是"那条倒着从下游流往上游的河流"。他与米坦尼划定边界，并三次接受了臣服于米坦尼的首领们的礼物。送礼之人包括一名未留姓名的亚述城首领，很可能是亚述纳丁阿赫一世（Aššur-nadin-ahhe I）。如果他的后代的记载可靠的话，亚述纳丁阿赫一世曾经接受过埃及赠予的 20 塔伦特黄金。亚述在这 100 年间的记载可能大幅拔高了实际收到的黄金数额，不然就是引用这个数字的亚述乌巴里特一世（Aššur-uballit I）故意夸大了数量，借机在信中羞辱法老埃赫那吞，让他慷慨解囊，也送这么多礼物给自己。毕竟，亚述乌巴里特一世的前任宗主米坦尼（亚述人称之为哈尼迦尔巴特）国王也收到了 20 塔伦特黄金。不过，无论数量多少，埃及的黄金都令亚述统治者魂牵梦萦，这也成为了

亚述与尼罗河边遥远的埃及王国开展外交活动的重要动机。

亚述乌巴里特一世是亚述第一位采用国王头衔的统治者。在掌权的 30 多年里，他将亚述王国建设成了一个全新的强大的国家，功绩显赫。在统治的末期，他甚至远征到巴比伦，只为在那里安排一位令他满意的国王就任（见第五章）。亚述乌巴里特一世与埃及第 18 王朝后期的法老的外交信函被称之为"阿玛尔纳信件"，这是根据信件的发现地点取的名字。其中有两封信可以追溯到亚述乌巴里特一世统治的早期，那时他似乎还没有完全从地方统治者成长为国际政治人物。他的第一封信是用亚述语写的，非常简短，尤其是考虑到送信的路途相当遥远。信使从亚述城出发，穿过整个叙利亚，然后沿着地中海海岸前行。接下来，他沿着西奈半岛的海岸线到达尼罗河三角洲，逆流而上，到达首都埃赫太呑，也就是现在的阿玛尔纳。两地的直线距离是 1450 公里，但陆路至少有 1800 公里。

亚述乌巴里特一世的使者带来了一份见面礼，觐见法老时他将正式呈上这份礼物。作为首次示好，亚述乌巴里特一世送来了一辆战车、两匹马和一块青金石。青金石是一种珍贵的深蓝色宝石，产自遥远的阿富汗。除了与埃及建交之外，亚述乌巴里特一世的第一封信最关心的是保证他的使者迅速返回亚述：

> 不要耽搁我派去访问的使者。他访问之后就应该离开并回到这里。他只需了解你的为人和你的国家，然后便启程回来。

亚述乌巴里特一世的第二封信言辞更加优美，但语气同之前没有什么差别。这封信不是用亚述语写的，而是用当时国际政治的通用语巴比伦语写的。另外，这封信也较之前长了许多。亚述乌巴里特一世和大臣一直在研究与埃及过去的交易，而且如我们所见，为了确保能够收到与亚述礼物相称的回礼，他在信里到处摆事实，报数目：一辆配有两匹白马的战车——配得上国王的尊贵身份，另外还有一辆战车和一枚青金石印章。亚述国王明确指出自己想要的回礼：黄金，而且最好比之前收到的多。

> 黄金在你的国家就如尘土，人们只要把它收集起来就行。为什么要吝啬这点黄金呢？我正在建一座新宫。给我多送些过来作装饰。

接着：

> 我们两国相距甚远。我们的信使每次长途跋涉就是为了这样（糟糕）的结果吗？

对于初出茅庐的政治家亚述乌巴里特一世来说，与埃及维持外交关系可能主要是为了钱财。但埃赫那吞派遣代表团回访亚述城时，他的确非常高兴。虽然亚述乌巴里特一世坚持要求立即遣回自己的使者，但他对埃及使者可没这样的打算：

> 见到你的使者，我非常开心。当然，你的使者会与我同住，尽享尊荣。

在亚述精英和来访的显贵面前炫耀埃及派来外交官员，定会提升亚述乌巴里特一世的威望。在现有史料中，我们无从知道亚述乌巴里特一世的使者的姓名，但他一定身居高位，很可能是王室成员。例如，公元前 13 世纪被派往亚述国王图库尔提宁努尔塔一世王宫中的赫梯使者特里沙鲁玛（Teli-Šarruma）就是一位王子。哈尔贝（现叙利亚东北部楚埃拉丘）出土的文献证明，特里沙鲁玛是访问亚述的赫梯外交官之一。他带着四队马、三队骡子和六头驴，给亚述城送来了信件和礼物，带着十头驴子上路的阿姆鲁（现位于叙利亚境内）使者也是如此。

西顿（现位于黎巴嫩）的腓尼基使者则轻松得多，因为只需送信，他只带了一辆战车和三头驴，但这些信件非常重要，是埃及法老寄给亚述国王的。所有的使者、随行人员和牲畜都不用担心食宿问题。据哈尔贝出土的文件记载，只要各国代表团在亚述的领土范围之内，他们回国沿途的每个站点便都安排了补给。一个世纪前，亚述乌巴里特一世的使者从亚述城前往埃赫太吞应该也是如此情形。

## 流落深山，约公元前 1082 年

为了获得代用资料，古气候学家通过分析易受周围气候环境影响的物质来探索过去的气候状况。研究古代中东的气候有两种方法较为适用。第一种方法是用大钻头发掘古代沉积物，最好是从湖底提取（"湖芯"），收集其中的花粉和其他气候指示物，测量温度、含氧量、营养水平，以及收集木炭，并通过碳定年法来推定碳层的年代。第二种方法是用一个小钻头切入喀斯特洞穴形成物（洞穴化学淀积物），重建微观层次序列。随着水滴不断落下，微观层每年增加一层，因此它的化学性质年年都有变化。分析结果表明，相对凉爽的降水丰沛期在持续了约三个世纪之后，在公元前 1200 年左右便结束了。随后，气候变暖，雨水减少，这一相对干旱的时期一直持续到公元前 900 年左右。降水减少对于处在边缘的农耕地区来说是个坏消息，因为它让美索不达米亚北部地区传统的旱农种植变成了一场冒险的赌博。

1987 年，气候学家杰胡达·诺伊曼（Jehuda Neumann）和亚述学家西莫·帕尔波拉（Simo Parpola）就已经提出了气候变化和大规模迁徙之间的联系。当时，大迁徙破坏了中东大部分地区的稳定。值得一提的是，帕尔波拉让我们对一篇亚述年代记的文本有了更深层次的了解，该文本面世已久但残缺不全，其中有一则关于公元前 1082 年的记录：

> ［在国王提格拉特皮勒塞尔一世（Tiglath-Pileser I）统治的第 32 年，发生了非常严重的饥荒］，出现了人吃人的情况；……阿拉姆"家"掠夺［土地］，占领道路，征服并夺取了亚述［许多设防的城市］。［为了活］命，［亚述人逃离］到哈布里里的群山之中。［阿拉姆人］占领了他们的［房子？］和财产。

年代记中援引骇人听闻的吃人事件，反映了当时食物极为短缺的困境，乃至社会秩序都土崩瓦解。同样的场景在其他地方也出现过，比如国王亚述巴尼拔的铭文。该铭文记录了公元前 652 至前 648 年亚述巴尼拔的弟弟沙马什舒姆乌金（Šamaš-šumu-ukin）领导巴比伦叛乱的结果。然而，公元前 1082 年的饥荒并非发生在亚述，而是发生在其他地方，并且引发了阿拉姆人的入侵。这次入侵并非抢夺食物这么简单，他们是来争夺土地的。年代记中记载的事件具体发生在大扎卜河的山谷地带，因为其中提到的哈布里里区域就是位于阿尔贝拉以东、扎格罗斯山脉以西的哈里尔高原。在阿拉姆侵略者的追赶下，亚述人逃到了这里，山区保证了他们的安全并提供了相对稳定的经济条件。但随后不久，亚述也失去了对哈布里里的控制。公元前 10 世纪中叶，据国王亚述丹二世（Aššur-dan II）的铭文记载，他努力夺回了该地区，并洗劫了那里好几个定居点。另外：

> 我把精疲力竭的亚述［人］带回来了，他们［因为］贫困、饥饿和饥荒而放弃了［他们的城市和房屋］，并［流散到了］其他地方。［我将］他们［安置］在［合适的］城市和房屋中，他们在那里安居乐业。

公元前 883 年，亚述纳西尔帕二世在哈布里里地区建立了行省，亚述永久地控制了这一地区。

在干旱期开始和结束的时候，亚述的其他地方也发生过类似的事件。杜努沙乌兹比（现土耳其东南部迪亚巴克尔附近的吉里加诺）出土了一份公元前 1069 年或前 1068 年的私人法律文件，文中着重提到，亚述对底格里斯河上游区域的控制逐渐减弱。据国王亚述贝尔卡拉（Aššur-bel-kala）的王室铭文记载，当时阿拉姆人正在进攻这一地区。在这份法律文件中，一名男子与别人合伙，为他的经商之旅提供资金。该合同设定了一项独特的条款来保护合伙人的投资：如果此人"逃入山中"，则合伙人可获得其田产的下一次收成。公元前 882 年，亚述再一次恢复对该地区的管辖——只有亚述纳西尔帕二世才具备这样的能力。人们曾迁往底格里斯河上游河谷以北的舒布里亚的山区，这里的地形特点和哈布里里地区很相似，亚述纳西尔帕二世将他们安置回已经被荒废了几代的原定居点。关于此事，亚述纳西尔帕二世的铭文沿用了曾祖父亚述丹二世提及哈布里里的亚述人的说法，他写道：

> 我把精疲力竭的亚述人带回来了，他们因为饥荒跑到了别处，到了舒布里亚的山区，我将他们安置在图什汉城。

从这些材料来看，当时，大扎卜河、底格里斯河上游、哈布尔河区域、幼发拉底河区域似乎都脱离了亚述王国的控制。这并非因为日益干旱的环境危及了当地大规模的农业生产，而是因为这些经济相对稳定的低地吸引了饥肠辘辘的阿拉姆部落。这些部落在亚述语里被称为"家"，通常以创始人的名字命名，比如比特–阿杜尼，意为"阿杜尼家"。阿拉姆人曾经居住在叙利亚中部的比什里山等更为偏远的地区，约公元前 1500 至前 1200 年，这里的温度更低，气候更湿润，也曾有过农业耕种。此时，他们找到了一个经济基础更稳固的地方，并在此定居，每一个部落都发展成了一个小型区域国家，而当地的亚述人则被迫迁移到海拔更高的地方。从公元前 10 世纪中叶开始，这群人想要"回归故土"的想法到底有多迫切，这个问题有待讨论。不过，从亚述政府的角度来看，拯救这些"精疲力竭"的飞地居民，为亚述发动对阿拉姆部落的解放之战提供了一个顺理成章的理由，而且当时，这些阿拉姆人已经在亚述的故土建立了小型区域国家。

## 一位不受欢迎的大使，约公元前 710 年

到了公元前 8 世纪末，亚述帝国控制的疆土大致被划分为65 个行省。这些行省由国王任命的总督管理。在那些臣服于亚述的权威，但仍受当地政府管理的附庸国，大使（亚述语中意为"可信之人"）代表了帝国的利益。和行省总督一样，他们一般通过信件和使者与国王沟通。

库美就是附庸国之一。和许多在名义上被允许保持独立的政体一样，这个小小的山地国家占据了一个亚述不便于直接控制的地方。腓尼基的提尔和阿尔瓦德因地处岛屿，远离地中海海岸，从而得以自保。而库美则位于小哈布尔河上游，现伊拉克与土耳其交界处以北的贝伊蒂谢巴普地区，是一个古老的城邦，建有一座祭祀风暴之神的神殿。贝伊蒂谢巴普地区有一处温泉，据说此处的泉水可以治疗各种小病痛，单凭这一点，此处便足以成为重要的圣所。此外，壮美的山地景观为风暴之神与巨石怪伍里库米（Ullikummi）等敌人战斗的神话提供了背景。这里经常发生的雪崩和滑坡被视为神力的显现。自公元前2 千纪初起，风暴之神的神殿吸引了许多远方王室的光顾，其中包括叙利亚的马里、安纳托利亚中部的哈图沙、亚述；公元

前 895 年，国王阿达德尼拉里二世（Adad-nerari II）在库美的圣所献祭。公元前 879 年，库美代表团作为亚述纳西尔帕二世的客人，出席了帝国中心卡尔胡的落成典礼。

公元前 739 年，提格拉特皮勒塞尔三世征服了附近的乌鲁布王国之后，库美的领土直接与亚述新建立的行省比尔图接壤。一开始，亚述帝国并没有试图兼并这个小国。从萨尔贡二世的信中，我们可以详细了解亚述与其附庸国之间的关系。这些附庸国仍然处于当地统治者的控制之下。当时（约公元前 710 年），阿里耶（Ariye）是库美的城邦领主。他与亚述帝国签订条约，建立了紧密联系。亚述为库美提供保护，作为回报，库美也必须承担一些义务：提供人力、马匹、木材以及当地的情报。在获取情报方面，库美具有得天独厚的地理位置优势：从亚述核心地域直达乌拉尔图中心——今土耳其东部凡湖——的崎岖山路，正好经过库美。尽管与亚述有约，但库美依然和乌拉尔图保持了密切关系，甚至为其提供人力和情报。库美这些行为并没有向亚述隐瞒，而是在亚述的鼓励和支持下进行的。因为亚述人认为，这不失为获取死敌情报的好方法。

为了确保库美对亚述的忠诚，亚述的核心策略是往阿里耶的宫中派遣一位长驻的大使。这个职位由亚述莱苏瓦（Aššur-reṣuwa）担任。在现存所有亚述大使写给萨尔贡的信函中，他的信件最多。信里经常描述木材运输这样的日常事务，但也关注亚述与乌拉尔图之间的间谍与反间谍活动，后者数千年之后读来依然令人胆战心惊。最刺激的一次，也许要数在千钧一发之际及时拆穿了乌拉尔图的阴谋——他们计划绑架库美境内的几位亚述官员。当时还是王子的辛那赫里布在向父亲汇报时，引用了阿里耶关于乌拉尔图的同谋、邻国乌库国王的报告：

> 乌库的统治者写信给乌拉尔图国王，称亚述国王的官员正在库美建造一座堡垒。乌拉尔图国王给地方总督下达

了如下命令："带上你的军队，前去库美活捉亚述国王的官员，把他们带到我这里来。"目前我尚未得知完整的细节；一旦我听到了更多信息，我会送快信给王储，请他们派兵给我。

对于库美来说，这次阴谋导致亚述变本加厉，愈发加强了控制。公元前714年之后，有一次，乌拉尔图的新王质问库美代表为什么没有来他的宫里。根据传回给萨尔贡二世的信息，库美作出了如下回应：

> 因为我们臣服于亚述，我们的上司是一名骑兵长。我们只剩下了库美的房子……别的地方我们都无法踏足。

这时，库美已经被亚述军队牢牢控制。虽然信中提及的领主阿里耶和他的儿子阿里扎（Arizâ）似乎一直忠于亚述，但并非所有的库美人都像他们一样忠心耿耿。和其他所有在附庸国任职的亚述大使一样，亚述莱苏瓦可以随时随地见库美统治者，也可以公然影响他的决策。公元前676年，埃萨尔哈东和提尔国王签署协议。在亚述签订的所有双边协议中，此协议极为难得地保留了原件。该协议概述了亚述大使的特权，其中一个章节片段略述了附庸国的统治者应当如何与亚述大使共事：

> ［当］你的国家的长老［召集大家］征求意见，大使［必须］在场……［如果……］，不要听他的，在没有大使的情况下［不要……］。你必须在大使的陪同下才能打开我写给你的信。如果大使不在，那就等他来再打开。

毫不足怪，许多库美人认为大使亚述莱苏瓦的所作所为是一种压迫和侵犯。亚述莱苏瓦则反过来认为一些库美人对亚述的利益构成了威胁。他写信给国王：

> 应当除掉四名男子。我在这里时，他们绝不能当着我

的面随意走动。他们在煽动这个国家。

亚述莱苏瓦变得非常不受欢迎，库美人甚至向萨尔贡二世和其他人请愿将他召回。他们抗议道，尽管亚述莱苏瓦非常令人憎恶，但他们依然会继续忠于帝国。因此，另一位官员在给国王的信中这样写道：

> 之前向您，我的主，上诉的库美人现在已经回来，他们找到我，对我说："整个库美都无法忍受这位大使。但是我们能够并且将会（对整个帝国）承担责任。"

然而，另一封信表明人们对亚述大使的仇恨影响到了库美领主的地位：

> 现在整个库美都反对阿里耶；他们……还谈到要杀害［大使］。

亚述莱苏瓦大使最终的结局如何，目前尚不得而知。但关键在于，对于帝国来说，一个失去了领导能力的附庸国统治者毫无价值。

根据现有的史料，我们无法得知这些敌对情绪是否导致阿里耶最终被推翻，但类似的事件在附庸国常有发生。附庸国臣民一而再，再而三地废除拥护亚述的统治者，转而支持其他不接受亚述霸权的王位觊觎者。在这种情况下，亚述通常会迅速出手干预，且频频考虑是否要吞并这个国家。不论是大使还是当地统治者，也不管是尚在谋划还是已经行动，只要是反对亚述的代言人，便足以为库美的独立地位画上句点，哪怕亚述尊崇风暴之神的神殿也无济于事。此后，这座城邦在史料中销声匿迹。我们可以据此推断，这块弹丸之地变成了亚述比尔图行省的一部分。对亚述帝国来说，扶持一圈缓冲国来对抗乌拉尔图是有利之举，但如果这种间接控制的方式不被附庸国所拥护，那么下一个最佳的解决方案就是直截了当地彻底废除当地政府。

## 手足之争：沙马什舒姆乌金，巴比伦国王，公元前648年

公元前672年，亚述巴尼拔被提升为亚述王储，与此同时，他的哥哥沙马什舒姆乌金被任命为巴比伦王储。他们的父亲埃萨尔哈东既是亚述国王也是巴比伦国王，但他希望南部的领土由独立政府管辖。正如他在铭文中所说：

> 我把沙马什舒姆乌金，我的儿子和后代，作为礼物献给了马尔杜克神（Marduk）和扎尔帕尼图女神（Zarpanitu）。

整个帝国都要宣誓尊崇国王任命儿子亚述巴尼拔和沙姆什舒姆乌金为继任者的决定，各行省总督和附庸国的统治者也要代表各自的臣民立誓。效忠条约的文本被刻在大泥板上，上面盖有亚述神的三个圣印。第一个圣印造于公元前19世纪，第二个造于公元前13世纪，最后一个造于公元前700年左右。当时应该抄录了约200份效忠条约，并分发到了各地，其中有十份手稿散布于亚述城（只有一块残片）、卡尔胡（八份），还有一份最近才出土于库拉尼亚（现土耳其哈塔伊地区的塔伊那特丘）。2008年，蒂姆·哈里森（Tim Harrison）领导的加拿大团队在库拉尼亚一座小神龛的内殿里发现了当地总督的泥板抄本。根据效忠条约的指示，它显然被当作一个神圣标志摆在那里：

> 你应当守护这块盖有众神之王亚述神的圣印的契约泥板，把泥板放在你面前，就如同面对你的神。

埃萨尔哈东对继承人的安排传遍了整个帝国，人们也可以

直观地看到这一消息。通常，亚述王室的石碑只展示国王的形象。但是，在沙马勒（现土耳其哈塔伊省金基力）和巴尔西普丘（现叙利亚阿赫玛尔丘）竖立的石碑上（见图 8），埃萨尔哈东将自己的形象摆在前面，两位王储的形象略小，位于石碑的左右两侧。其中，沙马什舒姆乌金穿着传统的巴比伦王室服装。此外，王室印章上的图像紧跟现实状况进行了一番调整，将继承安排广而告之。按照惯例，印章通常展现国王杀死狮子的场景，而更新后的设计将这个主题重复了三次（图 10）。以上种种均表明，埃萨尔哈东将和两位王子一起掌管帝国。当时的信件也确实证明，两位王子都参与了重要的政治和宗教事务。

古代亚述简史

图 10. 印章印记，刻有三幅国王勇斗雄狮的图案，此图案是亚述王权的象征。出土于尼尼微

公元前 669 年，埃萨尔哈东去世，亚述巴尼拔登上亚述王位，沙马什舒姆乌金也按计划成为了巴比伦国王。但亚述国王

自称霸主，而哥哥只是一个附庸国统治者，他们之间的关系迅速恶化。很多巴比伦官员直接听命于亚述巴尼拔，他掌控着巴比伦的外交事务；巴比伦也没有单独的军队。亚述巴尼拔有时甚至公开宣称是他任命了巴比伦国王。公元前 652 年，沙马什舒姆乌金试图冲破弟弟及其帝国的重重包围。我们并不清楚他发起叛乱的原因，他是否在南方待了二十年后入乡随俗了？然而，显然并非所有的巴比伦人都支持独立。巴比伦国内效忠亚述者和本土派系之间存在着深刻的分歧，而本土派系却死心塌地地跟随那位有亚述血统的领导人。伊朗的埃兰王国和南部阿拉姆部落的首领都支持沙马什舒姆乌金，并提供了他急需的军事援助。作为回应，亚述巴尼拔向南进军。

紧随其后的便是长达四年的血战。一些亚述国内的国务信件和国王亚述巴尼拔的铭文记载了战争的始末。这场冲突极大地破坏了巴比伦的稳定，并引发了严重的饥荒，被围困的城市情况尤其严重。人们被迫遗弃自己的孩子，在食物价格飞涨时以极低的价格卖掉他们。法律文献纳入了专门针对这种情况的条款，以保护买家在未来不会遭遇索赔。最终，亚述一方取得了胜利，但巴比伦和整个帝国都付出了巨大的代价。沙马什舒姆乌金的叛乱重创了亚述帝国的威望。于是，其他附庸国也敢再碰一把运气，比如埃及等一些国家便成功逃离了帝国的控制。

亚述巴尼拔和沙马什舒姆乌金有一个姐姐叫沙鲁亚埃提拉特（Šerua-etirat）。根据各种信件记载，她在父亲的朝廷中曾担任要职。沙鲁亚埃提拉特试图调解两位弟弟之间的冲突。当时的文献并未记录这一故事。后来，公元前 4 世纪的一张埃及莎草纸用阿拉姆语和世俗体文字记载了一篇关于此次冲突的文学作品，我们才得以了解详情。在这个故事中，沙鲁亚埃提拉特坚定地站在亚述巴尼拔的阵营。她恳求沙马什舒姆乌金与弟弟和解，但劝说无果。然后，她建议沙马什舒姆乌金和他的孩子们一起自杀。有趣的是，她将沙马什舒姆乌金的闹剧归罪于他的学者，因此他们也要一同自裁谢罪。毕竟，正是他们向沙马什舒姆乌金的头脑里灌输了关于巴比伦王权的想法，直接导致了眼前的危机。在故事中，沙鲁亚埃提拉特说道：

> 如果你不听我的话，如果你不注意我讲的话，那就离开贝尔（神）的房子，离开马尔杜克（神）的房子。让我们为你建造一座……的房子，修建一座……的房子。扔掉焦油、沥青和芬芳馥郁的香水。带上你的儿子、女儿，以及使你傲慢自大的学者。当你看到他们如何（深深地）受到你的伤害时，让大火将你同他们一起烧了。

沙鲁亚埃提拉特建议弟弟聚一个火葬用的柴堆，然后焚烧自己、孩子和学者。在亚述巴尼拔的铭文中，沙马什舒姆乌金最终葬身火海，而这似乎可以和沙鲁亚埃提拉特的建议联系起来。

如今，这个故事被称作"两兄弟的故事"，是几部讨论公元前7世纪亚述宫廷生活的阿拉姆语作品之一。另外一个例子是"圣人阿希卡（Ahiqar）的故事"，记载于埃及南部象岛出土的一片公元前5世纪的莎草纸，与一位服务辛那赫里布和埃萨尔哈东的学者有关。这两则故事都参照了历史事件，并提供了一些准确的内部信息，这说明它们来源于宫墙之内。这些文学作品均用阿拉姆语写成，着重反映出阿拉姆语在当时广为流行，甚至在宫廷中也是如此。数个世纪之后，埃及仍流传着这些故事，印证了国际化的亚述帝国宫廷文化的持久魅力。

# 第五章
# 外国人在亚述

本章关注在亚述城生活的外国人以及他们到达这里的方式，进而了解亚述与外界的互动。文中前两个案例探讨了公元前2千纪亚述与美索不达米亚南部的政治和文化联系。第三个案例展示了亚述开展的外交活动——安纳托利亚的一名统治者受邀参观亚述城，不管他是自愿还是被迫。最后两个案例关注的是亚述城的外来居民，他们被迫从伊朗迁到这里，就是为了凸显帝国时期，亚述核心地域的文化日益多元化，环境日益国际化。

## 榜样人物：沙姆什阿杜，亚述城的征服者，公元前18世纪

尽管国王沙姆什阿杜并非生于亚述城，但他在扩张战争中征服了这座城市，并在公元前18世纪内统治了这里33年之久。拥有如此辉煌的战绩，沙姆什阿杜便自诩为"宇宙之王"。虽然亚述城为不断扩大的亚述疆土添上了浓墨重彩的一笔，但他本人并没有选择在此定居，而是任命长子伊什麦达甘（Išme-Dagan）为亚述城的总督，后者住在亚述城附近的埃卡莱特。不

过，亚述城和这里的神祇对沙姆什阿杜而言非常重要，值得他的特殊关照。他重建了亚述神的神庙，并且依据美索不达米亚南部的传统，为神庙建筑群增添了一座雄伟的塔庙。瓦尔特·安德烈在挖掘亚述城的过程中，发现了这些建筑的遗迹，也发现了纪念沙姆什阿杜修建神庙这一功绩的铭文抄本。

公元前 13 世纪的亚述国王沙尔曼纳瑟尔一世和公元前 7 世纪的亚述国王埃萨尔哈东在记录自己的修葺工作之前亚述神庙的建筑历史时，重点提及了沙姆什阿杜的事迹。他们在铭文中使用的都是沙姆什阿杜这个西闪语名字的亚述语版本：沙姆什阿达德（Šamši-Adad）。同时，他们也遵从沙姆什阿杜在铭文中所提出的要求：

> 神庙破旧之时，愿国王们，我的儿子们，修缮这座神庙，用油脂抹洗我的黏土和碑铭，供奉祭品，并使之完好如初。

亚述统治者习惯于寻找先辈留下的奠基文献，并将它们和自己的文献存放在一起。亚述神庙中发现的埃萨尔哈东的铭文中有这样一段相关描述：

> 我的祖先、亚述神的代表乌什皮亚，最早建造了早期的亚述神庙。神庙变得破旧后，我的祖先、亚述神的祭司、伊鲁舒玛（Ilu-šuma）之子埃里舒姆（一世）重建了神庙。126 年过后，神庙再次变得破旧了，我的祖先、亚述神的代表、伊鲁卡布卡比（Ilu-kabkabi）之子沙姆什阿达德（一世）重建了神庙。434 年过后，神庙在烈火中被焚毁，我的祖先、亚述神的代表阿达德尼拉里（一世）之子沙尔曼纳瑟尔（一世）重建了神庙。580 年过后，内殿，我的主亚述神的住所，……破败，老旧，过时了。我忧心忡忡，惶惶不安，对修缮神庙一事犹豫不决。在占卜师的碗里，

沙马什和阿达德两位神坚定地回复我："是"，他们在肝脏上写下了对重建神庙、修缮礼拜堂一事（的回复）。

最后一段指的是，为证实众神确实支持计划中的建筑项目而进行的献祭占卜（见第三章）。

在沙姆什阿杜为亚述神庙撰写的铭文中，神被称为恩利尔（Enlil），这是按美索不达米亚南部的大神取的名字。亚述神似乎被认为是恩利尔神的一部分，他的信徒沙姆什阿杜时在铭文中以及其他场合就是这样描述自己的。舒巴特恩利尔，意为"恩利尔之位"，是沙姆什阿杜给新王国的首都取的名字，此地现位于叙利亚东北部哈布尔三角地区雷兰丘。在沙姆什阿杜为亚述神庙撰写的铭文中，他称自己是"统一底格里斯河与幼发拉底河之间的土地"的人。公元前18世纪，中东地区总体上形成了大规模的跨区域政体。例如，当时卡奈什的统治者在安纳托利亚中部建立了一个领土国家，即所谓的赫梯古王国的雏形。地缘政治形势的变化对于亚述城的商行来说并非利好消息。强大的新兴国家强征的额外费用大幅缩减了利润空间，最终，他们放弃了安纳托利亚所有的贸易殖民点。

在其漫长的统治生涯行将结束之际，沙姆什阿杜将势力范围扩展到了底格里斯河流域以外的扎格罗斯山脉西侧，征服了后来构成亚述核心地域的土地。因此，他的疆土为公元前13世纪亚述王国的边界奠定了基础。不过，沙姆什阿杜的王国只是昙花一现，寿命甚至没有超过它的创造者本身，沙姆什阿杜去世后，这个国家便迅速瓦解了。尽管亚述城依旧由他的儿子伊什麦达甘统治，但他也不得不依靠南方的盟友来维持政权，甚至曾三次逃往巴比伦城。在伊什麦达甘去世后不久，亚述城重归本土统治者管理。

虽然后来的亚述国王们习惯性地视沙姆什阿杜为他们的祖

先，但接手他那短命王朝的统治者们却并不这么认为。因此，我们在普祖尔辛（Puzur-Sin）的铭文中看到：

"在我的主，亚述神的授意下，我摧毁了他曾经创造的罪恶的事物：他的祖父沙姆什阿达德的墙和宫殿。沙姆什阿达德是一场外国瘟疫，他不是亚述城的骨肉，他摧毁了亚述城的神庙。"

前文指明了孙子的身份：

"当我，普祖尔辛，亚述神的代表，亚述贝尔沙美（Aššur-bel-šamê）之子，摧毁了沙姆什［阿达德］的后代阿西努姆（Asinum）创造的罪恶的事物……并为亚述城重新确立了合适的秩序。"

这篇铭文在善与恶之间，亚述人与外国人之间，沙姆什阿杜的防御工事、宫殿与亚述城的神庙之间，制造了对立。征服者、他的继承人、他们所创造的东西遭到了全盘否定。

的确，沙姆什阿杜是一个外国人，他对亚述城的统治并非与生俱来的权力，而是征服所得的奖赏。他与恩利尔神的亲密关系早就表明了他的南方出身背景。此外，他的祖先名单可以与另一位统治者的家谱相对应，后者通过征服开拓了一大片疆土。如今，巴比伦国王汉穆拉比因一块石碑而闻名，碑文内有一长串法律条令，证明他"正义之王"的身份。这块石碑就是所谓的《汉穆拉比法典》。汉穆拉比和沙姆什阿杜很可能同属一个氏族。因此，这位亚述城的征服者来自如今的巴格达地区，即迪亚拉河与底格里斯河交汇的地方。

尽管沙姆什阿杜并非亚述人出身，但他在一份被称作"亚述王表"的文献中具有突出的地位。"亚述王表"记录了亚述城的统治者及其相应的统治时间。它不仅将沙姆什阿杜和他的儿子伊什麦达甘列入本土统治者的名单，还将他们（和汉穆拉比的）那些从未踏入过亚述城的祖先们也纳入了名单。这是为了通过混淆沙姆什阿杜的出身，给他统治亚述提供合法依据，还是后来的亚述统治者宣布著名的"宇宙之王"及其祖先就是尊敬的先辈？现代学者对此持不同意见，他们的观点很大程度上取决于"亚述王表"的编撰史的再现方式。沙姆什阿杜的最后一位继承人阿西努姆，以及在沙姆什阿杜的王朝结束后恢复亚述城本土统治的普祖尔辛都没有被收录在王表文本中。这表明，该文本的编纂时间肯定还要靠后，应当是在沙姆什阿杜可以被顺利编入亚述历史的更为成熟的时机。不论真实情况如何，每新增一个亚述统治者的条目，王表就会定期更新。王表存留了几份抄本，距今最近的一份写于公元前 8 世纪末沙尔曼纳瑟尔五世（Shalmaneser V）统治时期。"亚述王表"是重建整个中东古代年表的重要资料来源。

至少在公元前 13 世纪，国王沙尔曼纳瑟尔一世在自己的建筑铭文中提到沙姆什阿杜对亚述神庙的修缮工作时，完全把这位征服者当作亚述的统治者以及现任国王的直系祖先。此时，没有人想要抹除沙姆什阿杜统治亚述城的记忆或痕迹。作为一个幅员辽阔的大国的前任统治者，这位杰出的先辈当时成为了亚述国王们的榜样。为表示纪念，他们采用了沙姆什阿杜的头衔"恩利尔神任命之人"和依照惯例的"宇宙之王"。

## 马尔杜克那丁阿赫（Marduk-nadin-ahhe），来自巴比伦的王室书吏，约公元前 1328 年

对于公元前 14 世纪的第一位亚述国王亚述乌巴里特一世而言，与巴比伦维持和平关系非常重要。根据巴比伦编年史记载，他把女儿慕巴里塔特舍鲁阿（Muballitat-Šerua）嫁给了巴

比伦国王布尔那布里亚什二世（Burnaburiaš II），进而巩固了与南方邻居的良好关系。夫妻俩的儿子，即亚述乌巴里特一世的外孙，将会继承巴比伦的王位。然而，在公元前1328年，布尔那布里亚什二世去世，巴比伦人反对新任统治者卡拉哈尔达什（Karahardaš），他们处决了他，并将纳兹布伽什（Nazibugaš）推上王位。纳兹布伽什被称作"无名者之子"，也就是说，他原本与王室无关。我们并不清楚这件事的来龙去脉，但从亡君的外祖父亚述乌巴里特一世随后立即入侵巴比伦的举动可以看出，卡拉哈尔达什与亚述的关系可能正是他在巴比伦不受欢迎的原因。亚述军队很快就除掉了篡位者。随后，亚述乌巴里特一世安排他的另一个外孙库里伽尔祖二世（Kurigalzu II）登上了王位。

巴比伦人肯定划分为两个阵营：支持纳兹布伽什的叛乱者和合法王室的支持者。书吏马尔杜克那丁阿赫很可能卷入了这场冲突。他出身显赫，家族成员曾担任高级行政和学术职位，服务过好几代巴比伦统治者。他后来选择离开巴比伦，在亚述首都亚述城安置新家，并在那里成为了亚述乌巴里特一世的王室书吏，地位尊贵。他的职位似乎与后来的"大学者"（见第三章）一职对应，职责大致与国王的顾问团相似：撰写王室铭文和其他官文，在学术问题上为君主提供建议，甚至可能还要教王室成员写字。马尔杜克那丁阿赫是亚述宫廷中已知的最早的王室书吏，据推测，这个职位可能就创立于此时。在亚述臣服于米坦尼之前，亚述乌巴里特一世的目标是确保王国实力强大。为国王的学术顾问设立一个引人注目的职位非常符合这一目标，如果新任命的王室书吏出身于曾服务巴比伦王室的家族，则更是锦上添花。

我们对马尔杜克那丁阿赫的了解，源于他在搬入亚述城的新住处时所写的铭文。现存只有原始铭文的抄本，在结尾处，他向巴比伦之主、马尔杜克神提出了请求——亚述乌巴里特一世在位期间在亚述城拥挤的神庙区域为马尔杜克神建立了一座神庙：

> 愿我的主马尔杜克神检查那所房子，并因我的麻烦而将其授予我。愿他允许（它）屹立不倒，延续到我的子辈，孙辈，我的后代和后代的后代，这样我和我的家人就能永远尊敬我的主马尔杜克和女主人扎尔帕尼图。或许，在马尔杜克的命令之下，有人可以纠正我那些曾经背信弃义的［亲戚］和祖先。愿我的主［马尔杜克］保佑亚述乌巴里特富贵长寿，他爱怜我，他是宇宙之王，我的主。

在铭文中，他不同寻常地提到了自己的麻烦和背信弃义的家庭成员。不难看出，在得到亚述乌巴里特一世的保护和赞助，并在亚述城安置新家之前，马尔杜克那丁阿赫在巴比伦陷入了冲突。他希望自己和家人能永远留在亚述城，显然没有让自己或后代再次回到家乡巴比伦的打算。

这位流亡者在马尔杜克的神庙旁建了一座房子，这当然少不了王室的庇佑，因为在拥挤的亚述城中，居住空间非常宝贵，而且在神庙区域内建造一座新房子需要清除现有的建筑物。据"亚述神祇目录"（见第二章）显示，马尔杜克神庙似乎是亚述神庙建筑群扩建的一部分。这就意味着，马尔杜克那丁阿赫那座"建在马尔杜克神庙的阴影下"的房子就在距离神庙非常近的地方，甚至有可能在神庙内部。这说明这个巴比伦人可能当过祭司，而且极有可能负责马尔杜克及其配偶扎尔帕尼图的祭拜仪式。

尽管地理位置如此金贵，这座房子仍建了两个侧厅，一个通向外界，另一个通向私人生活空间，在最里面的房间之下有一个地下墓穴，房子整体符合亚述精英的住宅的典型标准，甚至自家还有一口井。建筑铭文的第一部分写道：

> 我，马尔杜克那丁阿赫，是一名王室书吏，马尔杜克乌巴里特（Marduk-uballit）之子，乌舒尔阿那马尔杜克（Uššur-ana-Marduk）之孙，受到神和王的祝福，本性谦卑顺从，主对我很满意。我将房子建在马尔杜克神庙的阴影下，以尊贵的身份住进了这里。我在此处打了一口冷水井，我在我的主马尔杜克神无尽智慧的指引下将其归为己有。我凭借聪明才智，小心谨慎地在房子下面用烧砖建了屋子，无人知晓此事。我完成了整座房子的建造，包括接待区和住宅区。我不会允许愚蠢之人占有（它）。

最后一句岂不是暴露了这位巴比伦名人针对亚述邻居的沙文主义思想？

## 王室人质和亚述城的意外游客，公元前 1112 年

新版铭文按时间顺序叙事（因此叫做"亚述年鉴"），总结国王在位时每一年的作为，直到最后组成一篇完整的文本。在已知的最早的年鉴文献中，提格拉特皮勒塞尔一世详细描述了公元前 1112 年，他率领远征军深入安纳托利亚的过程。在凡湖以北的曼齐克特平原——公元 1071 年塞尔柱帝国苏丹阿尔普·阿尔斯兰（Alp Arslan）歼灭拜占庭军队的著名战场，亚述国王也同样取得了胜利。他击败了由 23 位当地统治者组成的联盟。提格拉特皮勒塞尔一世在最后写道：

> 我活捉了纳伊利（即安纳托利亚）的所有国王。我怜悯他们，饶了他们的性命。在我的主太阳神的面前，我解开了他们的链子和脚镣，让他们在我伟大的神面前发誓永世为奴。我把他们的王子当作人质。我向他们强征了 1200

匹马和 2000 头牛作为贡物。我让他们回到各自的领土。

战败的统治者不得不臣服于亚述的最高权威，并与他们的新霸主缔结条约。他们要矢忠，并将子女送去当人质，以此作为履行条约的担保。条约规定，他们需定期向亚述运送牛和马，亚述急需这批牲畜组建战车部队。从公元前 9 世纪末开始，骑兵队也急需牛马（见第六章）。来自安纳托利亚的人质将在亚述王宫中长大，而他们的存在对亚述而言有两重目的。在亚述，他们以自身性命确保自己的家族和国家对亚述忠诚。而回到家乡后，如果他们顺利当上统治者或者身居其他要职，那么在亚述王宫的经历将会使他们与亚述人更加合拍，从而能够保证他们在家乡的作为更值得亚述信赖。

公元前 7 世纪初，当几位质子按照亚述的意愿回到家乡进行统治时，这一点得到了充分证明。王室铭文中记载到，公元前 703 年，辛那赫里布任命贝尔伊布尼（Bel-ibni）为巴比伦国王，称他"像小狗一样在我宫里长大"（考虑到时间问题，此处或许是指他父亲萨尔贡二世的宫殿）。另外，埃萨尔哈东任命塔布亚（Tabua）为阿拉伯人的女王，称她"在我父亲（辛那赫里布）的宫中长大"。被送往亚述王宫时，这些王室人质还是儿童，明显有利于实现灌输"亲亚述"思想这一目标。不过，他们到底是人质，还是受保护者，这一点很难讲清楚。有时，外国统治者将亚述王宫视为子女的避风港，特别是在本国发生剧变的时候。例如，在对手比特亚金部落的首领麦洛达赫巴拉丹二世（Merodach-baladan）宣布自己为巴比伦国王时，巴比伦南部部落比特达库里的首领巴拉苏（Balassu）便将自己的儿女送往萨尔贡二世处寻求保护。

关于安纳托利亚之战，提格拉特皮勒塞尔一世的铭文还写道：

我带来了达厄努国王塞尼（Seni），他不肯服从我的主亚述神，如今只能戴着枷锁和脚链来到我的亚述城。我怜悯他，让他活着离开这里，以彰显伟大神祇的荣耀。

由此可见，这位安纳托利亚的国王需要受到特别的教训。不同于剩下的 22 个盟友，他被带到了亚述城。铭文中所提及的"不肯服从"是否意味着他拒绝矢忠，因此被带到亚述城以作惩罚？又或者，安纳托利亚的其他统治者也受到了同等对待，而参观首都是一种特殊待遇？不管真实情况如何，在亚述城逗留数日后，塞尼就被送回了家。在亚述城，他要歌颂众神，也可能要赞美亚述和亚述国王。在参观了亚述王都之后，塞尼会清楚地了解亚述国王的实力。

参观亚述中心地区是外国统治者被迫臣服于亚述霸权的典型经历。从亚述纳西尔帕二世开始，王室宫殿就成了震慑投降者的特定意象。这里既能看见军事征服和受降的混乱场面，也能看见王室典仪和呈纳贡物的有序场景，二者皆为与亚述交手的方式，显然后者才能吸引外国访客。

## 亚述城的一个伊朗家庭，公元前 715 至前 614 年

在第三章中，我们已经了解到亚述城里住着大量埃及人，公元前 671 年亚述人征服孟菲斯之后，他们就搬到了这里。不过，在美索不达米亚和叙利亚–巴勒斯坦的闪语世界之外，他们并不是第一批定居亚述城的外国人。早在 40 年前，亚述人在今伊朗西部的哈马丹地区建立了两个行省之后，米底地区的人们向西迁移了 500 公里，并于公元前 715 年穿过扎格罗斯山脉到达了亚述城。

公元前 716 年，萨尔贡二世建立的哈尔哈和基什西姆两个

行省最初的状况非常不稳定，国王与该地区的总督和下属的通信也证明了这一点。当地政府要与恶劣的气候作斗争，必要的基础设施建设常因天气原因被耽搁。一年当中总有一部分时间，扎格罗斯山脉的积雪会切断新行省与亚述核心地域之间的联系。早在公元前 715 年，新成立的行省就起义反抗刚刚起步的亚述政府，帝国军队随后又返回那里。根据萨尔贡二世的铭文记载，当地的军事镇压非常血腥，有 4000 名敌人被斩首，另外有 4820 人被选中迁至他乡（见第六章）。因此，一些当地人来到了亚述城。

基什西姆腹地珲迪尔的一个大家族搬进了通往亚述城西北部的大城门内侧的一座宅子。由于在拥挤的城里找到合适的住处变得日益艰难，他们便在这个略显尴尬的位置定居下来。1906 年，瓦尔特·安德烈在考察这座城市的防御工事时，发现了这些建筑。这些房屋保存完好，因为它们倚靠的城墙在公元前 614 年之后坍塌了，将这些建筑盖在了下面。这些房屋，尤其是屋子里的文献，使我们得以了解居住在那里的伊朗家族。公元前 7 世纪 20 年代，这个家族有三代家庭成员和 21 名奴隶，至少一共有 35 名定居者。两份法律文献记录了家长穆达米克亚述（Mudammiq-Aššur）对六个儿子的遗产分配，我们可以从中了解到这个家庭的详细信息。这是一个富裕之家，有两座相当大的房子，占地面积分别为 240 平方米和 320 平方米。他们住的房子比同时代的葡萄酒商人杜里亚述的宅邸（见第三章）还要宽敞。

自从米底人到达亚述城以来，家族的男性成员就开始（和当地的名人一样）在亚述神庙中担任职位。但由于他们的头衔依照原籍取名为"珲迪尔人"，因此我们尚不清楚他们的具体职位是什么。他们制造某种纺织品，可能是一种地毯。如果猜得没错的话，他们可能将一种手工打结绒毯的工艺引进了亚述的核心地域。这个家族也参与陆上贸易，但与杜里亚述的葡萄酒商行不同，他们的目的地并没有出现在文本当中。车队随行人员签署了往返行程长达 7 至 12 个月的劳务合同，所以他们从事的应该是长途贸易。根据这个家族的起源，他们的贸易伙伴最有可能是伊朗故乡。毕竟此时，米底中心哈尔哈和基什西姆已被征服者萨尔贡二世分别改名为卡尔–沙鲁金，意为"萨尔贡的港口"，和卡尔–内伽尔，意为"内伽尔神（Nergal）的港口"（沿用贸易点的传统名称；见第二章），以此纪念它们在古代丝绸之路重要路段的陆上贸易中所起的重要作用。

埃及人独特的文化遗产，包括名字、神祇和物质文化，在他们到达亚述后的数十年间仍然存续。而比埃及人先两代抵达亚述城的伊朗家族，至少在公元前 7 世纪下半叶，只取祈求亚述神祇保佑的亚述名字。而且，在他们住宅的遗迹中，找不到任何带有伊朗特色的物品。虽然这些证据似乎表明这个伊朗家族已经接受了亚述人的生活方式，但我们依然可以清楚地看到，居住在亚述城的米底人保留了他们伊朗身份的某种特征——他们依然从事自己独特的职业（无论其本质如何），并且还与故国有贸易往来。

这些材料并没有告诉我们，在公元前 614 年米底攻陷亚述城后，这个家族的命运如何。很多人会把米底人迅速围城与这个米底家族联系起来——他们居住在亚述城的重要城门内侧，占据地理位置优势，可以帮助攻城者破城。毕竟在前一年，巴比伦军队对亚述城突袭失败之后，亚述城为预防再次遭受袭击，巩固了防御工事，增加了粮食储备。在这样的情况下米底人还能迅速成功，着实令人吃惊。

# 两名女战俘被卖身为奴，约公元前 645 年

目前为止，我们已经知道，亚述帝国的城市里到处都有奴隶。在亚述社会中，拥有奴隶是财富和社会地位的象征。奴隶主通常属于城市的精英阶层。在本节中，我们将重点关注一对奴隶母女，并追溯她们以奴隶身份来到亚述城的来龙去脉。和亚述的许多奴隶一样，她们是外国人。不过，土生土长的亚述自由民在迫不得已的情况下也可能卖身为奴来抵偿债务。如果他们自己或其他人能够代表他们还清债务，他们就可以得到释放。我们在现有史料中遇到的大多数奴隶都是居住在奴隶主家里的用人。女奴的孩子仍旧是奴隶，无论他 / 她的父亲是谁。不过，这位父亲通常就是奴隶主。如果奴隶主想要承认他的后代，他可以领养这个孩子，只有这样奴隶所生的孩子才有继承权。但这种情况很少见，除非奴隶主没有合法的儿子，同时还按照婚姻合约征得了妻子的同意。

公元前 664 至前 648 年，亚述军队多次入侵并劫掠伊朗西南部的埃兰王国。埃萨尔哈东统治下的短暂的和平期过后，在亚述巴尼拔统治早期的大部分时间里，两国处于交战状态，王室铭文、尼尼微宫墙上的装饰，以及国务信件中均有记载。亚述城出土的一份私人法律文件记录了一对母女的命运。她们在战争中被俘，从埃兰被押解至此地。卖身文件（记录两人售价 1 明那［约 500 克］银子，这是公元前 7 世纪中叶的均价）将她们描述为"国王给予利巴里（即亚述城）的来自埃兰的战利品"。宫墙装饰多次描绘了在战争之后，行政人员登记并分发战俘等战利品的情景。但在现有史料中，我们很难追溯每个战俘后来的命运。这两名埃兰的女战俘是一个罕见的例子，凸显了战争对女性的影响。

奴隶买卖合同上面的日期已经消失，但它的背景表明，娜

娜亚伊拉伊（Nanaya-ila'i）和她的孩子是在公元前 646 年苏萨遭遇洗劫时被掳走的，当时亚述人抢得了大量的战利品。文件指出，她们作为分给亚述城的一部分战利品抵达当地时，归十名男性共同所有，随后他们将这对母女卖给了一个名叫马努基亚述（Mannu-ki-Aššur）的人。通过姓名和职业可以确定，卖家是一群神庙的工匠，其中包括面包师、厨师、纺织工人、金匠、铁匠和牧羊人。虽然他们都为亚述神庙服务，但他们的确没有什么共同之处。不过，他们十个人由于军队的原因与埃兰战俘联系在一起，我们可以推测他们组成了一个工作小组（*kiṣru*，意为"结"），为帝国履行兵役等义务。作为亚述城分遣队的一分子，他们可能参与了对抗埃兰的军事行动（很可能是作为非战斗后勤人员参战；见第六章），并从留给亚述城的部分战利品中获得了埃兰俘虏作为奖励。由于共同拥有奴隶对于他们来说没有太大的用处，除了卖掉她们再分摊收益，他们显然也没有更好的法子。所以，埃兰战俘一到亚述城就被卖掉了。

从那时起，娜娜亚伊拉伊和女儿便成为了马努基亚述的家奴。她们的命运与那些在亚述城定居的米底人或埃及人有云泥之别。尽管后者对被迫迁至亚述城一事几乎没有发言权，但一旦到了定居地，他们就被"算作亚述人"，和其他的自由居民享有相同的权利，履行相同的义务。与娜娜亚伊拉伊和女儿那样的战利品不同，他们并不是奴隶。娜娜亚伊拉伊意为"女神娜娜亚是我的神"。这当然不是她的本名，只可能是她沦为亚述战俘后重新获得的名字。这个名字故意提及了亚述巴尼拔大肆宣传的娜娜亚女神雕像回归一事，1000 多年前，该雕像被掳至埃兰。文中没有提及她女儿的名字，说明她当时还很小，依然需要母亲照顾。她的年龄可能不止四岁，因为从文中的描述来看，她既不是婴儿（需要"喂奶"或"哺乳"），也不是刚学会走路的小孩儿（与母亲"分开"，即断奶）。

除了名字被剥夺之外，娜娜亚伊拉伊还可能会失去很多构成她之前身份的东西。我们对她原来在埃兰的社会背景一无所知。不过，至少孩子还在她的身边。只要孩子们年纪尚小，亚述出售奴隶时通常都会这样做。在这个案例中，让母女待在一起是明智之举，这可以让外国奴隶更容易融入新环境。埃兰语与亚述当地通用的亚述语和阿拉姆语等闪语族语言毫无关联。因此，娜娜亚伊拉伊在新环境中无法和他人流利地交流。她的女儿年纪还很小，学习当地语言更容易一些，可以帮助母亲融入新环境。

　　在亚述城的新生活里，这两名埃兰奴隶负责主人马努基亚述一家的日常事务。鉴于马努基亚述来自亚述城，我们推测他可能住在一栋宅子里——类似于葡萄酒商杜里亚述（见第三章）或者已经讨论过的米底家族的住宅，除此之外，我们对男主人一无所知。他的家里可能有一群奴隶，但这两名埃兰人肯定不算为数几十人的家庭中的成员，这一点和舒尔木沙里的杜尔-卡特里穆豪宅里住的人不一样（见第三章）。娜娜亚伊拉伊和女儿可能要做许多家务，包括磨面粉、烘焙、烹饪和清扫，可能还得纺羊毛和编织纺织品来为主人家赚钱。我们可以想象，在经历了战争和被虏至亚述带来的创伤之后，她们安静地生活在这里，也算是一种慰藉。但是，若不是过早离世（如常因分娩造成的死亡），娜娜亚伊拉伊的女儿可能会目睹另一次入侵，即公元前614年米底对亚述的征服。她很可能再次被当作战利品，而这一次，米底军队可能会将她带回到东边的伊朗。

# 第六章

# 亚述对世界的统治：探路的帝国

亚述帝国于公元前9世纪成形，是随后统治地中海和中东地区的波斯帝国、罗马帝国等一系列帝国的探路者。亚述帝国在意识形态、基础设施和组织架构方面的创新为继任者提供了基础和模板。建立一个帝国并不简单，而维持内部团结一致更是难上加难，但亚述沉着地应对了这个任务。最后一章专门讨论亚述帝国管理和意识形态的关键，正是它们助力亚述帝国在三个世纪里成功把控住自己的根基。亚述的宫殿艺术、王室铭文以及《圣经》都重点描绘了战争，我们将借此机会仔细研究传说中的帝国军队。绝对王权的意识形态，创新的长途邮驿服务，以及覆盖整个帝国的移民安置计划，都是维系帝国凝聚力的强大工具。最后一部分谈论亚述国王从公元前14世纪开始组建和维护的王室图书馆。在19世纪中叶，勤勉的考古学家奥斯汀·亨利·莱亚德重新发现了亚述图书馆，此后，它为我们了解亚述的文化历史做出了卓越贡献。就算对书籍的热爱曾在创立图书馆的过程中起过某些作用，但这肯定不是唯一的动机。

## "亚述神的行伍"——一支你不大想加入的古老军队？

公元前 14 世纪，当亚述成为领土大国时，它的武装部队主要包括应征的农民组成的步兵部队，和持弓箭的贵族家庭成员组成的战车部队。战车部队里的第二名成员，即驾车者，显然是战士的副手。驾车者总是被当成次要人物，而战士们则不一样，他们名声赫赫，通常不需要档案文件作进一步证明，凭军衔便能确认身份。那个时代的战车部队可以说是"半路出家"，因为队员们需要花费大量时间来练习技能。不过，我们目前还不清楚他们是常备军，还是只在国王有召时才会集结起来——后者的可能性更大。从纳税人当中征召的战士只能在夏季服兵役，因为这个时候农民不需要干农活。他们被按照十进制（10，50，100）组成单位，如此形成的社会结构足以与家庭的重要性抗衡，让人们铭记国家对个人生活的影响。在当时的亚述，整支武装部队都是以这种方式组建起来的。

公元前 9 世纪中叶，亚述军队从一支以临时动员的征兵为主的军队转变成了一支主要由全年服役的战士组成的军队。沙尔曼纳瑟尔三世建立了常备军，长期驻扎在易受攻击的边境区域。在此过程中，他还将长达一个世纪的征战中被俘的专业战士吸收到亚述军队中来。同时，他创建了亚述的第一支骑兵部队。将战败地区的战士整合到常备军中成为了一项惯例，他们主要被归集到战车部队和骑兵部队中，也就是那些受最专业训练的战士所在的部队。在提格拉特皮勒塞尔三世领导下，军事扩张使亚述的疆域增加了一倍，此时的常备武装力量规模庞大，亚述便不再需要征召纳税人临时服役了。因此，那些原本应征入伍的人大多被派去服务民事，比如修建公共建筑。此时，由于不再依赖需要按时务农的劳动力，军事行动也不再局限于夏季。如此一来，亚述军队便有了更长的作战时间前往更远的目的地，例如埃及。

在公元前1千纪，亚述军队人员众多。王室铭文颇有诗意地称他们为"亚述神的行伍"。不同的军团可以保留和发展自己的习俗和特色。亚述军队并未被锻造成一个牢固的统一体，相反，各个独立分部为赢得王室的认可和支持，彼此之间的竞争相当激烈。这一策略旨在压制武装部队的力量，防止其相对于国王和国家而言不受约束。这种方法非常管用，而且成功维持了亚述内部的稳定和王朝的长久，功不可没。军队的不同部分下设由军官领导的军团，其中至少有一部分军官是从普通士兵中晋升的。基础指挥部有50人。人们可以区分出哪些是国王亲自指挥的"王室队列"，哪些是他交予他人执掌的军队。虽然军队驻扎在边境战略地区的要塞，但各行省并没有永久驻防的军队。无论是临时动员或是从其他地方借调，各行省总督控制军队的时间都很短。高效的防御系统将常备军主体集中在沙尔曼纳瑟尔三世统治期间建立的四个战略边境位置上。

与亚述军团一同作战的还有从邻近地区和内部边缘地区（草原、沙漠、山脉）来的辅助部队。这部分军事力量非常重要，他们主要充当之前由应征士兵组成的步兵。亚述帝国与某些辅助部队之间建立了长期联系。不过，当时的政治和机遇肯定也会影响辅助部队的使用。因此，正如尼尼微西南宫墙上的"拉基什之围"所绘，公元前701年，辛那赫里布在犹大王国征战时集结的武装力量包括辅助部队的投石兵，这些训练有素的步兵用当地特有的弹弓作武器——《圣经》中大卫（David）战胜歌利亚（Goliath）的故事便是最好的例证。在宫墙的装饰中，我们通过衣着便能轻易地将辅助部队与亚述军队区分开来：后者穿着统一的制服，戴着典型的锥形头盔；而辅助部队总是穿着自己特定的服装。在亚述艺术中，战争是成年人的事情：战士们都是一副年富力强的成年男性模样，胡须浓密（除非他们是宦官，见第二章），肌肉发达。

在专业分工方面，帝国军队由战车兵、骑兵和步兵组成，步兵又分为远程弓箭手和近战长矛手。长矛手被称为"持盾和矛者"，即手持装甲盾和长矛的人，通常被简称为"持盾者"。这些士兵非常类似于希腊的装甲步兵。战车兵是依战车取的名字，而骑兵则因骑马作战而得名（意为"张开双腿的人"）。所有这些部队都由职业士兵组成。各种文献史料表明，战车、骑兵、步兵的比例为1∶10∶200，步兵又以2∶1的比例划分为弓箭手和长矛手，这是理想的平衡状态。但是，军队也会根据具体目标召集武装力量，并相应地派遣合适的军队。行军过程中，亚述军队住在临时搭建的防御营地内的帐篷里。搭建营地是非战斗后勤人员的任务之一，他们当中有些人是应征入伍的士兵，占军队的很大一部分比例。每个行省中心都会储备粮草作为军需物资。在国外时，军队和牲畜以觅食为生，因为行军过程中要将大宗物资减到最少。

从公元前2千纪末到前1千纪，亚述军队一直在使用载有弓箭手的战车，装备和战术使用也几乎没有变化。一方面，在美索不达米亚和叙利亚的平原上，战车在速度和机动性方面的双重优势使它长期以来都是优秀的攻击武器。另一方面，骑兵在公元前9世纪沙尔曼纳瑟尔三世的统治下才成为正规军。战车的构架轻而且易碎，又缺乏悬架，在山地区域驾驶这种昂贵的移动工具毫无可能，因为地形对车轮的磨损会让战车完全困在原地。战车只能拆卸后再运上山地，如此一来，它们便不再是危敌的利器，而成了麻烦的重负。发明适应恶劣地形的战车的尝试促成了骑兵的出现。这类战车将用于崎岖不平的托罗斯山脉和扎格罗斯山脉地区——自公元前9世纪乌拉尔图、曼努亚、米底兴起以来的兵家必争之地。沙尔曼纳瑟尔三世时期，卡尔胡附近的巴拉瓦特的神庙大门上的青铜装饰最早对亚述骑兵的描绘显示：骑手两两组队，像战车部队一样行动（一人"驾车"，一人射箭），但他们不会像战车那样受到地形的限制。

战车部队在平原上依旧能大展身手。但到了公元前 8 世纪中叶，更经济、更灵活的骑兵部队在战场上取代了轻型战车部队。当时的战车配有装甲，由三人操控：驾车者、战士和保护其他人的"第三人"。到了公元前 7 世纪，战车规模依旧维持在数百辆的水平，但是此时战车部队的装甲甚至更加繁重。战车不仅配备有四匹马，车上还出现了第四个人来加强防护。这些像坦克一样的战车比以前的样式要高得多，车轮直径接近两米，既可以近距离射击敌方弓箭手，同时又能一石二鸟，有效地展示武力并恐吓对手。

战车部队、骑兵部队和大部分步兵都使用弓箭进行战斗，他们用的是传统的复合弓：弓呈三角形，弓长 110 至 125 厘米。因此，弓是亚述军队最重要的武器，这一事实应该能反映出他们在激战中所有的战术构想。然而，文本史料的片面性使得再现特定战役的构想本身就存在问题。

海战则处于相对次要的地位。第一支亚述舰队建于公元前 694 年，部署在波斯湾。战船由尼尼微的叙利亚工匠建造，腓尼基和爱奥尼亚（可能是希腊人的总称）船员操纵，沿底格里斯河航行到巴比伦，再经陆路运到幼发拉底河的一处河湾，然后从那里航行到波斯湾，对伊朗的埃兰国的海岸发动突袭。如宫墙上一贯以来的装饰图案所示，这些船可能是双层桨作战船。在地中海，亚述帝国需与腓尼基附庸国，尤其是与提尔合作。直到公元前 677 年，亚述吞并西顿并将其设立为亚述港口，更名为"埃萨尔哈东的港口"，帝国才建立自己在地中海的海军力量。亚述对西顿的控制，为从陆路入侵埃及提供了后卫力量。

另外，围攻战是亚述军队的一个重要战术，围攻带来的威胁更是重中之重。在弹射器（公元前4世纪初才开始广泛使用）或者其他任何可以在安全距离之内部署的重型火炮出现之前，攻城的唯一选择是在对方防御范围内攻克或摧毁其防御工事。宫墙装饰对围攻的描绘（图11）展示了一个壮观的兵工厂：破城锤、攻城战车、云梯、移动攻城塔以及挖掘隧道的各种工具。设计这些图像就是为了创造亚述人战无不胜的深刻印象。人们对亚述帝国的普遍看法与这些图像传达的印象相差无几，亚述人也因此被视为一个不顾一切进行征服的民族——这一点完全如创作者所愿。例如，鲁珀特·马修斯（Rupert Matthews）和戴维·安特拉姆（David Antram）合著的《你不会想要成为一名亚述士兵：一支你不大想加入的古老军队》所传达的中心思想正是如此，这本描述亚述的童书实为罕见，且妙趣横生。

图 11. 围攻尼罗河畔埃及设防城市之战及其战果：库什的努比亚士兵被俘，埃及平民遭流放。来自国王亚述巴尼拔建于尼尼微的北宫

然而，如果在没有内应的情况下，完全依靠武力攻下一个设防的城市，成本会非常高。因此，正如问询神谕的例子（见第三章）所示，亚述军队会尽可能避免围攻战，而是利用各种方法说服被围困的人投降。如果接受投降，亚述会兑现大赦的承诺，人口迁居不算惩罚。如果不接受投降，城墙外的果园和棕榈树种植园里的树木会被砍伐一空。因为这些树需要很多年才能结果，所以这种方式将长期持续地破坏受困者的生计。最终，防御者将目睹被选定的战俘或人质被处决。处决方式是刺刑，不过显然大部分围攻都无须走到这一步。如果受困者没有屈服，例如，和在亚述巴尼拔和兄长沙马什舒姆乌金长达数年的巴比伦争夺战期间的巴比伦城和尼普尔城一样，那么饥荒和疾病很快会使围城生活变得恐怖和绝望。

## 神圣的国王：绝对君主制

公元前 879 年，亚述纳西尔帕二世将王宫从亚述城迁至卡尔胡时，新宫的王座厅里的装饰图案进行了精心设计，有意传达两条至关重要的意识形态信息。首先，所有土地归亚述纳西尔帕二世统治。我们之前已经强调了王宫里两种画面之间的对比：一边风平浪静，井然有序，来访者觐见国王，呈献贡品，展示了国王与忠实盟友之间的互动；另一边则腥风血雨，混乱不堪，大军围攻和征服敌人，展示了国王应对抵抗的强硬手段。其次，王座厅要强调的是，尽管离开了亚述神庙，但国王作为被神选中的代表，和神的关系仍然紧密牢固。

为此，一个引人注目的场景在王座厅中出现了两次（图12），一次是在长方形大厅靠长边墙的入口对面的墙上，另一次是在尽头的王座平台之上。参观者进入大厅时，目光会直接被描绘亚述纳西尔帕二世与亚述神的对称的纹章图像所吸引。

国王由带翼神侍守护，按照典型的礼拜礼仪举起了右手，这一场景在亚述神的两侧各出现了一次。亚述神作为众神之王，乔装成超脱肉体的人形现身，他留着胡子，戴着亚述统治者独有的像土耳其帽一样的头饰，持着国王的首选武器——弓和箭。图像周围还有一个张开双翼的圆盘，强调神的超凡来世，圆盘下方有一个神秘的标志，即今天所说的"神圣之树"或"生命之树"（尽管它看起来并不像是一棵树）。这幅充满象征意义的图像强有力地传达了一个观点：国王不需要亚述神庙也能和神交流。他们之间的联系十分牢固，神圣的国王本人就是与神沟通的中间人。在亚述神的保佑之下，国王的权利至高无上，不容置疑。

图 12. 国王与亚述神思想交融。来自国王亚述纳西尔帕二世建于卡尔胡的西北宫的王座厅

然而，人们无须前往卡尔胡的王宫觐见国王就能看到这幅令人敬畏的图像。沙迪卡尼（现位于现叙利亚东北部哈布尔地区阿贾贾丘）地方长官的红玉髓滚印（图 13）证明这幅图像被制成易于携带的艺术品，传向了整个帝国。这个印章上刻有穆舍兹布宁努尔塔（Mušezib-Ninurta）的楔文铭文，他是宁努尔塔埃利什（Ninurta-ereš）的儿子，萨玛努哈沙尔伊拉尼

（Samanuha-šar-ilani）的孙子。他们是统治沙迪卡尼城的一个古王朝的成员。萨玛努哈沙尔伊拉尼与亚述纳西尔帕二世生活在同一时代，亚述国王的铭文证实，公元前883年，他作为亚述盟友助其夺回了哈布尔地区。他的孙子可能是亚述纳西尔帕二世的继任者长寿的沙尔曼纳瑟尔三世的同时代人。铭文以阴文形式被刻在印章上，也就是说，使用印章时，印出来的文字是反着的。这也说明，该文本不属于原始的印章设计，它可能是在很久之后才加上去的。有可能是亚述纳西尔帕二世将这个珍贵的物品作为礼物送给盟友，因为这枚印章仿制了亚述纳西尔帕二世的卡尔胡王宫的王座厅里的纹章设计图。

图 13. 刻有楔形文字铭文的红玉髓滚印，其图案仿制了亚述纳西尔帕二世的王座厅里的图案

到了（至少）公元前7世纪，在王室的意识形态下，国王既与凡人有云泥之别，又凌驾于众人之上。在一篇谈论人的创造的文作学作品中，众神在创造了人类之后单独创造了国王：

埃阿（Ea，智慧之神）对贝莱特伊里（Belet-ili，创造女神）说："你是贝莱特伊里，是伟大众神的姊妹；是你创造了人类（*lullû amēlu*）。现在塑造国王吧，他是策士

（ *šarru māliku amēlu* ）！ 让他看起来仪表堂堂，拥有完美的容貌与身躯！"然后贝莱特伊里塑造了国王，即策士。

神圣的王室家族在亚述社会中享有非常特殊的地位，其中只有男性成员才有资格获得王位。虽然有篡位和继承之争，但直到帝国终结，所有的亚述国王都来自这个家族的男性后裔，该家族因此成为了历史上当权最久的王室之一。

## 长途快速通信

快速通信是确保疆域辽阔的亚述帝国保持凝聚力的一个关键战略，它在国王与各行省总督以及附庸国王宫里的大使之间搭建沟通的桥梁。帝国通信网络经过精心策划，创建于公元前9世纪，被称为"国王之路"。各行省总督要维护设在本省战略关键位置的驿站，这是帝国通信系统的经停点和交叉点；每当帝国版图增加新的行省时，将新的行政区域连接上"国王之路"就成了重要挑战之一。驿站要么位于原有的定居点内，要么其本身就是定居点。驿站配备有必要的农业基础，为职员、使者和赶路的牲畜提供补给。中世纪伊斯兰世界的驿站是一个很好的比较对象，因为它们都是沿着长途路线建造的，目的在于给旅客及牲畜提供短期的住处和保护。但两者间的重要区别在于，亚述的驿站只为国家服务，并不对商旅开放。

因此，只有那些获正式任命的国家公职人员才能够使用"国王之路"的资源。帝国的要人都会收到一枚复刻的图章戒指，上面刻有公认的帝国标志（国王杀狮子的画面；见图10），这是他们官职的象征，也是他们代替国王行事的工具。他们用这枚戒指来封印信件，所有传递公函的人，比如驿站的工作人员和国王的秘书，便能凭此枚封印立即判定这是国家要事，并按规定严肃紧急地处理。

信息要么只能通过信使传信进行交换，要么通过使者交换（他们不一定带着信件）。如果信息非常敏感，或者需要当场作出决定，派遣使者奔赴全程传信是首选的通信手段。国王的"朋友"（见第三章）经常担任他的使者。第一种方法要快得多，因为每一名信使只需从本站走到下一站，中间只有一站地的距离，等到了下一站，信件便交给了新的信使，因此信息传递过程中没有耽搁时间。公元前 9 世纪，亚述断开了信件和信使之间的联系，这在当时是一项相当激进的举措。在电报出现以前，近 3000 年来，这一传递系统为通信速度设定了标准。

信使和使者都带着成对的骡子上路，尽量避免骑手因牲畜跛脚而耽搁了行程。骡子是母马和公驴的后代，这些不育的杂种动物躯干似马，四肢类驴，通常比马和驴都长得高。骡子比马和驴要晚成熟五年，但工作寿命长达 20 年。养骡子是一项昂贵的投资，因为它们无法繁殖后代，身体发育缓慢，并且需要大量精细的训练。但骡子比马更强壮，适应力能力更强，并且继承了驴子步履稳健和自我保护的本能，对于亚述帝国而言，这些优点轻易便抵消了昂贵的花销；而且，它们还会游泳。这类动物在军事上至今仍有用武之地，比如英国和美国的军队都会使用骡子。

国王的通信者只有在需要中央政府参与决策或传递重要信息时才会使用昂贵的通信系统。国王任命了一批重要官员，代表国王在地方行使权力，这也意味着他们时常要依靠自己的判断开展工作。他们的主要职责是：无论何时何地，在国王不能出席的情况下代表国王行事。因此，他们大部分的信件涉及的是突发状况而不是常规事务，例如：出现良机，发生灾难，或是那些让地方官员大受惊吓或六神无主的情况。许多信件都谈的是难题、小问题和挑战。

目前已经发现了大约 2000 封公元前 1 千纪的国务信件。从公元前 8 世纪初阿达德尼拉里三世统治时期到帝国终结，这两个世纪的信件数量在时间上分布不均。大多数国务信件都来自萨尔贡二世统治时期，共计约 1200 封。其中大部分信件都属于尼尼微的王室档案，在萨尔贡二世的继任者辛那赫里布统治时期，它们被转移到了那里。但还有一小部分信件是在卡尔胡出土的。这些文献是历史学家研究古代帝国如何运转的最佳材料之一。

## 把他们算作亚述人：重新安置计划

帝国的所有人，无论其出身，都"算作亚述人"，亚述王室铭文如是说。《圣经》中引述了一条信息，称亚述国王辛那赫里布可能在公元前 701 年围攻耶路撒冷时向城里的人传达过这个消息。辛那赫里布在力劝他们放弃奸诈的附庸国国王，也就是他们的犹大国王希西家（Hezekiah）之后，说道：

> 与我讲和，来我这里。之后你们每个人都可以吃到自己的葡萄藤和无花果树上结的果子，喝自己水池里的水，直到我将你们带到一个属于你们自己的地方——那是一片有着谷物和新酒、面包和葡萄园、橄榄树和蜂蜜的土地。选择生路，活下来！（列王纪下 18:31—32）

亚述帝国这种大规模的重新安置策略通常被称作"驱逐"（鉴于该词引发的各种与实际情况毫不相干的联想，如边缘化和灭绝，此处实属用词不当）。实际上，"驱逐"可以被视为一种特权而非惩罚。人们可以同家庭与财产一起迁往新居（见图11）。他们并非是在战火纷飞或国破家亡时，无奈之下远走他乡，而是经过一番精挑细选，才被选中来到这里。这通常发生在一场战争过后，他们的家园被夷为平地的情况下。亚述史料详细地列出了被重新安置的人口的名单，其中提到了城市精英、工匠、学者和军人。根据帝国的需要，重新安置政策将社区团体分成了两拨：必须留下的人和必须离开的人。为了帝国的经济文化利益，来自新征服地区的专业人士最常被安置在亚述的核心地域，为帝国创造知识和财富。

另一方面，名誉扫地的亚述人不会被杀，而是被流放到殖民地为国家服务，从而反省思过，救赎自我。复杂的移民循环精心策划并执行了数年，人口被重新安置到帝国边境区域，他们既取代了别人的位置，也被其他移民所取代。例如，撒马利亚的居民在公元前 722 年被征服后，于公元前 716 年迁移到了在米底领土内建立的哈尔哈和基什西姆行省——现位于伊朗哈马丹地区。这两个行省的居民反过来定居在亚述城（见第五章）。公元前 720 年，叛乱被镇压后获得赦免的一部分人从亚述城迁往哈马特（今叙利亚哈马）。而哈马特这时也发生叛乱，但最终被镇压，哈马特的居民因此被迁移到了撒马利亚，结束了这个循环。这个庞大的移民计划错综复杂，多地同时进行，还涉及了巴比伦与安纳托利亚地区，以上案例只是它的冰山一角。根据王室铭文的记载，我们可以计算出，在公元前 9 世纪中叶到前 7 世纪中叶，亚述帝国重新安置了3,500,000~5,300,000 人，其中 85% 的人定居在亚述中部——这是一个庞大的数字，尤其是考虑到当时的世界人口数量只是今天的一小部分。对于所有这些人来说，重新安居意味着能有一个更好的未来，同时也有利于帝国本身。当然，他们的搬迁同时也可以有效地降低他们反对中央集权的风险。

移民以及他们的劳动力和才能对国家来说极为宝贵。他们的迁居经过了精心策划和组织。旅程安全舒适，他们才能以良好的身体状态到达目的地。按照宫墙装饰的描绘，男人、妇女和儿童成群行进，通常坐车或骑牲畜赶路，从来没有桎梏束缚他们。公元前 8 世纪，一名官员写信给国王提格拉特皮勒塞尔三世，谈论一群来自叙利亚西部的移民在旅途中的补给：

> 关于阿拉姆居民，国王曾写信给我："为他们的旅程做好准备！"我会给他们食物、衣服、水袋、一双鞋和油。我现在还没有驴子，一旦有了，我将会派出我的车队。

从他写给国王的另一封信中可以清楚地看到，一旦移民到达目的地，国家也会给予他们支持：

> 关于阿拉姆居民，国王说道："他们要有妻子！"我们找到了很多适婚的女性，但是她们的父亲不愿意让她们结婚，说道："除非他们给聘礼，否则我们不会同意的。"给他们聘礼，这样阿拉姆人就可以结婚了。

这段话强调了国家积极促进新邻居与当地融合的举措。亚述的重新安置政策的最终目标，是创造一个具有共同文化和身份的"亚述人"同质群体。

## 知识与权力：王室图书馆

如果说王宫雕塑的发现使亚述大受欢迎，促成 19 世纪中叶亚述相关的书籍畅销，亚述文物展厅内人潮拥挤，那么，尼尼微王宫里的大量档案以及图书馆的复原和解读，则预示了一个叫亚述学的新学科的建立。几个世纪以来，亚述的核心藏品慢慢被收集起来，现在以最狂热的王室收藏家的名字命名，叫做"亚述巴尼拔图书馆"。图书馆里曾藏有大量的蜡板（见第二章），但公元前 612 年，尼尼微王宫遭大火吞噬，又加上时间的摧残，蜡板已经完全消失。不过，大约有 20,000 块图书馆收藏的泥板幸免于难，现在归为"库云吉克藏品"（以尼尼微王宫所在的定居土丘命名）的一部分藏于大英博物馆。虽然其中很多内容已经公之于众，但图书馆的馆藏规模非常庞大，现在我们仍然无法全面地概述馆藏内容。但可以确定的是，只有极少数文本可以算作文学作品，其中包括著名的《吉尔伽美什》。而已经公布的馆藏文献主要记载的是占星术和祭祀占卜的仪式指南和预测准则。这些藏品的主要作用是为国王的学术顾问提供王室决策所用的材料，并保证神支持国王和国家。这些文本包含了举行仪式所用的详细的指南，或者是大量关于预兆的参考文献。

所有的亚述国王——至少公元前 8 世纪和前 7 世纪是如此——都学过楔形文字，其他那些注定要管理帝国事务的人也一样。然而，亚述巴尼拔对神秘深奥的知识的痴迷远远超出了基本的读写。在他的铭文中，他声称自己接受了全面的学术教育。此外，在尼尼微北宫的宫墙装饰上，他腰带间别着笔，而不是更为常见的刀。不过，亚述王室图书馆的起源可以追溯到公元前 14 世纪国王亚述乌巴里特一世统治时期，那时，他那位来自巴比伦的王室书吏马尔杜克那丁阿赫（见第五章）可以大展身手，可能已经启动了这个项目。公元前 13 世纪，图库尔提宁努尔塔一世洗劫巴比伦时，从当地带回泥板，充实了亚述的馆藏。到了公元前 7 世纪，王室图书馆已经成为有史以来馆藏最丰富的楔形文字图书馆。

王室图书馆基本上是当地亚述人抄录、编辑和创作的产物。不过，亚述巴尼拔也集中利用帝国对巴比伦，可能还有埃及的控制来收集图书馆文献。这种收集文献的工作非常有组织性——国王派出搜索队去查找珍贵的学术作品，并将它们占为己有，必要时还会诉诸武力。列出了 2000 块泥板和 300 块写字板的记录证明这些都是在巴比伦叛乱结束后，公元前 652 至前 648 年（见第四章），从私人收藏中被整合到王室图书馆中的。除此之外，巴比伦人也被征召加入大规模抄录泥板的项目中。一部分人是受命而来，劳动有偿，其他人则是被迫参与了这次活动。一份行政文件记载，"戴着脚镣"的巴比伦战俘们在胁迫之下抄录泥板，其中包括支持叛乱的尼普尔总督的儿子。从这一记录中可以大致了解身处尼尼微的政治犯们的待遇，它也证明巴比伦的城市精英都接受过良好教育。知识渊博的绅士学者亚述巴尼拔绝对不是特例。

到了公元前 7 世纪初，尼尼微、卡尔胡、亚述城这些亚述的中心城市都住着来自世界各地的著名专家。如果没有他们，亚述国王的一些不朽成就，比如建造和装饰那些宏伟的宫殿和神庙，或是收集亚述巴尼拔那座著名的图书馆的馆藏，是不可能完成的。无论他是出于对知识的渴求，以及为了帝国利益而希望控制和使用这些知识财富，还是身为一名富有的收藏家沉迷于揽集好物，在今天，王室图书馆是亚述巴尼拔，或者说是亚述最恒久的纪念碑。

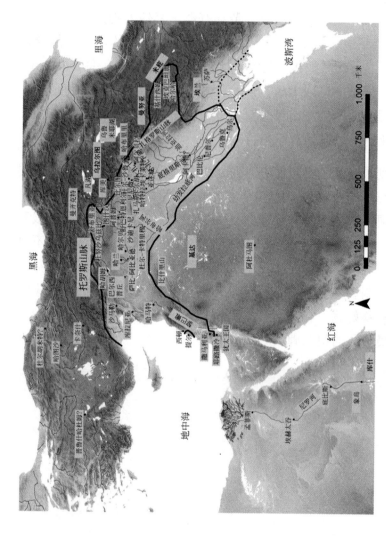

地图．约公元前 670 年的亚述帝国，以及本书先后提及的所有地点

# 年表

## 亚述城统治者

……

| | | |
|---|---|---|
| 乌什皮亚<br>公元前 3 千纪末 | 建立亚述神庙 | |

……

| | | |
|---|---|---|
| 埃里舒姆一世<br>公元前 19 世纪 | 扩建亚述神庙 | 卡奈什的亚述<br>商人<br>Ib 地层 |

……

| | | |
|---|---|---|
| 沙姆什阿杜<br>公元前 18 世纪 | 征服亚述城；<br>重建神庙 | 卡奈什的亚述<br>商人<br>II 地层 |
| 伊什麦达甘<br>公元前 18 世纪 | | 巴比伦国王汉<br>穆拉比 |

……

| | | |
|---|---|---|
| 普祖尔辛<br>公元前 17 世纪 | 将亚述从外国统<br>治中解放出来 | |

......

亚述纳丁阿赫一世
公元前 15 世纪

......

## 亚述国王

| | | |
|---|---|---|
| 亚述乌巴里特一世<br>公元前 1356—前 1322 年 | 第一位亚述国王 | 王室书吏马尔杜克那丁阿赫 |
| ...... | | |
| 阿达德尼拉里一世<br>公元前 1300—前 1270 年 | | |
| 沙尔曼纳瑟尔一世<br>公元前 1269—前 1241 年 | 彻底击败米坦尼 | 第一任哈尼迦尔巴特总督伊巴什伊里 |
| 图库尔提宁努尔塔一世<br>公元前 1240—前 1205 年 | 征服巴比伦 | |
| ...... | | |
| 亚述尼拉里三世<br>公元前 1200—前 1195 年 | 继位之争 | 最后一任哈尼迦尔巴特总督伊里帕达 |
| ...... | | |
| 宁努尔塔阿皮埃库尔<br>公元前 1189—前 1178 年 | | |
| ...... | | |
| 提格拉特皮勒塞尔一世<br>公元前 1114—前 1076 年 | 发生饥荒，导致移民 | |
| ...... | | |

亚述贝尔卡拉
公元前 1073—前 1056 年

……

| | | |
|---|---|---|
| 亚述丹二世<br>公元前 935—前 912 年 | 开始夺回失地 | |
| 阿达德尼拉里二世<br>公元前 911—前 891 年 | | |
| 图库尔提宁努尔塔二世<br>公元前 890—前 884 年 | | |
| 亚述纳西尔帕二世<br>公元前 883—前 859 年 | 公元前 879 年：<br>新都卡尔胡 | 大学者加布伊拉尼埃利什，王宫总管内伽尔阿皮库姆阿 |
| 沙尔曼纳瑟尔三世<br>公元前 858—前 824 年 | 恢复古代边界 | |
| 沙姆什阿达德五世<br>公元前 823—前 811 年 | | |
| 阿达德尼拉里三世<br>公元前 810—前 783 年 | | 行省总督内伽尔埃利什 |

……

| | | |
|---|---|---|
| 提格拉特皮勒塞尔三世<br>公元前 744—前 727 年 | 开始征服新领土 | |
| 沙尔曼纳瑟尔五世<br>公元前 726—前 722 年 | | |
| 萨尔贡二世<br>公元前 721—前 705 年 | 公元前 706 年：<br>新都杜尔–沙鲁金 | 大使亚述莱苏瓦 |

| | | |
|---|---|---|
| 辛那赫里布<br>公元前 704—前 681 年 | 约公元前 700 年：新都尼尼微 | 犹大国王希西家 |
| 埃萨尔哈东<br>公元前 680—前 669 年 | 公元前 672 年：与所有臣服者签署协定 | 公元前 680—前 612 年：第三章提到的人 |
| 亚述巴尼拔<br>公元前 668—前 630 年 | | 巴比伦国王沙马什舒姆乌金 |
| 亚述伊特尔伊拉尼<br>（Aššur-etel-ilani）<br>公元前 629—前 627 年 | | |
| 辛沙鲁伊什昆<br>公元前 626—前 612 年 | 公元前 614 年：亚述神庙被毁 | 巴比伦国王那波珀拉萨尔 |
| 亚述乌巴里特二世<br>公元前 611—前 608 年 | 公元前 612 年：尼尼微沦陷 | |

## 亚述城统治者

| | | |
|---|---|---|
| 波斯国王居鲁士二世<br>公元前 538—前 530 年 | 第二座亚述神庙<br>（"神庙 A"） | 乌鲁克的亚述人社区 |
| …… | | |
| 鲁特–阿索尔<br>公元 1 世纪 | 第三座亚述神庙<br>（"帕提亚式"） | 东方教会 |
| …… | 约公元 240 年：亚述神庙毁灭 | 萨珊王朝国王阿达希尔一世 |
| | | 圣马太和圣贝赫纳姆 |

# 斑斓阅读·外研社英汉双语百科书系典藏版

**更多内容**

**历史系列：**

**文化艺术系列：**

**自然科学与心理学系列：**

| Cosmology | 认识宇宙学 |
| Cryptography | 密码术的奥秘 |
| Darwin | 达尔文与进化论 |
| Dinosaurs | 恐龙探秘 |
| Dreaming | 梦的新解 |
| Emotion | 情感密码 |
| Freud | 弗洛伊德与精神分析 |
| Global Catastrophes | 全球灾变与世界末日 |
| Human Evolution | 人类进化简史 |
| The History of Time | 时间简史 |
| Jung | 简析荣格 |
| Prehistory | 走出黑暗——人类史前史探秘 |
| Psychiatry | 浅论精神病学 |

**政治、哲学与宗教系列：**

| Animal Rights | 动物权利 |
| The Bible | 《圣经》纵览 |
| Buddha | 释迦牟尼：从王子到佛陀 |
| Continental Philosophy | 解读欧陆哲学 |
| The Dead Sea Scrolls | 死海古卷概说 |
| The European Union | 欧盟概览 |
| Existentialism | 存在主义简论 |
| Feminism | 女权主义简史 |
| The New Testament | 《新约》入门 |
| The Old Testament | 《旧约》入门 |
| Plato | 解读柏拉图 |
| Postmodernism | 解读后现代主义 |
| Shakespeare | 读懂莎士比亚 |
| Socrates | 解读苏格拉底 |
| The World Trade Organization | 世界贸易组织概览 |